Praise for *Murphy's Law*

"Sean has a razor-sharp wit to match his intellectual curiosity. Consistently a treat to read."
—Jake Sugarman, *Salon*

"Sean Murphy's sharp, insightful writing is as delightful as seeing a really good movie; you find yourself thinking about it for days afterward as your previously held assumptions and beliefs are challenged. The fact that he can shine a light as thoughtfully as he does on subjects ranging from music to politics and sports to literature makes *Murphy's Law, Volume One* a real treasure; the kind of book you can dive into anywhere and find the minutes turning to hours as he leads you to places you never suspected you could get so caught up in."
—Robert Rodriguez, *The Beatles* author and co-host of the *Something About The Beatles* podcast

"While there aren't many political views that I agree with Sean on, there aren't many things he writes that I don't love. He makes me think by being reliably provocative, and he is occasionally quite convincing. Either way he is invariably amusing, thoughtful, and speaks past my brain directly to my soul -- a talent that is rare but very needed in these times."
—Mike Shields, Senior Republican Operative, CNN Contributor

"Sean Murphy's work is a joy to read. He instantly and easily draws the reader into his world with authenticity and humor. It's clear that Sean understands people -- we often find a piece of ourselves and our lives in his words. At the end of each story I read, I wish there was more, yet still feel satisfied with the little gems of wisdom he imparts."
—Cat Beekmans, *Elephant Journal*

"The musicians who Sean Murphy writes about set out, like so many of us, to change the world. Sean has the eloquent gift of letting you feel like you're in the studio with them and then sitting front-row, best seat in the house, feeling the impact, watching them perform.

Sean's musical insight is a peek behind the curtain, a gift and rare view everyone wants to see."
—Cerphe Colwell, Legendary Washington, DC DJ

Praise for *Not to Mention a Nice Life*

"The world of work, life, and love changed seismically in the early 2000s and Sean Murphy's narrator Byron, like everyone else, has been scrambling to keep up ever since…or wondering whether keeping up is even possible. In *Not to Mention a Nice Life*, Murphy's masterful storytelling takes us on an honest, searing, sardonic ride through the decade that wasn't."
—Jeremy Neuner, co-author of *The Rise of the Naked Economy*

"It's early in that lamentable decade of the 2000s, and while the good times continue to roll in corporate America, they won't be rolling for much longer—and no one knows it better than Byron, the Everyman narrator of Sean Murphy's witty and wise firecracker of a debut. If you liked Joshua Ferris's And Then We Came to the End, you'll love *Not to Mention a Nice Life*. Byron might not have a future, but Sean Murphy certainly does."
—Greg Olear, author of *Totally Killer* and *Fathermucker*

"Murphy has provided a wry sendup of the manners and mores of 21st century American culture, which inspects all the Prufrockian frailties and foibles we carry through life."
—Martha's Vineyard Times

"Sean Murphy has cleverly transformed Byron from Lord to dot-com schlub. Instead of chasing minotaurs through labyrinths, he hunts for meaning among the cubicles. *Not to Mention a Nice Life* is a wry, acerbic, and terrifying critique of the notion that there is really nothing left to critique. Modern Corporate America is less an enemy than a state of reality. They have won. We have lost. Byron, like the rest of the 99%, is left with layoffs, failed stock options, and the slight possibility of love. Read this very funny book. Like, right now. And then pour yourself an ice-cold laudanum."
—Sean Beaudoin, author of *Wise Young Fool and Welcome Thieves*

"Sean Murphy's *Not to Mention a Nice Life* offers a voice rarely seen—that whisper of human suffering that comes from an insular heart. It's as if the photo negative suddenly spoke, and claimed to be the real image, the real person behind the living color and magnetism of what we find in our everyday moment-to-moment existence. As Byron moves into and through his "Terrible Thirties," and the dot-com boom of wild heights and terrifying drops, we move with him…but we also get to watch, and be that cautious eye which only has to watch, and doesn't have to be. Which is both blessing and curse in this romp of Americana, half *Fight Club*, half *Catcher in the Rye* for the middle-aged. Regardless, I'm hooked—and want to stay that way."

—Jesse Waters, author of *Human Resources*

Praise for *Please Talk About Me When I'm Gone*

"*Please Talk about Me When I'm Gone,* which pulled me in from the first page and never let go, is a mosaic love letter from a son to his lost mother, so everyone in the bereavement club should read it. But this memoir is also a thoughtful, compassionate meditation on being alive. I nodded in recognition, dog-eared pages containing lines I loved, felt my eyes well with tears. In the end you should read it for the reason anyone reads good writing: to feel less alone."

—Jenna Blum, NYT best-selling author of *Those Who Save Us and The Stormchasers*

"As an oncologist treating a difficult and often fatal group of cancers, I witness firsthand as patients and their 'villages' cope with the diagnosis. So many decisions, so much emotion, and everyone does it a bit differently. No one path will serve; instead it is a truly individual course we choose. Sean Murphy's book is a great new resource for patients and families, and frankly for us all."

—Dr. John Marshall, Chief, Oncology at Georgetown Hospital

"As both the President of a colorectal cancer non profit, and more importantly a son who also lost his mother to this disease, I found this memoir emotional, educational, and edgy. I highly recommend this read for patients, survivors, caretakers, and physicians alike.

Congratulations Sean, for this amazing story, your mother would be proud."
—Michael Sapienza, President and Founder, Chris4Life Colon Cancer Foundation

"Sean Murphy brings a poetic voice and insightful contemplations to the largely unexplored territory of dying and death. With deep compassion and philosophical curiosity, he processes his individual grief while confirming the universality of loss."
—Roy Remer, Director of Volunteer Programs, Zen Hospice Project

"In some moments of profound experience, we see and feel in extraordinary ways. That is what happened to Sean Murphy after his mother's death. He has had the courage to look honestly at death, and the talent to express his love and grief in a way that will comfort and sustain his readers."
—Steve Goodwin, author of *Breaking Her Fall*

"Sean Murphy writes of his loss in a way that is compelling and insightful. Anyone early in the process of grief should hear his message—that you never get over the death of a loved one, and that's as it should be."
—Elizabeth Rogers, Social Worker, Advanced Illness Management Program

"An extremely moving, beautifully written, heart-felt and touching chronicling of the life and death of a parent."
—Charles Salzberg, author of *Devil in the Hole*

"When I started Sean's book, I read a section and said to myself, 'I'm going to email Sean to tell him how amazing that sentence is.' Then as I read a little further I thought, 'No, I'm going to email Sean to tell him what an amazing depth of knowledge and perception he's giving us.' And then, yes, you got it, on the very next page he wrote something that made me think, 'His Mom is looking down on Sean with unending love for what he just wrote. This is one amazing book!"
—Donald R. Gallehr, Director Emeritus, Northern Virginia Writing Project

VOLUME ONE

MURPHY'S LAW

SO THAT HAPPENED

SEAN MURPHY

Sean Murphy

Bright Moments Books
Reston, Virginia
Printed in the United States of America

Paperback ISBN: 978-0-9898805-3-4
eBook ISBN: 978-0-9898805-4-1

Visit Sean Murphy online: http://seanmurphy.net

For all my teachers, inside and especially outside the classroom.

"The only thing I deeply, avidly, wanted was a lucid, unillusioned eye."

—Milan Kundera, *Testaments Betrayed*

TABLE OF CONTENTS

INTRODUCTION

Short version: here's a collection of previously published pieces culled from the last decade or so.

Longer version: I've always been writing. Before I figured out—learning as I went—how to do it with some degree of competence for an actual audience (however modest), I was struggling to integrate my discipline for fiction writing and my lifelong passion for celebrating things that moved me. Most of these early attempts, which I'd sardonically refer to as love letters to nobody, are contained in the various journals I kept, starting in grade school.

I'm not inclined to revisit those journals very often, hopefully for all the right reasons, but I'm certain that one theme resurfaces, equal parts aspiration and mission statement: immerse myself as much as possible in art and express why it inspires me and why it matters. I suspect just about any critic or commentator has a similar backstory; it's a deeply personal impulse, but the desire to share or advocate is a kind of quid pro quo. For any happy, hopeless soul who gets emotional about the books, movies and music they venerate, it seems a measured appraisal is the least we can do for these kindred spirits and would-be allies who expand and occasionally save our lives.

If I bring anything to the table, it's incorporating that graduate school preoccupation with historical perspective and context and the sincere ardor of a fan. I couldn't, and wouldn't spend my adult life running blindly down the rabbit hole of academia, agonizing over topics most people couldn't care less about; my goal became combining criticism and advocacy; covering my world in writing.

Two things happened in my mid '20s that helped put me more steadily on the same path I find myself treading today. First, I opted not to pursue a PhD, a decision that bewildered friends, family and, at times, myself. It wasn't that I didn't have the heart for it; graduate school, while challenging, had also seemed natural, inevitable. But I had what at the time was an unsettlingly difficult time choosing the topic to which I'd dedicate several years of my life. I look back now and recognize that this reluctance to tether my intellectual facilities—such as they were—to a single, necessarily abstruse subject upon which I'd become an *expert*, was not only a sign that I wasn't meant for academia, but might be considered a badge of honor rather than weakness.

For my twenty-sixth birthday I requested and received a copy of Milan Kundera's *Testaments Betrayed.* If my fiction suffered from the subsequent obsession with this great man's work (too soon, too good, too *much*), my introduction to Kundera's writing about writing was as formative and influential as anything I'd yet come across. Shortly thereafter, something similar ensued with Martin Amis: I devoured—and imitated, badly—his novels, but in his non-fiction I recognized a style blending confidence and sophistication that made most other contemporary criticism seem stiff, clichéd, soulless. To this day I maintain the best arbiters of literature are those who create it, not because they've mastered the craft but have dedicated their lives *attempting* to master it, and often been confounded.

I still kept a journal and I sent a million emails: arguments, snapshots, half-assed analyses, attempts to convince, love letters to anyone who'd listen, all lost in the electronic ether. Not many people were reading my work, and I still wasn't sure how to more formally achieve what I felt most passionate about: reading, listening, watching, and *responding.* That compulsion informed my aspirations before, during and after college, and it's still the primary imperative of my writing life.

A breakthrough of sorts occurred in August, 2006. Arthur Lee, the alternately maligned and misunderstood lead singer of the biggest band that never was, Love, passed away. I read the various obituaries with sadness, but felt compelled to bear witness in some way, my own way. I spent the entire weekend wrestling with a tribute to him, uncertain (and not especially concerned about) who might read, much less publish it. An online site I read and admired, *PopMatters*, was one of the places I pitched. They accepted, and thus began a ten year-and-counting relationship. I remain grateful for that first byline and offer gratitude to both Sarah Zupko and Karen Zarker for their enthusiasm and support.

Toward the end of the decade, and just as the presidential race turned from contested to comical, thanks to the spectacle of Sarah Palin, I began writing more about politics—a neurosis honed from innumerable email arguments with old college friends, and the inexorable result of being raised, and remaining, just outside Washington, D.C. With some degree of ambivalence, I began blogging. At that point, it still seemed an obligatory, if solipsistic endeavor, and most of the blogs I encountered at that time left me cold. I learned quickly, however, that blog writing could combine the joys and intimacy of journal writing with the rigor of a work intended for an intelligent audience.

Personal essays were not foreign territory, but a sustained examination of life and how it's lived (including death and how to live through it when it rocks your world) turns out to be the best real-time training for getting one's mind—and pen—around an unfettered attempt to make sense out of profoundly personal things. It not only seems possible, but oddly appropriate to embrace the audacity of putting it *out there*, so to speak. Best intentions clash against execution and at a certain point it's out of your hands: other people will determine if the work in question works. It's at once intimidating and liberating, the way it should be for anyone who puts words on paper.

While constructing most of these pieces, I had one distinct objective: write only about things I cared about and, hopefully in the service of both readers and myself, try to do a subject justice. That simple, that impossible. But what does that *mean*? For me, in a few thousand words or less, make a case, render a verdict, or interrogate an issue that, once written, can withstand time, trends and repeated viewings. Any honest writer who hopes their work will resonate must respect, in advance, anyone who'll take the time to check them out.

I'm grateful you're checking me out. And to those who have been around for a while, particularly the beloved friends and family who have been there all along, I cherish your loyalty and goodwill. I leave you with a promise and a warning: there's more where this came from. So, to be continued.

ONE: RUMINATIONS IN REAL TIME

WILLIAM DOWD AND SOME THOUGHTS ABOUT THE HARPSICHORD

A life well spent?

That's the goal, isn't it? For any of us. Not necessarily to be enshrined in a newspaper's obituary (although few people would protest such a proposition), but to have affected even a few lives, to have left the world better; or failing that, different, than it would have been. Leading a life that is, in some way(s), directed outward as well as inward, cultivating a passion and then sharing it; assisting others in discovering or enjoying that passion. Not an inconsiderable accomplishment, by any standard.

Of course, some shoot higher. For instance, William Dowd (who died this week, aged 86, in Reston, VA—which makes me wish I'd met him). Dowd's life's work was reviving the craftsmanship of harpsichords (a skill perfected in the 17th-century, when harpsichords were the electric guitars of their time). What prompted this singular ambition? After serving in World War II, interested in music but not properly trained, he fell in love with the quaint instrument after attending several classical music concerts. Along with lifelong friend and partner in crime Frank Hubbard, the two men engaged in the modest mission of (in their own words) "reviving single-handed the whole baroque orchestra."

More from Dowd: "They were (no longer) making anything that was remotely like an antique harpsichord. We discovered a resonant, flowering sound which we liked. We, with the enthusiasm and rash brashness of the young, believed we knew how to bring back the authentic instrument upon which the early harpsichord music was all based."

Over 800 harpsichords later, Dowd's handiwork is scattered across countries all over the world, and arguably comprise a collection of the most frequently played—and appreciated—instruments. Says his wife, Pegram Epes Dowd: "Men like that came back from World War II, and they believed there was nothing they could not do. They really were risk takers. I think it was very heroic."

It seems somehow appropriate that in assessing the work of what could fairly, if somewhat inadequately, be described as a quintessential 20th-century man, one is obliged to discuss a type of music (and the instrument upon which most of it was composed) made several centuries before he was born. It goes beyond the obvious, but essential, actuality that Dowd was keeping alive music that cannot (and fortunately, for the foreseeable future, *will not*) die; his life is necessarily larger (in scope, in ambition, in consequence) because he devoted his energies toward a force that endures simply by virtue of *being*. It is not a stretch, then, to propose that Dowd will continue on through the music played on the instruments he assembled.

We shall not see his like again. That this encomium is offered up so frequently is, for once and in a refreshing exception, a demonstration of the power of cliché: that we've had so many individuals deemed worthy of this praise says much about our potential as human beings. It is, nevertheless, more than a little bittersweet to consider the larger implications of Dowd's ambition. Will we have enterprising craftsmen dedicating their best years to the refinement of harpsichord construction in the 21st century? Will we have people even *listening* to harpsichord music? The answer, obviously, is yes; at least to the second query. But it still warrants consideration: even though every generation necessarily mourns the inevitable passing of its so-called best and brightest, when it comes to artistic endeavors, once we lose advocates (not to mention the actual artists) that part of our world becomes a little bit smaller. Over time, these losses constitute erosion that simply can't be replicated.

Progress in virtually every other earthly endeavor, from medicine to science to sports, is always pulling us forward to the future:

advancements are the currency of innovation and they render the old ways irrelevant, dispensable. The opposite might be said to be the case with art: innovation does occur, and it is welcome and inexorable, but entire periods of time are contained within particular artistic movements; these eras are a very real way in which we can assess ourselves. Put more prosaically, no one is going to lament the loss of, say, 20th-century (to say nothing of 17th-century!) medical practices; our collective progress means less pain and more salubrity for us all. The art being created today (and that will be created tomorrow) is, to be certain, as valid, meaningful and useful as the works enshrined in museums and box sets. Indeed, our art today naturally says as much about us now as art from yesterday speaks of the way we lived, then. Still, while we celebrate the exceptional life and achievements of William Dowd, we should also hope that his work serves to inspire an individual, not yet been born, who will find himself drawn irretrievably toward a past he is able to apprehend, miraculously, through the music.

December, 2008

THERE'S JUST MEANNESS IN THIS WORLD

As obstreperously opposed to the death penalty as I remain, it's nevertheless difficult to feel uncomplicated emotions regarding the execution of John Allen Muhammad.

I—and any individual living in or around the D.C. area—was in the line of fire, so to speak, during this disturbed man's killing spree in the fall of 2002. I was one of the people looking over my shoulder while I pumped my gas. I was the guy debating whether or not that Home Depot run should be postponed. I was the guy who thought: as if getting killed on my morning commute was not absurd enough, I have to worry about *this*? I was, finally, the guy who decided that, not unlike it feels when you step onto that plane, if your number is up, your number is up. It was not defiance, and it was not any kind of bravery; it was simply a refusal to stop living my way because I was afraid of dying.

Crimes of passion are easier to analyze. Momentary lapse of reason; a boiling point reached due to betrayal or provocation. Manslaughter is a similar case (ever notice how manslaughter is also mans laughter?). These things, however tragic or repugnant, have some sort of cause and effect, you can see where point A picked up a gun or a knife or put a drunk-driving key in the ignition, and made its indelible way to point B.

But a serial killer? (And let's not sugarcoat it. Sniper? That depiction sterilizes things too much by half. Imagine if someone you loved was the random victim of this depraved sociopath, would it not be more than a little insulting to say they were killed by a *sniper*? Unless you are killed in action in a war—itself a complicated and appalling scenario—it's simply inappropriate to use the term "sniper" to describe a citizen deciding that it is, on any level, tolerable to put innocent civilians in the crosshairs).

And then there are the sociological implications. Did this killer have a terrible, tortured life? Perhaps. Is there ever a circumstance where it's acceptable to take out random, unknowing human beings to...*what?* Prove a point? Strike a blow against an uncaring world? Inscribe one's name in the permanent record? Find perverse meaning in an otherwise meaningless universe? To paradoxically feel alive by taking another person's life? All of the above? Some? None? The answer to this question, of course, is that it's an affront to any reasonable code of conduct declaring oneself the arbiter of life and death. End of story.

And so, is it the place of society to determine, once the evidence has been counted and corroborated, that this human insect—this remorseless, yet undeniably disturbed—shell of a man deserves to die? Is it justice? Is it an Old Testament type of quid pro quo? Is it a plain matter of ensuring that he would never hit the streets and take another life? All of the above? None?

Was there any benefit, on any level, in ensuring this man remained alive? Did he have a book to write, entreaties to make of the families he destroyed, wisdom to impart from the dark depths of his fractured heart? Had he descended to a spiritual place that obviated the possibility of redemption? More to the point, did he care? Who gains from his eradication from this planet? And more to the point, who cares? Do we require answers, or insight, when it comes to a human being who—for whatever myriad reasons—determined that his pain, or confusion, or nihilistic impulse, compelled him to kill other human beings?

Are we going to shed a tear for this psycho?

Of course not. At least not until our eyes are dry from the ceaseless drops they should shed for the friends, relatives and families of the folks killed by his hand.

Will it provide closure for any of these people? Obviously not. Just because the murderer is dead does not mean the people he murdered will return to life. And perhaps it's because his death will not restore their lives that the concept of capital punishment seems so absurd, so barbaric. But is there a refined or compassionate way to deal with a person who forfeits his claim on those conditions?

The best answer I can come up with is that there is no answer.

No answer for how to deal with an unapologetic murderer. No answer for the innocent lives he stole. No answer for where that hatred emanated from. No answer for how to handle such a monster in a lawful society. No answer for how I would feel if someone I loved had been cut down for no conceivable cause. No answer for the human condition that goes back as far as Cain slaying Abel. No answer for how we got here. No answer for where we're going. No answer other than we all must, in some fashion, hold one another accountable for what we do. No question about right and wrong.

The only remaining question is: what else can we do?

November, 2009

NEW YEAR'S EVE: THE VERTIGINOUS EVENT

New Year's Eve is that vertiginous event where you're recalling—or trying to forget—the past while anticipating—or dreading—the future, but at the same time living utterly in the moment.

This year is slightly different, because we're not only reflecting on the last twelve months, but the last ten years. I'll join the clichéd chorus and marvel at how fast it goes. Ten years, already? Exactly a decade ago I was up in the Big Apple, determined to see in the new millennium even if meant going down with the ship. Remember how terrified people were about Y2K? The clocks would stop, the computers would crash, Reality TV would disappear, et cetera. Of course, we made it through in one piece. If Reality TV is the price we had to pay for surviving the infamous *fin de siècle*, then so be it.

Through a combination of dumb luck and the audacity to hope (abetted by a full night of celebratory end-of-the-world cocktails) my friends and I stumbled right out into the middle of Times Square, which had been on total lockdown for more than two days (we ran into people who'd stood in place for 36 hours or more, pissing into cups and freezing to death in slow motion under their multiple layers): the folks who wanted to witness history in real time were packed in barricaded city blocks, behind ropes and more cops than there are donuts (or cops) at a Krispy Kreme convention. Long story short: a few of us were simply trying to get back home to watch the New Year (or obliteration of the planet) happen on TV, like any reasonable American would do. As it turned out, we ended up watching the ball drop less than five hundred feet in front of us. Once in a lifetime, one in a million. We not only lived, but lived to tell about it. And, despite the awkward oversight that enabled us to slip not-so-innocently under a chained line to mingle with the crowd, the security was stellar that whole weekend. Cops were *everywhere* and they had things under control. But it was more than that: once the clock turned to 2000 the craziest (and coolest) city in the world was partying like it was...well, 1999. And there was nothing but love and happiness amidst that spectacle. People were happy, perhaps exhilarated to still be alive. Hugs and high-fives abounded, and I did not see a single act of violence or ill-will as midnight lurched toward the hangover of the century. Good times, to be certain.

And I remember thinking: what a great time to be alive. What a positive omen for a new century. Of course, things didn't quite pan out as predicted that evening. In the same city, less than two years later, everything changed forever. (In cities all over the country, less than one year later, the worst president in the history of America weaseled in on a technicality, ensuring that the idiotic and apathetic would ruin it for the rest of us, as usual.) It seemed like the rest of the decade was one calamity or crisis after another, testing even our capacity to absorb the inexplicable. And we still managed to make it, scarred and scared, to another decade. Another chance to make good on the work that needs to be done. For all of our sakes, let's hope we do better this time around.

I went into 2009 prepared to deal with the inevitable passing of my best furry friend, and could not have imagined it would end up happening many months sooner than expected. That hurt. It still stings, every single day, but as anyone who has experienced any kind of loss knows, the harder it is, the better it was. It's never enough to compensate for the pain by acknowledging the profundity of the love, but it helps. That was the big event for me this past year and it feels right to remember that, now, while celebrating that he was with me for just about a decade. Bittersweet, to be certain, but as Big Head Todd would say, more sweet than bitter.

And, as always, it's a hell of a lot easier to keep these things in perspective by considering the (increasing) number of our brothers and sisters who are struggling just to *be*, here and overseas. And for entirely too many people (inside our borders but especially beyond) every year is only about one thing, survival. Here's hoping better times (financially, spiritually) are on the horizon for all, but mostly for those that need it the most. Don't be cynical: find a charity you can feel good about supporting, endorse the efforts of our great artists, tell your parents you love them, appreciate—and savor—the friends who always have your back. Be good to strangers and be better to yourself: you deserve it.

Friends, family, health, music, movies, books, good food and drink, and happy memories yet to be made. Those are some of my favorite things, and I am blessed to have enjoyed all in abundance throughout the 2000's. Here's toasting much more of same, for as long as all of us are able to keep the party going.

December, 2009

ON THE DEATH OF AN INDESTRUCTIBLE DOG

Check it out: I have three separate, visible scars on my right hand. All of them are from Quinzy's teeth. The largest scar is from a bite he gave me, *while I was petting him.*

I feel quite confident in saying there has never been another dog that was anything like this Shih Tzu, who I am proud to have liberated from a rather disconsolate puppy mill almost exactly 15 years ago. But I am not the hero in this story; not even close. That person would be the woman who became his mother (and shortly thereafter, her husband, who became his father), who "inherited" him because the woman who was my mother could not handle him. At the time I was surprised and more than a little disappointed that the same woman who had already raised two human puppies decided, in a moment of anxiety-induced weakness, that she was not up to the task. The woman who insisted she wanted a "grand-puppy" (based on her love of Otis, the first Shih Tzu in the family) and, at that time without a human grand-puppy, was looking for somewhere to direct that abundance of love and affection she had in reserve. Fortunately, my sister was on the case and within a year my mother was able to dedicate herself to the proposition of spoiling my (human) niece.

I would have taken Quinzy myself but the complex I lived in at the time did not allow pets. I contemplated rolling the dice but realized (wisely) that it would be devastating for all involved if the little guy got settled in and attached, only to find himself (and/or myself) ejected from the apartment. And so it was that the woman who at one time had been my fiancée was now, abruptly, the mother of the puppy my mother owned for less than 24 hours. And just like that, Otis (himself only two years old) found himself a rather reluctant older brother.

Quinzy? My mother had picked out the name long before we picked up the pup. Growing up just outside of Boston she could attest that one way to sniff out transplants and fake New Englanders was the way they pronounce the town of Quincy: If anyone says it the way it looks (kwin-see) they are suspect; everyone else knows it is actually—and correctly—pronounced kwin-zee. She felt that was a great name for a little dog, and I tended to agree. I especially liked the added touch of spelling it with a Z, as it reminded me of the fact that Led Zeppelin did not spell their name the correct way (Lead) because they knew (correctly) that Americans would invariably pronounce it Leed Zeppelin. To see a two pound, eight-week old Shih Tzu named Quinzy is difficult to describe or surpass, even if he had the all-but obligatory (and quite noisome) case of puppy-worms. Little did any of us know what we were in store for...

Long after he was house-trained Quinzy still had accidents. As a person whose carpets and floors bore the brunt of too many of these incidents to count, I used to call them "on purposes". Quinzy was a character. Theories abound, from the lazy to the elaborate: he had a screw loose; he was mildly retarded; he was the utter distillation of pure Id; he was the inevitable result of a very irresponsible and poorly run breeding factory ("puppy mill" is at once an appropriate and completely inadequate euphemism for the conditions in which so many of our best friends are bred: when I first took my mom to inspect the pack, I made the mistake of sitting down on the carpet while scores of Shih Tzus—literally—bound hither and thither, and ended up with a urine stain on my shorts that I could never fully eradicate). Like recalcitrant literary figures before him including Whitman, Thoreau and Kerouac, Quinzy marched to his own funky drummer and sucked the marrow out of life --and he wasn't afraid to kill something in order to get that marrow (of which more shortly).

Quinzy's "condition" was mostly innocuous (says the man with the scars) and often cute: there was undeniably some type of faulty wiring, or he was part feline, or he was the first of an evolutionary leap forward—even though he often acted like the opposite. When he was being pet his tail would wag, indicating happiness, but he would growl, indicating displeasure. After a while it became clear that it was his way of purring (part cat? based on his hunting prowess and the environment he was born into, this possibility is not totally far-fetched). When he was young he had a freakish ability to jump: his hang-time was more impressive than most adult white males. He was a born predator and while he was seldom without some type of stuffed animal lodged in his snout, he much preferred actual game. His success rate was astonishing considering he did not live on a farm. In his prime (and his prime was pretty much his first year through his thirteenth when he finally began to slow down a tad) he was able to capture and kill several birds. Let me repeat that: *he was able to capture and kill several birds*. I know leopards with less-impressive track records. His mother, ever sensitive and not supportive of these feral proclivities, felt obliged to tie a bell around his collar so that the birds in the backyard had half a chance. Please keep in mind: we are not talking about a retriever or what some people may unkindly (if not inaccurately) call a *real* dog: this was a twelve pound Shih Tzu. You know, *Shih Tzu;* that is Chinese for *Sissy Dog.*

One of my favorite Quinzy stories (and I have dozens: buy me some beers and I'll keep you laughing for hours) is the brawl he got in with an opossum that had the temerity to live in the wood-pile behind the townhouse. His mother recalls him coming in from a late-night tinkle and laying down beside her. It wasn't until she saw (or smelled?) the blood that she realized he was injured. Inspecting him, she saw a substantial cut under his throat; he hadn't barked or cried, he just came back in as if nothing had happened. Naturally a trip to the vet was necessary and it was later discovered that a family of opossums had set up shop behind the wood-pile. Opossums are pretty big, and have rather sharp teeth. They're also kind of nasty, especially if they are protecting their brood. Needless to say, the next time Quinzy stepped into the backyard (and every time for a long time afterward) he ran *directly* to the wood-pile and frantically looked for his foe so he could finish what he started. Fearless, idiotic and inimitable.

Quinzy bit people. He pissed and pooped with impunity. Another favorite of mine is the electric blanket story. I was taking care of him (and Otis) one weekend during the middle of winter. It was frigid outside and while I was snug inside my bed (and electric blanket) I realized the two poor pups, although snuggled together in their "nest" in the living room, probably would welcome a little extra warmth. I brought them into my room and in short order they were wrapped around me and, presumably, grateful. A few minutes later, just as I was drifting off, I felt what seemed like liquid on and around my legs. Impossible, I thought. And then I remembered the Quinzy factor. I threw the cover off and flicked on the light. Sure enough, this contemptible swine had taken an enormous piss, soaking my sheets, blanket, comforter and *himself.* It made me recall the old trick we used to always play (unsuccessfully) where during slumber parties we waited until someone fell asleep and put their fingers in warm water. Leave it to Quinzy to perfect that adolescent scenario, much to my chagrin. Yet, as always, when you looked down at him he didn't betray the least bit of guilt or even comprehension that he'd done anything wrong. And I sincerely believe it never occurred to him that he had. That was the difference; he was never *bad*, he just *was.*

Years and at least one scar later, I would tell people, watching his growl/purr in disbelief that I was almost entirely certain he was expressing deep joy and gratification. Except he still might bite you. Many years later, I've had enough experience with dogs (my own and others) that there is no canine I can't trust and not a single one I won't snuggle. But with Quinzy, even after a decade and a half, there was always, *always* the awareness that you didn't want to get your face too close to his, just in case...

You could not help but love him.

I used to say (and I was more than half-serious) that while I did not believe he could ever die, if and when he did, the medical community needed to study him and find the cure for cancer. I've never seen a dog that simply did not show any signs of weakness or age for so long. He was not hyper; he just went at the world in a way that Auggie March would fully endorse. So with apologies to Saul Bellow, I'll take the liberty of embellishing that famous first paragraph from his masterful novel: "*I am an American, (puppy-mill)-born—...and go at things as I have taught myself, free-style, and will make the record in my own way: first to knock, first admitted; sometimes an innocent knock, sometimes a not so innocent. But a (dog)'s character is his fate, says Heraclitis, and in the end there isn't any way to disguise the nature of the knocks by acoustical work on the door or gloving the knuckles (or muzzling the snout).*"

Quinzy treated the world like his bitch and while I couldn't (and wouldn't want to) necessarily emulate that approach, it's hard not to admire and respect it. I've never met a human—much less an animal—that slurped so much ecstasy out of every second he was allowed to enjoy. Quinzy got his eyes, ears, snout and occasionally his teeth on anything and everyone within his reach and he never hesitated and he never slowed down. Until he slowed down.

But we never thought he would die. We actually thought he would live forever. Or at least shatter some canine records. I still reckon that scientific minds should study his DNA and come up with the antitode for illness, aging and depression. He was the most *alive* dog I've ever known and I've known a lot of dogs. Dogs, if nothing else, are very alive and adept at living (they are dogs, after all).

I won't get carried away and claim that the scars on my hand, which I can see right now as I write these words, are the ironic gifts Quinzy left me. But in a way I could not appreciate until this very second, perhaps he was giving me something I couldn't fully fathom, since I'm a human. Did he understood and appreciate that he had been rescued from abandonment or a premature appointment with the veterinarian's least-loved needle? Who knows? Who cares? What was he supposed to do, *thank* me? He did more than that anyway, and he did it without guile or the expectation of gratitude, since he was a dog. He showed me how to live a less contrived, more memorable life. He left me with a part of him that I can easily keep in my head and my heart. Finally, in his own incomparable fashion he ensured I had a visible reminder or three I'll carry with me until the day I finally slow down myself.

September, 2011

WHITNEY HOUSTON AND THE WAGES OF FAME

Sadly, only the most optimistic or naive observers didn't see this coming.

Indeed, it is fair, if harsh, to wonder how it took so long.

I make it a habit to avoid any and all "reality TV" shows, but it did not demand sustained viewing of her and then-husband Bobby Brown's public spectacle to see that all was far from well in her world.

On the other hand, who felt comfortable making a prediction? For every Amy Winehouse there is a Keith Richards. For every Jimi Hendrix there is an Eddie Van Halen. Some of our rock stars have the combination of good genes, dumb luck and, perhaps, destiny keeping them from snuffing themselves out.

It's a shame: so much talent, so much unrealized potential. Same old song and dance, really.

Except for two things.

One, it seems fair to suggest that Houston more than fulfilled any hopes and expectations. She was on the top of her game—and the world—for a good, long ride, and there is no question her music will be listened to for a very long time. By any reasonable measure, she did what she was put here to do.

Two, it's difficult to get too worked up with pity and disappointment for someone who had everything and couldn't hold it together. There is no judgment in that view (indeed, I have a tremendous amount of sympathy for anyone, rich and famous or not, who struggles and ultimately loses a drawn-out battle with demons they can't control), but it is difficult in some ways to behold our very American tendency to instantly beatify our celebrities when they die, particularly when they die prematurely and as a result of their own appetite for destruction. It seems to me this default mechanism overlooks and, ironically, perpetuates the same dynamic that helps people nullify themselves.

Listen: I understand, and get it, that Houston's dying on the eve of the Grammys (I'll resist the urge to comment on what an exorbitant, appalling festival of ostentation and egotism that ceremony is, and save it for another time) made the occasion tailor-made for overblown, egocentric mini-tributes. In fact, the way we signal our solidarity with bumper stickers, sweet nothings on national TV or pink ribbons does much to signify how we simultaneously take the path of least resistance and make any unfortunate situation as much about ourselves as possible. It doesn't require a cynic to see a bunch of millionaires in designer dresses and suits nodding their heads in somber acknowledgment of yet another tragedy and find the routine more than a little hollow. How many of these preening pop stars put their considerable money where their bleach-toothed mouths are and get involved? How many of them are helping fund drug treatment clinics? How many are doing public service announcements? How many are on board to help educate the fans who buy the tickets? More likely, they are hustling to get their own reality TV shows.

Look: it's on every individual to make whatever choices they should make and be accountable for the good or ill that results. Still, it speaks volumes to behold Hollywood—an insular community looking to traffic and exploit any opportunity to say how much they care—partake in this scripted, soulless ritual. And of course our mainstream media is no less culpable. In fact they are too often a prurient posse of hucksters and hypocrites, at once breathlessly reporting each misadventure and then, once the damage is done, sugar-coating it and sanitizing it. I'm certainly not suggesting it would have been fair or appropriate to lead each Houston obituary with a detailed exegesis of her substance-addled spiral. I do maintain that we should all be disgusted with this familiar formula, and don't kid yourself: once the proverbial dust settles (and the accolades and feel-good statements and montages have been aired) there will be no shortage of dirt seeping out. Every lurid anecdote and embarrassing setback will be cataloged, all in the name of an insatiable public's right to know. In this we are all culpable.

(Would legalizing drugs help? Would more rock star money assisting free clinics make a difference? Would cancelling one of these narcissistic fame orgies and donating those millions to charity do some good? Of course. Will any of these things happen? Of course not.)

There is no easy answer. The only thing that's certain is that what we're doing now isn't working. And I'm not talking about the regular, and regrettable body count of pop stars dying by their own hand (intentional or not). I'm talking about the uncountable numbers of human beings (in America and around the world) who, for a variety of all the usual reasons, fall prey to forces and vices that take hold of their lives. Yes, it's a very sad day when a beautiful and gifted songbird gets silenced. And if the wage of super-stardom doesn't need to be tragic, the cause and effect of our hero—and money—worshipping society makes it more likely. It's a sad day every day when the people we don't know and won't produce cry-on-demand tributes for slip away, unnoticed. No one will eulogize them because few people know who they are.

February, 2012

BACKS TO THE FUTURE

Take a guy.

Let's say he is about my age: old enough to own a place and pay almost all his bills sometimes; young enough to understand that he is not getting any younger. Add a dose of fresh alienation—not enough to be unhealthy, of course, but enough to enable him to function in a world full of imbecility and indifference and all those unattainable happily-ever-after's awaiting him on the other side of his flat screen TV. Take this guy and give him enough stability so that he has no excuses, but plenty of alibis. Most likely, he is utterly average in every regard, except for the fact that, unlike almost everyone he knows, he is aware of it. Finally, add the oncoming collision of the big Five-Oh (When? *Someday,* we don't say) and there's no choice but to buckle up and insert all applicable clichés, complacent epiphanies and the half-earned angst that are smirking impatiently, just offstage.

It's time to pay tribute. Yes, at this point it would seem appropriate to tip the bottle and pour out some beer for our dead homeboy. But we don't because we are not drinking beer. Also, he is not dead, and we are not in a music video or even a bad movie, and above all, we are too cynical, self-conscious, or married to imitate such affected gestures. Unless we were being ironic, but it's too early in the evening for that type of commitment, so we'll stick to doing what we do best: retelling stories that never happened exactly the way we insist on remembering them. (Plus, our class couldn't even pull it together for a formal reunion. *Been there, done that,* we don't say.) No harm done, a little bullshit and bourbon on the rocks never hurt anyone. Besides, I am increasingly aware that it is because these stories are so obviously embellished that we need them to be true. Add a few hours and more than a few drinks and once again, here we are: backs to the future, looking in the mirror for someone who should be standing alongside us.

This is not exactly what they mean by flashing back, and yet I'm trying to stay in the moment, knowing I can if I try hard enough. But first I need to make sense of that old saying, how does it go? If I knew now what I didn't know then? No. If I knew *then* what I did know, now? I don't know. I'm here, but now—and not for nothing—I'm recalling the mistake I didn't make, over two decades ago.

Remember Love Boat? Not the TV show, but a blunt laced with PCP, also known as angel dust. *The boat.* This was the holy grail of illicit drugs, and considering the fact that all drugs were illicit, period, even a dumbass underclassman knew this was Filed Under Fucked Up. I didn't know much but I knew that alcohol was off limits, marijuana was out of the question, and Love Boat was officially off the charts. This was the stuff that longhaired actor took an accidental hit of and then quickly found himself perched on a rooftop, trying to fly (or perhaps that was the surreptitious tab of acid in his fruit punch, same difference). We saw that movie in the '70s and it scared us even straighter. Nevertheless, every so often when we were shooting hoop after school, some older brothers would show up, commandeer the court and show us all the things we knew we could never do. Inexorably, one of them would see us seeing them, raise his eyebrow and say the dangerous words: "You lookin'?"

Most likely, the question never presumed a possible transaction, and was more an offhand (but not ironic, because nobody knew what irony was at that age) way of reminding us, at once, who they were, who we were, and most significantly, who we would never be. But some other kids were in on the action; they had to be. Why else would we constantly be on the receiving end of these perfunctory solicitations?

Eventually, we agreed that it could only be one group of unusual suspects: the freaks. Older students, the rock concert t-shirt wearing army of outcasts; the rebels who at one time had been athletes, or nerds, or drama dorks, and then popped through the pimple of post adolescent purgatory and found themselves born again as deadbeats. The ones, we belatedly recognized, who saw through the self-immolation of Izod shirts and feathered hair, the ones who shirked intramural activities and the safety of numbers, the ones who could no longer belong to any Key Club that might accept them as members. The ones who never even got hassled by the jocks because they simply were not worth the aggravation; a cafeteria-style ass kicking would not earn a striving sophomore any status. These were the guys, everyone knew, who dared to flick their middle fingers at student governance, decorum and the future: they were going nowhere and seemed to be in a real hurry to get there. These were the ones, we decided, who had the audacity, when the brothers asked if they were looking, to say *yes*.

Just say no? Remember, this was a world before computers and consoles and cell phones and even CD players. Not an innocent era, by any means, but a time when some of us read books because we couldn't think of anything better to do. A time when growing pains were the physical kind and the one thing everyone agreed upon was that we couldn't get older quickly enough. A time, most likely, that comprised the formative years so many adults feel an almost unbearable longing for, mostly because whatever it is they were feeling can't ever be felt that way again. Sentimental? Shit, I still find myself craving the same things I hoped for then: a pretty girlfriend (remember going steady?), a decent report card (also known as a performance review), to be considered cool by the types of people who are considered cool, and mostly to be accountable, at last, and free to do whatever the hell I want when I grow up. Someday.

We didn't know how much we did not know, but we knew what everyone else seemed to understand. Such as, the U.S.A. could kick some Soviet ass if it had to (ask *Rocky IV*), that God existed (and, assuredly, was a Capitalist God), that he who dies with the most toys wins, and we all knew exactly what we'd become after graduating from our first- or second-choice colleges: some of us would be practicing L.A. Law, some of us would be sporting Top Gun bomber jackets, some of us would get wealthy on Wall Street, and the rest of us would have the old-fashioned types of jobs that you could actually describe in one or two words. What we were *not* going to be was forgettable. We did not know where we were headed, but we were emboldened by an instinctual understanding that our parents' wallets would insulate us from too much reality, or at least break our fall if any of us tripped climbing up that American ladder.

Not quite everything we believed turned out to be wrong, and life is usually kind enough to wait a while before it reveals some of the answers to questions you never knew needed to be asked. But even before graduation we were disabused of at least one illusion that took us down a notch or two: it wasn't the freaks who dared not to just say no, it was us.

Not me, you understand. I was too chickenshit, or at least too Catholic, to dabble in the dust, and while I reckon there was a vague contentment underlying that decision, I am even more relieved, looking back. See, I went to college, and I saw the reefer (smoked it too), smelled the 'shrooms (ate them too), saw the unsnorted remnants of white powder under the noses of blissed-out fraternity boys (fortunately for all involved, I did not have the funds for that type of fun). And, obviously, the alcohol. None of us were ever the same after those first dozen or so hangovers: no matter what it dished out, we kept going back to the unwell, looking for something to…what, exactly? Provide pleasure? Instigate adventure? Derail inhibition? Seek fleeting solace from the cold, cruel world? Sure, all that crap, but something else as well. There is a reason the most expensive advertisements are still allowed to promote an activity that kills more kids each year than any boogeyman on amphetamines—or Nancy Reagan for that matter—could ever conceive in their darkest dreams. There is something that alcohol almost, but never quite, delivers, that keeps everyone in the game. Just like back in the day, there's safety in numbers, and it would sure seem Un-American to cast aspersions on something so many people need to believe in.

Nevertheless, I saw a handful of buddies brought low, churned up and rehabbed before they turned twenty-one, and every year at least one friend or acquaintance finally finds something else to look forward to on Friday afternoons. What I'm saying is, I'm lucky. Because I never pushed my luck and ended up biting something that bit back and wouldn't let go. But if I knew then what I know now, I may have unwittingly joined a few of the guys—who got better grades than I did—when they took trips across town in a borrowed car.

Get this: not only were some of the guys we knew in on the action (and for the record, as far as they knew the freaks never touched the stuff—more irony wasted, like everything else, on the young), their escapades were abetted by a teacher. Put another way, a teacher at our school was paying them to make drug runs. To an adult, today, this shouldn't seem shocking; indeed, it is practically expected. But that is only because we are too well acquainted with irony, which merely proves that we no longer have the capacity to surprise ourselves, if we ever did.

In any event, it turns out that the mastermind of these Love Boat runs was quite possibly the least likely culprit and therefore (in hindsight?) the most obvious. Mr. X., as he was not known, since this is not his name, was at the time—and still, in my mind—ageless, simply an *adult*, although he could not have been much older than thirty. If this story were depicted in a movie, the car the kids borrowed would have been nice, perhaps ironically nice, instead of the unremarkable piece of shit it actually was. And, crucially, Mr. X. would be played by George Clooney, or a lesser star that still emanates the slick celluloid charisma no real people can ever obtain. In the movie, the teacher would have a tragic flaw: a college football injury that derailed his obvious path to the pros, or some type of self-loathing resulting from a dark secret that he finally confronts in the end. Or something similarly redemptory, and ridiculous. In truth, Mr. X. was a mess—not quite morbidly obese, but working on it with the inimitable dedication of a junk food enthusiast. To look at him, even then, it seemed exceedingly improbable that he was once a varsity wrestler (in another state, in another world) and an offensive tackle. Well, it was a little easier to imagine him as an offensive tackle. And he had the pictures to prove it. Nonetheless, those days behind him, he had really gone to the (hot) dogs, a second-rate high school jock who had peaked at age seventeen, then metastasized into a third-rate high school geometry teacher. At least, looking back, he'd had the educational upbringing (in another state, in another world) to have sufficiently mastered mathematics. Today, after TV and YouTube had their way with him, he would have been fatter sooner, and the best he could have hoped for was teaching P.E., although (again, ironically) the gym teachers are in better shape today than they were then. Hopefully they are dressing better as well.

Even today, it's difficult to determine which revelation is the most unsettling: that one of our boys was casually smoking Love Boat with older, cooler guys (it was enough that, as a junior, he could hang with the senior wrestlers, the ones who walked through the locker room like Greek gods with acne), that he could dabble without fear of addiction (he could hit it and quit it, precisely what the rest of us, with our after school special sensibilities, were terrified of being unable to do), or that the assistant wrestling coach, and teacher (!), was a more than recreational user. He was crazy, and brazen, enough to loan his car, and his funds, to a group of varsity lettermen so they could cross the bridge into D.C. and get the goods. Or maybe they snuck right across town, in broad daylight, to the basketball court, near a neighborhood that was verboten even before rap music, MTV and guns were invented.

You know how this story ends: nothing happened (wait for the movie). The star athletes went off to school on scholarships and our boy, we assumed, grew out of his bad habit or, with his willing accomplices removed from the scene of the crimes, had no one to instigate further misdeeds. At least that was the way it seemed, until he stopped coming to school. Mr. X.? Long gone; no idea where, not even worth Googling. Besides, unless he found Christ or Jenny Craig, the smart money says he's currently kickin' it in his oversized coffin. Full disclosure: it's not his fault that I never understood parallelograms or gave a good shit about the Pythagorean Theorem (remember that? Me neither), but he certainly didn't do much to stem my apathy.

In any event, everyone had plans before graduation; everyone had plans for after graduation as well, but that's a different story altogether. Some of the guys were still pilfering liquor from their parents' supply—that eternal fountain of youth; some guys (the smart ones, the lucky ones) were still trying to get laid for the first time before high school ended. Allegedly, some of them succeeded. Some people were busy doing whatever it was everyone did before you could live your entire life online. The rest of us, bored and boring, not knowing enough to be careful what we wished for, felt begrudgingly grateful to stand on the ostensible threshold of adulthood. We posed for pictures, we put on the caps and gowns, and eventually, inevitably, we strolled across that stage.

But one of us wasn't there that day: our boy, who need not be named, and in the interest of fuller disclosure, was only on the periphery of my circle (mental note: that would need to be addressed in more detail for the movie), did not appear in any of the pictures. As it happened, he'd made the transition from underling to ringleader without too much difficulty, and dove headfirst down that rabbit hole. Those of us who weren't doing the things he shouldn't have been doing were just as surprised as everyone else when he vanished overnight, like one of the Communist Dissidents we had read about.

While we were mostly content to snatch the occasional beer from our parents' stash, his folks had already put him on double-secret probation for acts we never knew about. And so one day, just like that, he was gone. We later learned he'd been sent to one of those discreet asylums that only upper-middle class parents and pop stars from the cover of *People* magazine can afford.

Nobody acknowledged it as we clowned around for the cameras, but his absence was unavoidable, a blemish on our collective accountability. Our friend wasn't there, but he was with us, his story an uncomfortable reminder of how human we actually were. By not being there, he was ensuring that none of us, in the name of good dumb fun, became unwitting apprentices to the Sorcerer who preys on impressionable punks. That eternal trickster, offering a free line of credit (called Experience) that is recouped later by its alter ego (called Regret), always with interest accruing at the speed of stupid. Overflowing with post-adolescent pride, we believed we had stared down this malign specter that, with one angel-scented spell, might have sent us careening into an early adulthood. Or, even worse, toward some of these lives none of us would ever have imagined ourselves growing into.

December, 2013

BORNE CEASELESSLY INTO THE PAST

i.

When I first read John Steinbeck's *Travels with Charley: In Search of America* I was not quite old enough to drive. Still, I felt I could appreciate his somewhat elegiac ode to a world that was quickly disappearing, literally and figuratively. Literally in the sense that old things were becoming new, being torn down, refurbished, modernized; figuratively in the sense that airplanes had become more accessible (affordable) and *de rigueur* as a mode of business travel, while highways continued to get people from Point A to Point B a hell of a lot more efficiently. As a result, people who found themselves on the road were missing (intentionally) the long haul through less-traveled paths, and missing out (unintentionally?) on interacting with the places one doesn't see, and the people who populate those less-known places.

And that was in *1960*. What is there to say, over a half-century later, about the things we do and the things we don't see?

Perhaps more to the point, how many of us, given the opportunity, would be interested in an old school trek from coast to coast, stopping to sniff the sights and taste the sounds made by towns that time has forgotten? In this era of two-weeks paid vacation, where *staying-employed* is the new promotion, would anyone have the means, much less the inclination, to take an extended jaunt from coast to coast?

A leisurely circuit through several red states is, perhaps, too much of a good thing, so how about splitting the difference between automotive crawl and air-travel excursion, old school, train style? Quaint? As it happens, in 2014 you can't be whimsical enough: skinny ties and dirty martinis are back in the game, making TV watchers believe they're on to something that hasn't once again been marketed and served up on a cynical (if tasteful) platter, new school, *Mad Men* style.

Still, some types of nostalgia, let us concede, are better than others. If the archaic Old-Fashioned—which I remember only senior citizens ordering when I waited tables in the late '80s and early '90s—now doesn't seem quite so…old fashioned, less ancient fads like Zima remain mercifully buried beneath the basement of our collective consciousness, at least until some hipsters dig those cases up.

Nostalgia, in short, is arguably the most irresistible elixir. Amtrak, in an impressive grasp for relevance—or at least recognition—seems keenly aware of this, and this spring they featured a series of promotions for a writer residency program. (*Travels with Siri*, anyone?) Good press and many applications ensued: the company claims to have received over 16,000 submissions from would-be road trippers enticed by a free 2-5 day trek. However calculated this potential escapade might be, it's interesting to contemplate how many of these aspiring Steinbecks have even been on a train before. In terms of wistful or aesthetic import, it hardly matters: everyone has likely been on a plane and planes, as we know, are hardly conducive to creativity.

Then again, is *anything* conducive to creativity these days? Even when we're alone, we are never truly isolated, at least in the sense that anyone who was sentient prior to Y2K can recall or comprehend. Once the Internet became ubiquitous and we could hear the siren-songs of new e-mails announcing their arrival, we typically had to walk into the other room to read them. Now, our machines are equal parts security blanket and business imperative: we are never without access to the wide, webbed world. And for people with a penchant for introspection, or a compulsion to compose, distraction is now a full-time adversary.

One wonders what Steinbeck would make of our sociological intersection, circa 2014. Innovation has advanced to the point where just about anyone can carry a miniature computer in their pocket, and Google Maps provide virtual road trips to places we can't pronounce. *At what cost?* Steinbeck might inquire.

Have our technological toys provided us with everything but perspective, making us increasingly oblivious to the realities of people we're not familiar with? Is this one possible explanation for a country, like ours, with unlimited access to all sorts of content, being as polarized (politically, psychologically, personally) as any time in recent memory? Has the anonymity—and security—of electronic interaction made us immune to and/or intolerant of opinions we don't share?

The country Steinbeck described, that awesome, even intimidating mid-century experiment, is now overdue for resuscitation. A society still unsettled and, at best, uncertain after our recent recession has definitive answers for questions that are not being asked by the appropriate people. Highways, tunnels and bridges that once signaled our arrival as a genuine global model to be envied have become a sullen indictment of our myopic priorities.

Perhaps it's not prospective authors who most need some quiet time on a train, but the politicians who are too preoccupied by 24 hours news cycles and sound bites substituting for policies. Assuming, of course, most of these cretins consider such things; further proof that we don't manufacture cities, or elected officials, like we used to.

Since poets are likely to remain our unacknowledged legislators, here's hoping as many of them as possible are able to take a tour of the places that otherwise glisten from below when seen through the window of an airplane. Riding a train is, of course, a paltry approximation of what Steinbeck experienced, but there's something to be said for a brief, backward glance at an invisible America.

ii.

Most of the time, it's a blur of trees or water or dark (as in, when it's nighttime or when you're asleep) so the only times you tend to look are when you're aware—instinctively or otherwise—of being alongside something you're not accustomed to seeing. Driving through the ass-end of deadbeat towns, back alleys that no one remembers; the kind of real estate that seems vaguely mortified about its dirty laundry being aired to mostly upper middle class commuters.

Look: a ramshackle white building with the painted black letters *House of Flowers*. Except the only thing visible is an assortment of junked cars and worthless tires, begging the question: does anyone frequent this place? (Does anyone *sometimes* this place?) How about the name: was it, at one point, an actual house that sold flowers? Is it now? Is the name intentional or ironic? Both? Neither?

A few clicks along the tracks and there is another in a series of dirt clearings strewn with trash. There is a large green bag that had been filled with bricks. Naturally, the bricks broke through their confinement and have formed a makeshift wall around the plastic that only briefly concealed them. Rained upon, rusted, growing mud and moss, they are incapable of fulfilling their intended purpose. Kind of like certain types of people.

More things contemporary eyes don't see or understand: sprawling pipes standing three stories high, tarnished kettles with nothing left to hold inside, barbed wire encircling works in progress that had their plugs pulled by design or default. Most of these monuments are graveyards for machinery that has decayed in direct proportion to the time passed since industrious hands operated them like so many human ants.

Dozens of bridges, covering creeks and sporting graffitied coats of many colors; one big backyard that never gets raked, watered or mowed; limbs of trees at the end of the line, immobile and out of time. Warehouses, 18 wheelers, school buses, cinder block cathedrals and stolid electrical grids, genetically indifferent to the power they provide.

You lose count of the burned out buildings, all harboring grudges against the good old days, hoping for central heating. Their shattered windows have blinded them, denying a jealous glance toward the other side of town, or even across the street at their regentrified brethren. These broken properties are like the broken people who enlist in the military or throw themselves at the not-so-tender mercies of the types of churches named after obscure saints: they need to be torn down and rebuilt from the roots up. A new lease on life, an extreme makeover that only requires forfeiture of the souls they once possessed.

Through it all, the trees remain impervious; the trees adjust to the death rattles and reclamation projects—they are planted on firm ground. The trees grow, get green when Nature calls, and mostly are kind enough to offer no comment. They are uninterested in passing judgment on the concrete and the cars and the punks with their spray painted patois. Quietly and in some cases long-sufferingly, they provide cover for the plants and animals, offering window dressing for the inquisitive eyes barreling by at the speed of surround sound.

And then, of course, there are the neighborhoods. New ones and especially the old ones: Oddfellows and American Legions and taverns with Christian names. Fences and grass and street signs, an arithmetic formula found in translation. There is money here. Little league fields, churches and bicycles in repose. The rain feeds the lawns and the sun warms the driveways of four car families. The birds circle the well-stocked feeders and can't quite believe their good fortune. Even the worms are relieved to burrow in safer soil, praying that once they are eaten and shat out they can fertilize the earth they once called home.

This is the calm calculus of civilization, just out of earshot from the neglected intersections that choke and sigh but no longer scream. Sometimes docile dogs and curious cats sneak past their security gates and wander too close to a reality their caretakers keep them from. They sniff the fear and sense the dread and understand the choice was never theirs to make. The wise ones, inherently aware of the whim that separates fate from fortune, run safely back to masters who speak a language they've learned to understand.

July, 2014

THE PROBLEM WITH THE HOMELESS PROBLEM

There is a man who sits near the pumps at the gas station I drive by each day. The man is very obviously from somewhere else and has about him a certain look—the meek, awestruck eyes, the apprehensive gestures—that indicts him as someone who speaks little if any English. A *stranger.*

He remains respectfully distant from the customers—who incessantly fill their tanks, like bees returning to the nest before heeding the urgency of their instinctual obligations—but near enough to the action to remain in plain view. He sells flowers. Actually, he doesn't seem to *sell* anything; he pretty much sits there, on an upturned milk crate, often from early morning until well in the evening, after the rest of the weary warriors have commuted past him, home from work and their worries of the wicked world. He silently plies his wares, content to play his part in the charade: he is not accomplishing much, he is begging, and the milk crate and collection of fading flowers at his feet communicate an inexpressible anguish. *Please help me*, his unscrubbed face, his unlaced sneakers, his oversized slacks, his filthy, fidgeting fingers—everything but his voice—all ask, saying what he cannot, and will not, say for himself.

***

Hey brother, can you spare a life, the woman moving past me does not say.

I'm in too much of a hurry to stop (like always, like everyone else getting on and off the subway), but there is something so familiar about her that I'm compelled, despite everything I've learned, to pause and look back: she is still there, off to the side, shabbily clad, immediately recognizable by her contrast to everyone around her; she wants to approach one of these businessmen, but all of them are walking too fast, too deliberately, too purposefully. Getting from Point A to Point B so we can get paid.

Automatically, the doors move aside and sweltering air earnestly greets everyone headed its way. It takes about five seconds (as always) to feel the heat and then the money dread: if it weren't for the money, it wouldn't take much—in a strange city, lost, alone. Broke. That's how shit like starvation and sleeping on grates gets started. Quiet in the corners, huddled under bridges, working the frenzied crowd for a friendly face, hoping for the handout that never comes.

I don't have any lives to spare, but I'll dig deeper and give 'til it hurts.

This hurts me more than it hurts you, I don't say.

***

Who *was* he?

I think the same question each time I see him (once a week, sometimes more, occasionally double-shifts: the same man in the same spot, holding the same sign that tells everyone who he is, now—prompting the question: who did he used to be, at some point in the past?) at the intersection he has stood at for several months now. The cardboard sign he holds both question and answer: Homeless veteran (the explanation), can you put some pocket change in this plastic cup (the question). The sign says he is a veteran. Okay. And even if he isn't actually a veteran, he has been homeless long enough to be a veteran; or if he is not actually homeless, he has been acting the part long enough to earn the title. Either way, it is time for a promotion.

And so, I think, this is the problem with the homeless problem: it wasn't (some of us learn—too late) the ones who hustled or even approached you who were down and out; they were the ardent ones, half the time they weren't even *homeless*; it is the ones you never see, even when they're sprawled on the concrete right beside you, the ones who *are* down, the ones who *are* out, the ones who have nothing to ask for, nothing to say, nothing to do except wait, sit it out until time or the whiter man's burden delivers them that eventual, inevitable verdict. It was the ones you could afford *not* to be afraid of, the ones who could not even hurt themselves, because they'd already dug as deep inside as their ashen fingers could reach, the ones too dead to tear out their hearts, but not dead enough to unloose their souls, the ones who learned (too late) that death was only impatient for the fools who failed to acknowledge it, it had all the time in the world for those who the world owed nothing except the decency of an overdue release.

Could that be me?

A primal foreboding, an ancient fear. Who knew how it happened, who could make sense of it? And yet. These people do not wake up one random morning, on the streets and out of their minds. Or do they? If you believed the signs the man on the corner held, the government did this to him—and could do it to anyone else: that was his message, his mission.

The problem with the homeless problem is that these people who don't see you and can't see themselves are all chasing something they can no longer name: memories. Or, even worse, it is the memories that are chasing them, speaking in tongues they long ago ceased to understand.

***

A memory:

Newark Airport. That shithole. A place has to be exceptionally beautiful, appalling, or incomprehensibly pointless in order to be easily remembered years after a brief visit.

When I was a kid, (I couldn't have been much older than ten) my father and I had a layover in Newark Airport. Even then, I was perceptive enough to understand that this was no place I ever needed to return voluntarily.

An unassuming older man (at any rate, he was noticeably older than my old man, which made him *old*) sat in one of those impossibly plain plastic chairs, with his pants leg rolled up. It wasn't until we got closer that I realized two things: he was alone, and he was scratching at a series of scabs on his shin. For some reason he looked our way at the moment we passed him, and after sizing us up, he stood and amiably approached my father.

"Sir, did you need someone to help you and your son carry your bags?"

"No thanks, we're okay," my pops replied, looking ahead and picking up the pace.

The man was persistent. In the space of fifteen seconds—my father denied him three times—my emotions slid from the appreciation of possibly having someone carry my suitcase for me, to the vague, uneasy suspicion that my father was being somehow rude, a *jerk*, to the unsettling awareness of recognition. I sensed something I'd seen plenty of, but never before in any person older than myself: fear. I saw it in his eyes, and felt it in my insides.

As we walked away my old man waited until we were at a charitable distance, then looked at me meaningfully and offered the somber assertion: *That's as low as you can go*. I asked him to elaborate, as was my style, and he was either unwilling or unable to add anything to his observation, as was his style. It wasn't that I didn't understand what my father was saying, I understood him perfectly. It was because I understood him that I needed him to say more, to talk to me a little longer about it, about *anything*, anything to interrupt that silence and the sudden thoughts that accompanied it.

***

It's easy to believe that people like this exist for our sakes: they are dying lessons on how not to live, warnings of what *could* happen if you weren't careful and found yourself scratching at scabs in the world's ugliest airport. Or enlist, get used up and ask not what your country can do for you, because you've already received the answer. We forget, or we don't allow ourselves to entertain the idea, that these people have histories; that these shadows and signposts don't happen to serve a purpose for anyone else; they were once actual people themselves.

I realize, now, my father was wrong about one thing. That's not as low as you can go. You can go lower, a whole lot lower. But perhaps it's more disturbing to see the ones that are on the way down, it's somehow easier to accept the ones at the bottom of the ocean; it's the ones who are sinking, who are still within reach, who are drowning noisily in front of you, who sometimes have the temerity to ask you to hold out a hand. These are the ones we can scarcely tolerate, because every so often we look at them and see ourselves.

November, 2014

OVER/UNDER THE VOLCANO

I still have hangovers, thank God.

Everyone who has known an alcoholic knows that as soon as you stop feeling the pain, it's because you are no longer feeling the pain; you are no longer feeling much of anything.

So, I welcome the horrors of the digital cock crowing in my ear at an uncalled for hour, am grateful for the flaming phlegm in my throat, the snakes chasing their tails through my sinuses, the smoke stuck behind my eyelids, the shards of glass in my gut, and the special ring of hell circling my head. Because if it weren't for those handful of my least favorite things, I'd know I had some serious problems.

All of us can think of a friend whose father (or mother for that matter), we came to understand, was in an entirely different league when it came to the science of cirrhosis. The man who falls asleep fully clothed with a snifter balanced over his balls, then up and out the door before sunrise—like the rest of the inverted vampires who do their dirty work during the day in three piece suits. Maybe it was a martini at lunch, or several cigarettes an hour to take the edge off. Whatever it was, whatever it took, they always made it out, and they always came back, for the family and to the refrigerator, filled with the best friends anyone can afford.

Our friends' fathers came of age in the bad old days that fight it out, for posterity, in the pages of books, uneasy memories and the wishful thinking of TV reruns: the '50s. These are men who have never opened a bottle of wine and have no use for imported beer, men who actually have *rye* in their liquor cabinets—who still have liquor cabinets for that matter. These are men who were raised by men that never considered church or sick-days optional, and the only thing they disliked more than strangers was their neighbors. Men who didn't believe in diseases and didn't drink to escape so much as to remind themselves exactly what they never had a chance to become.

Theirs was an alcoholism that did not involve happy hours and karaoke contests; theirs was a sit down with the radio and a whiskey sour, a refill with dinner and one before, during and after the ballgame. Or maybe they'd mow the lawn to liven things up, tinker under the hood of a car that had decades to go before it could become a classic. Or perhaps friends would come over to play cards. Sometimes a second bottle would get broken out. This was a slow burn of similar nights: stiff upper lips, the sun setting on boys playing baseball, mothers sitting on the couch watching TVs families did not yet own, of forced smiles battling bottled tears in the bottom of a coffee mug, of amphetamines and affairs, overhead fans and undernourished kids, of evening papers and a creeping conviction that there is no God, of poets unable to make art out of the mess they'd made of their lives.

It was a hard time where people did not live happily ever after, if they ever lived at all. It was a time, in other words, not unlike our own.

***

When I lucked into my first so-called real job I got in the habit of referring to the time—admittedly too long—spent in the service industry as the *bad old days*. It wasn't because I had no fun (I did) or that I thought there was any future in it (I didn't). It wasn't that I felt joining the corporate world (grad students and waiters refer to it as the real world) was any type of instant ticket to peace or fulfillment. But it did remove one from the front lines of a scene with too many lives on the fast track to nowhere. Most people there fail to understand where they are, and where they are not going.

And when I think of the place some people never find a way to leave, it makes me remember one person in particular. More than the implicit slights suffered or the stalled potential each day I strapped on an apron, when I think about what I could never afford to lose, I think of Izzy. That, of course, was not his real name, but it was what everyone called him. When he and I first met I would have sworn he was in his forties, but in fact he had only recently turned mid-thirty-something. Not old in the nine-to-five arena but ancient in the restaurant business. A lifer who had never been promoted to general manager, he was a satellite drifting through the soiled orbit of a franchised business. He was never handed his own place to run, and he seemed entirely satisfied with that arrangement. In fact, as I came to see for myself, he counted on being an assistant behind the scenes, the hardened soldier who could close up shop and count the checks. We were often the last two left, hours after the final customer had called a cab or rolled the DWI dice. After a shift that started at 4 PM Izzy would set up camp in the sweltering office in the back of the kitchen, going about the unexciting but excuses-free business of book-keeping.

When Izzy showed up for his shift the following afternoon he always looked like someone had scraped him off the bottom of a greasy skillet. Red eyes blurred, his neck shrieking in silent agony from the burn of a blunt razor, the cigarettes and coffee escaping in sluggish waves from every inch of his sagging skin. Head bowed not in deference but disdain of the daylight; he could scarcely formulate the words being signaled from bruised brain to long-suffering lips. He would step up to the bar, shake his head and ask me to call him an ambulance. Then he'd disappear into the men's room for a minute or two, emerging like a televangelist with a badly ironed shirt. He could barely tie his shoe, but after his magic act in the crapper he would be ready to plate a thousand entrees and run laps around the building in his wingtips (managers who wear comfortable shoes are never taken seriously, but they don't realize until it's too late it's not because of the shoes).

For the next eight-to-ten hours, in between return trips to the powder room (occasionally he may have even used the toilet); Izzy was constant, awkward motion. All the waiters were in awe of him and all the waitresses were repulsed by him (especially the ones he had slept with). Izzy could sweat out more alcohol in a single shift than most of us could drink in an entire weekend, and he never missed a day of work during the two years I knew him. Even if you didn't catch him ducking into the bathroom you always knew he had recently refueled because he would suck his teeth like someone trying to extract snake venom. The lip smacking and teeth licking were, to me, the black and blue collar stage of development between rock star and burnout, the line so many in the service industry straddle before they get out or go under.

None of this fazed me, which isn't to say it was not unsettling, but grunts in the trench don't offer advice to their sergeants, so I mainly focused on my own unsavory habits. But I could never figure out how Izzy, when he retreated to the office each night to match receipts, guest checks and time sheets, was able to polish off an entire bottle of peppermint schnapps. When he finally went home, closer to sunrise than midnight, that bottle he took back with him would always be empty. At first I figured he was trying to impress or even intimidate me (full success on both fronts), but after months of the same scenario, I had no choice but to acknowledge that his appetites and obsessions had, at some point, evolved from unhealthy to superhuman. That bottle was not something he wanted, and was no longer something he needed; it was simply something that he *required*, along with the bathroom breaks and the air his lungs inhaled. I worked dozens of shifts where I didn't see him eat a scrap of food, but he never went into that office without his bottle of schnapps. And at least once a week he'd arrive at work with fresh bottles he kept to stock the bar. I could never fathom the physics, or biology (or algebra) that enabled a man to drain a fifth each evening and still function, but I also learned the hard way in high school that some subjects would, for me, remain forever mysterious.

By the time he took his transfer to the next location (never a demotion but never an advancement) he looked like he could collect social security. How long can that lifestyle sustain itself? I asked myself, then, and ponder it now. Where is Izzy today? Is he in an assisted living facility somewhere, or at the bottom of a river? Will I find him patrolling an intersection one night, not embarrassed to ask for tips after all these years? Or did he take the hard way out and start a family; his bad habits replaced by baby bottles, dirty diapers and manicured lawns? Or most likely and equally unsettling: has he subscribed to an altogether different sort of salvation, whacked out of his skull with sobriety?

November, 2015

O'CONNOR AND COLTRANE: SAINTS OF AMERICAN ART

I never, until this year, made the explicit connection between John Coltrane and Flannery O'Connor.

Why should I have?

One was an introverted white woman, a southern writer who tackled the Big Questions with a mordant élan and irony that's seldom been surpassed. In her short stories, the themes of identity, religion and salvation get interrogated by and through a series of characters that are, by turns, innocent, evil and grotesque. Above all, they are fallible: whatever their station in life, the issue that obsessed O'Connor was Grace and whether or not we could get good with God, regardless of where He placed us or what He put in our pathway.

The other was a quiet but prolific black saxophonist, a man born in North Carolina who migrated to the cultural center of the musical universe, New York City, where he then participated in some of the most beloved recordings of the '50s and '60s. In his songs, the quest was salvation through music: initially celebrated for his famous "sheets of sound", Coltrane continued to expand and grow, incorporating Eastern elements and extended improvisations. His live performances became legendary endurance tests, for the audience more than the performer. Coltrane was restless, but not because he was otherwise preoccupied or tortured; indeed he was the rarest of artistic breeds: focused and serene, uncomfortable only when he was unable to practice. By all accounts, his dedication to his craft remains unrivaled.

As Coltrane's masterwork, *A Love Supreme,* celebrates its fiftieth anniversary in 2015 (and has just been reissued, again, with never-before heard material), and I finally found the time to read

O'Connor's journal entries, collected as *A Prayer Journal* (first released in late 2013), the question became: how could I *not* have made the connection between these two icons?

While reading (and then re-reading) *A Prayer Journal*, which obliged me to revisit (again) O'Connor's selected prose, best or most easily found in *Mystery and Manners*, I could not stop thinking about Coltrane in general, *A Love Supreme* in particular. Considering them side by side, I was struck by one thing above all: these were artists who, due to circumstances as well as compulsion(s), cultivated an almost monastic approach to their art. Perhaps because illness claimed both of them entirely too soon (Coltrane died of cancer in '67, aged 41; O'Connor of lupus in '64, aged 39) theirs is a kinship forged in tragedy. Perhaps because they are both undisputed masters of their respective crafts who lived during roughly the same era it's easier to associate them. But it's their aesthetic sensibility that links them in ways few other artists of any genre can claim.

ii.

One need not be intimately familiar with O'Connor's oeuvre to appreciate the exceedingly brief but extraordinary—and revealing—meditations contained in *A Prayer Journal*. Of course, anyone who has read, and savored her work will find the material, written in 1946 and 1947 while she was studying at the University of Iowa's Writer's Workshop, at once affirming and revelatory.

O'Connor's unwavering allegiance to her craft leaves little to the imagination: she wrote, she talked about writing, she thought about writing and she wrote about writing. Allegedly, she ate and slept on occasion. "In my stories is where I live," she said, a statement applicable on a variety of levels. And so, the people who stand to be fascinated by this distinctly uneventful life are the very people who might be enlightened by reading about it: writers. O'Connor's monk-like commitment to her vocation could and should be a study guide for all aspiring scribblers. Never mind that dedication like hers is probably impossible to imitate today because of all the noise—electronic and digital—distracting us. There's also the fact that her work is inimitable: the style; the substance; the entire package is pretty much unparalleled in American letters.

I tend to feel uncomfortable throwing the *G* word around, but if any American writer of the last century could be called a genius, O'Connor is near the top of the short list. She didn't manage to write the great American novel (though she may well have, had she been given even a few more years), but her best collected stories go toe-to-toe with any of the great white males (and females for that matter). She also happened to approach perfection on at least three occasions, with "Revelation", "Everything That Rises Must Converge" and "A Good Man Is Hard To Find". It's the last of these three that most people know; like Beethoven's Fifth and the ceiling of the Sistine Chapel, its ubiquity tends to diminish its actual import. As a remarkable point of fact, it's even better than most people realize (and most people, if for no other reason than that they are told, recognize these things as immortal).

What O'Connor manages to do, in less than twenty pages, with "A Good Man Is Hard To Find" is lay bare the essence of what Dostoyevsky and, to a lesser extent, Tolstoy grappled with in their biggest (and sometimes bloated) novels: the nature of man, the existence of God, the possibility of Grace and the symbiotic tension between violence and love. When The Misfit declares (ironically, truthfully) "It's no real pleasure in life", he is (O'Connor is) succinctly expressing our fundamental philosophical and literary dilemma, post-Descartes. Beyond whether God exists (Tolstoy) or why God torments us (Dostoyevsky), and right to the darkened heart of the matter: we may betray God, but God betrayed us first.

As a reader and especially a writer, one can learn a great deal by studying her stories. Has any other writer so consistently applied mechanical precision with such emotional heft? Has any other author wrestled with the so-called big issues without using stick figures or preachy didactics? Take "Revelation", for instance: O'Connor fits notions of class, the dilemmas of southern identity, religious fervor, old-school bigotry and redemption into one story. In fact, she pretty much pulls it off on a single page (and that last page not only invokes, but obliges the use of such otherwise unforgivable words as "haunting", "chilling" and "moving"). More, the concluding image of "a vast horde of souls rumbling toward heaven" that includes the disenfranchised leading a troop of so-called respectable citizens—who of course have assumed their station by luck of the biological draw—whose "virtues were being burned away", might achieve the impossible, serving as an allegory to satisfy both the devoted and the faithless. Consider that. This type of writing, needless to say, is inspiring but is also intimidating. My initial (and in many cases, ongoing) reaction to reading an O'Connor story is to ask, in awe, *How did she do that?*

Yet aside from the singular example she sets, what should (can) one, living today, take from her hermetic life style in terms of practical application? Probably the same thing one might take from any worthwhile practitioner: whatever one can. It's that simple, and it's that unfathomable. For starters, one should be heartened (or, more likely, devastated) by the fact that even our greatest artists often struggle, and realize that the life they embark upon is likely to be painful and unprofitable. "What first stuns the young writer emerging from college," she wrote in 1948, "is that there is no clear-cut road for him to travel on. He must chop a path in the wilderness of his own soul; a disheartening process, lifelong and lonesome."

In her journal, she implored God to "give me the courage to stand the pain to get to the grace." O'Connor was not granted nearly the time she needed—or deserved—to continue perfecting her craft. But we are all fortunate she had the years, not to mention the fortitude and faith, to leave behind her unique, inexhaustible bounty. Her work is like her life: full of beauty, full of pain.

iii.

For those whose definition of genius is either too encompassing or excessively narrow, John Coltrane poses no problems: there isn't anyone who knows anything about music (in general) and jazz (in particular) who would contest that he's among the most prominent, impressive and influential artists to ever master an instrument. Furthermore, to put Coltrane and the skills he developed in their simplest perspective, it might be suggested that no one has ever done anything as well as Coltrane played the saxophone. Plus, he was an exceptionally gifted composer and bandleader and, by all accounts, he was a generous and gentle human being, as well. All of which is to say, if there is anyone worthy of celebration in our contemporary American Idol Apocalypse, Coltrane should serve as both antidote and inspiration.

Coltrane's prime years, the decade between 1957 and 1967, seem concise enough by typical human and even artistic standards. However, he recorded so much and went through so many profound changes, it's near impossible to convey the scope of his achievements—and impact. Early on, it was apparent that Coltrane pursued his dream with an intensity bordering on obsession. "He attacked his (musical) problems," Jimmy Heath once recalled. "He zoomed in until he solved it." Coltrane quickly but methodically cultivated an unsurpassed proficiency, and then he kept pushing. Like Charles Mingus and Dizzy Gillespie (and many others), Coltrane initially emulated the bebop progenitor Charlie Parker and listened to western classical music, especially the work of Stravinsky. Even in his formative years, though, Coltrane was already resisting the accepted (and acceptable) limitations and straining to explore the possibilities of his instrument.

It's worth quoting, in full, these observations by drummer Rashied Ali, (from an interview with Howard Mandel) who played with Coltrane in the last years of his life.

He never stopped playing. When I used to go to hear 'Trane, he would always be playing. He would be playing in his dressing room. He would be playing before he got to me. Just like a fighter would warm up in the dressing room, he'd come out in the ring and he'd be sweating from warming up, he would do the same thing in the dressing room. He would just play and play and play. He would break a sweat in the dressing room and then when he would come out on the bandstand, he had all that — I don't know where he got that energy from. He was relentless.

He always had an instrument in his hand. He was always playing something. He was always trying to be better than he was and it seemed like, you know, how could he get better? How could he do anything better than that, than what he's done already? And after playing all these years with all these different people…the man still had a vision that he could be better than he was and he was still practicing.

Of course, Coltrane's music was not universally embraced during the final years he was able to record and play. His solos became longer and (much) more intense, yet no matter how many listeners he alienated, it was apparent that in order to push the audience, he first had to push himself. Roscoe Mitchell, commenting on this spiritual searching, has likened Coltrane's later music to what he witnessed in churches growing up, with people transporting into religious trances. This—the music and the explanation—is where more than a few draw the line; it's just too *out there*; too much for the human ear. Coltrane contained multitudes, but his music, after 1964, was often uncontainable.

Coltrane knew where he was going, however, even if he couldn't quite define what he was looking for. His wife Alice remarked that Coltrane was following a "progression toward higher spiritual realization…and development." That type of sentiment can, and perhaps should, make people wary, but with Coltrane it was no pose, and this was no joke.

It was all over far too quickly. As is too often the case with our greatest artists, Coltrane fell ill and passed away long before his time should have come. It scarcely computes, even now, that the man making the music he recorded in early 1967 (particularly the shattering if cathartic *Interstellar Space*) was months from losing a battle with cancer. Where he would have headed had he lived is truly difficult to imagine. It remains more than a little startling, to consider the growth and refinement he demonstrated every few years, commencing in the mid-to-late '50s. Where he might have gone next is anyone's guess, but it's also safe to surmise that he took his instrument, and music, as far as anyone possibly could.

To understand the trajectory that took Coltrane from sheets of sound to *A Love Supreme*, it's instructive to consider his composition "Alabama", recorded in 1963. Inspired by the disgraceful 16th Street Baptist Church bombing, Coltrane said of his elegy: "It represents, musically, something that I saw down there translated into music from inside me." It is one of his enduring and devastating performances wherein Coltrane, already considered amongst jazz music's most emotional and sensitive players, manages to articulate the grief and the rage the occasion called for. A deeply spiritual man, Coltrane conveys the immutable senselessness of violence instigated by ignorance, but also hints at the redemption of peaceful power through unified awareness. As only he could, Coltrane crafts a solo that is angry, somber, and somehow hopeful; a subdued epitaph for the innocent dead, but also a rallying cry for the not-so-innocent bystanders who needed to join the cause. The Alabama bombing was a tipping point in the civil rights movement, and Coltrane captured that moment where confusion and rage inspired an outpouring of solidarity.

Another quote from O'Connor: "Dear God please help me to be an artist, please let it lead to you." It's clear that, for O'Connor, the journey was as important as the destination: being a good Catholic, she not only accepted that she'd have to suffer, she expected it. Coltrane's suffering, for some time, involved the self-imposed heroin addiction he finally kicked in 1957 (years of alcohol abuse undoubtedly contributed to his eventual liver cancer). The liner notes to *A Love Supreme*, written by Coltrane and addressed to the audience (Dear Listener, they begin) leave little doubt what the album was "about" and exactly what inspired its creation—and its creator:

ALL PRAISE BE TO GOD TO WHOM ALL PRAISE IS DUE. Let us pursue Him in the righteous path. Yes it is true; "seek and ye shall find." Only through Him can we know the most wondrous bequeathal. During the year 1957, I experienced, by the grace of God, a spiritual awakening which was to lead me to a richer, fuller, more productive life. At that time, in gratitude, I humbly asked to be given the means and privilege to make others happy through music.

It might be suggested we've never seen, in modern art, more abundant or eloquent evidence of Art leading to God than *A Love Supreme*. (And, if we can collectively embrace the notion that "God is Love", no ecclesiastical concerns need sully the discussion.) It serves as a consecration of sorts, a personal yet intensely spiritual expression: finally, Coltrane was able to filter all that intensity into a perfect chalice, never before, or after, was his vision so focused yet peaceful. The music—and message—is a force of nature the listener must let wash over them, while repeated listens will refresh and renew.

O'Connor wanted to jolt you with the violent shock of recognition, and achieve some type of artistic if not spiritual consecration; Coltrane wanted to transcend the insanity altogether, altering consciousness through a profoundly moving colloquy. That he attempted this is remarkable; that he was able to achieve it remains miraculous.

December, 2015

TWO: MUSIC

FOREVER NEVER CHANGES: REMEMBERING ARTHUR LEE

It's equal parts ironic and appropriate that Syd Barrett and Arthur Lee, two avatars of what we recall—mostly with fondness—as the Summer of Love, have gone on to that great gig in the sky within a month of each other this summer. Of course, any discussion of 1967 must begin and end with the Beatles: As has been well documented, *Sgt. Pepper's Lonely Hearts Club Band* moved the avant-garde to the mainstream at a time when our culture was perhaps most open to receiving it. All of a sudden, albums could—and quickly did—become statements, and rock music was elevated to the status of art seemingly overnight. So while *Sgt. Pepper* is the alpha and omega, it is as significant for the possibilities it created for others as for its own sake.

But as is always the case, the most interesting and enduring creations occur in the margins. Pink Floyd, darlings of the burgeoning London underground, arrived at Abbey Road studios in early 1967 and began recording their debut *Piper at the Gates of Dawn* at the same time the Fab Four were assembling the sonic puzzle pieces of *Sgt. Pepper.* Both masterpieces arrived in time to describe and define the Summer of Love, or at least its distinctly British component. Across the pond, another debut helped capture the sounds of that time: The Doors were to Los Angeles what Pink Floyd was to London, a lean and hungry band that had taken the time to cultivate a cult following and had a breakthrough single ("See Emily Play" and "Light My Fire", respectively) that shot them into the stratosphere. But the band that Jim Morrison hoped to emulate was the then heavyweight champion of the L.A. scene: Love, led by Arthur Lee, who was also a mentor to a young guitarist named Jimi Hendrix.

For a variety of reasons, some typical, some inexplicable, Love seemed to implode just as their ship was set to sail, and they never quite fulfilled their limitless and possibly unparalleled potential. While other bands made history during the Summer of Love, Love was busy living *through* incendiary months, and on the album that resulted, *Forever Changes,* Lee documented in real time and in living color the Daily Planet of the hippie scene, or at least its underbelly—which is perhaps the same thing. In other words, the album stands as the most accurate American version of the era, post Monterey and Haight-Ashbury.

Forever Changes failed to connect, though, and the band disintegrated shortly after its completion, with Lee soldiering on in increasing obscurity, his moment come and gone. How then, has his magnum opus, so insufficiently received, managed to inspire such loyalty and enchantment over the decades among its admirers? For starters, it is worthy of repeated listens; it deepens and intensifies well after you've made the initial connection. (Quick, when is the last time you listened to *Sgt. Pepper* all the way through? How deep do "Being for the Benefit of Mr. Kite" or "Lovely Rita" seem?) Although none of the songs on *Forever Changes* crept onto the paisley playground of its time, it is impossible to quibble with the confident brilliance of miniature gems like "Andmoreagain" or "The Good Humor Man He Sees Everything Like This", which showcase Lee's immutable gift: his voice, which had an almost extraordinary sensitivity and authority.

Sound like a contradiction? That's the genius of Arthur Lee, plainly put. For all his quirks and contradictions, Lee was a taskmaster in the studio. Listen to the demo version of "The Good Humor Man" and compare the sparse acoustic take with what the song would become with understated brass and strings, and the longing in Lee's delivery. If you don't get it, *Forever Changes* will never speak to you.

But it's not enough (nor should it be) to merely gesture toward an art work's ineffable qualities. What makes *Forever Changes* indelible is first and foremost its unmistakable honesty. The Los Angeles streets that broiled with heat and inspiration brought intimations of a severity largely absent from the rose-colored commentary that emerged from San Francisco. The songs on *Forever Changes* have a soul and sly élan that most of Love's contemporaries were incapable of conjuring. Lee described what he saw with deceptively simple, disarmingly straightforward lyrics that always evoked the feelings of an outsider. Lee, a black man, recognized what Chris Rock would later articulate, that no matter how many people profess to admire and envy you, few, if any, white folks would choose to trade places with you. This keeps the distance between what should be and what is foremost in one's mind; no amount of applause or plaudits or utopian hippie thinking can compensate for that disparity.

But the sad staying power of his somber vision is unassailable. The music on *Forever Changes* is by no means morose, though the merciful scarcity of saccharine free-love fantasia augments its staying power. Part of the album's perverse charm lies in its contradictions. For instance, it's most assured and ebullient songs are belied by Lee's lyrics. On this album, Lee—like Barrett on *Piper*—displays an uncanny facility for concision, capturing a larger truth somehow by *not* quite saying it. Lee's audacity, at 22, in employing non sequiturs creates an unfiltered vision, revealing a lack of cynicism and trust in his abilities as well as those of his listeners. "And I'm wrapped in my armor / But my things are material. / And I'm lost in confusions / 'Cause my things are material" The lines may not make immediate sense, but *Forever Changes* is a treatise from the trenches, capturing the dodgy promise that anything is possible. The Summer of Love, after all, was the American Dream redux, replacing all that boring humility, hard work and redemption of the Horatio Alger story with a strategically ingested tab of acid.

Lee not only captured what he saw on the street, he anticipated the darkness around the corner, so it's understandable that the more starry-eyed in his audience weren't trying to pick up what he was putting down. Though *Forever Changes* doesn't conform to the nostalgic picture of Summer of Love as drug-fueled ecstasy without consequences, Lee managed to relate the less sexy banality of the morning after before most hippies even knew what was about to hit them. You never know when you might awaken from your reverie with snot caked against your pants, as Lee sardonically sings about in "Live & Let Live". Lee depicts the big high and the lesser lows—or what the more pragmatic among us might call actual life. And it is this gray middle ground between compromise and revolution that provides *Forever Changes* its appeal. If it's hot or you're hungry or you have the rest of your life to sort out, then a concert or a hit record or the sudden insight to see through the charade may not be enough to get you safely to the other side. "All you need is love / love is all you need." Okay. "The news today will be the movies for tomorrow"? Ouch.

Stop and think about that, from Love's "A House Is Not a Motel." That could well be the most succinct—not to mention prophetic—articulation of the so-called counterculture, circa 1967. Youth protest at Vietnam any made-for-TV melodrama or sentimental movie soundtrack sprung from the money-making minds of Madison Avenue. It's pretty safe to conclude that the times aren't a changin'. "And for everyone who thinks that life is just a game/Do you like the part you're playing?" This question, from the optimistically named "You Set the Scene," is directed at the listener as much as the artist, and Lee's answers, which end the album, reveal he had no intention of turning his back on the promised land, even as it splintered into a billion bad trips. The full orchestral freak out that concludes the album and ushers it into immortality has a classic literary flourish, bringing full circle the motifs introduced with the innovative trumpet stylings that accompany the opening track, "Alone Again Or".

"The Red Telephone," which ends side one, is the album's centerpiece; its brooding, apocalyptic imagery captures that three-month moment of 1967, while remaining possibly more applicable to the here and now: "They're locking them up today; they're throwing away the key, / I wonder who it'll be tomorrow, you or me?" Those creepy chanted lines were prophetic, not only when you consider that Lee, who lived to be neither wealthy nor white, ended up imprisoned in the mid-1990s as a result of his own recklessness as well as California's controversial third-strike laws. The lyrics anticipate the aftermath awaiting Timothy Leary's disciples, those that ingested and distributed the chemical vehicles to Valhalla, who would end up pulling harder time than our white-collar charlatans face for fleecing employees and the country out of millions of dollars. The lines are also a commentary on Americans acting un-American, looking back to the internments of Japanese citizens and forecasting the so-called enemy combatants rotting behind bars without formal charges or legal counsel. I read the news today, oh boy. As Lee sings in the same song, "Sometimes I deal with numbers, / And if you want to count me: Count me out."

If Arthur Lee had been savvy enough to pull the businesslike burn out or the fortuitous fade away or—cleverest career move of all—die in some spectacular fashion in, say, early '68, it would be safe to bet that *Forever Changes* could have become a central part of the collective consciousness. That is the only rite of passage we ask of our best artists: Die so we can wake up and get around to appreciating what you accomplished. It's what we talk about when we talk about the lack of love and the fact that forever never changes. Hopefully, Arthur and his very American dream now have that chance, for all the right reasons.

August, 2006

ROKY ERICKSON: THIRTEEN WAYS OF LOOKING AT A GENIUS

Preface

You're Gonna Miss Me is an instant classic and will likely be regarded as essential years from now. Two critical things it has going for it: one, its subject, Roky Erickson, is a filmmaker's fantasy—the type of character who could never be adequately fictionalized because the story outstrips imagination, and two, instead of being overwhelmed by the material or trying to either sensationalize or sterilize it, director Keven McAlester, by simply standing in the right places at the right times, captures success, insanity, disintegration and redemption. It's almost impossible to imagine the viewer coming away from this documentary without a better understanding of popular music, mental illness, frailty and faith. It's likely viewers will better comprehend something about themselves, as well. What else could one ask for?

I. Pictures (Leave Your Body Behind)

There are a handful of artistic archetypes we know and love—or loathe—in cinema, literature, and music, especially rock 'n' roll music. To take just a sampling of some of the more obvious ones, there is the cautionary tale (see Keith Moon); the tragic hero case study (see Jimi Hendrix); the unrecognized master (see Shuggie Otis); the posthumously recognized master (see Nick Drake); the redemption song (see Brian Wilson), et cetera. And yet, has there ever been an individual who encompasses several of the above, creating an entirely unique category? Yes: Roky Erickson. Who? Exactly. Roky Erickson is indeed many things, all at once. The greatest singer not many people have ever heard. The saddest could-have-been-a-contender parable in the annals of rock. An authentic icon who, while written off even by those who at one time followed him, attracted artists such as R.E.M., ZZ Top, Julian Cope and The Jesus and Mary Chain to take part in the excellent 1990 tribute album *Where The Pyramid Meets The Eye* .

So, who was Roky Erickson? Envision a psychedelic era band that combined the darker energy of Love and The Doors with the bluesy kitchen sink vocal assault of Janis Joplin, alongside the musical proficiency of The Yardbirds or The Mothers of Invention. That amalgamation begins to approximate what the 13th Floor Elevators, from Austin Texas, sounded like before the Summer of Love. When they eventually (inevitably) headed up the coast toward the burgeoning Bay Area scene in 1966, they blew the minds, so to speak, of many of the groups who were still cultivating a more mellow, folk-based sound. The Elevators were heavier, edgier and more exotic, drawing on an electric blues foundation that at once assimilated the aggression of The Who and the more cerebral introspection of Dylan. It was anything but a simple, hit-seeking sound, yet their first album yielded a song, "You're Gonna Miss Me"—featuring the full range of Erickson's vocals and the trademark electric jug playing of Tommy Hall—that caused some excitement, reaching #55 on the charts.

Much like seemingly everyone else on the accelerating edge of the rock scene, Erickson found stimulation, solace and eventually (inevitably) distraction via the LSD he ingested like lemon drops. Along with his better-known acid casualty compatriots Syd Barrett and Brian Wilson, Erickson fell to earth. Chronic behavioral and legal issues ensued. Unlike Wilson, who headed for the relative security of his sandbox, and Barrett, who — after turning on and tuning in — dropped out entirely and disengaged from the outside world, Erickson returned to Austin and found himself the target of an overly enthusiastic police department anxious to make an example out of him. Popped for possession of marijuana joint and facing the possibility of serious jail time, Erickson's lawyer proposed the dubious stratagem of pleading insanity, which led to an eventual confinement in Rusk State Hospital for the Criminally Insane. He remained there for three years.

II. Roller Coaster

You're Gonna Miss Me traces the early adventures that led Roky to Rusk, and fills in the following decades, which have mostly been a tragic void for all but the most dedicated fans. Erickson may have been gone, but he was far from forgotten, as evidenced by the commentary provided by an impressively disparate array of musicians, including Billy Gibbons (of Texas legends ZZ Top), Patti Smith, Thurston Moore (Sonic Youth) and Gibby Haynes (Butthole Surfers). It is a documentary that unfolds like a mystery story, each anecdote and interview revealing another layer that helps explain who he was, who he became, and who he is now.

III. Slip Inside This House

Seminal scene number one: Roky Erickson, now under the exclusive care of his mother back in Texas (circa 1999), enters his modest and messy apartment. He turns on the radio. Then he turns on a second radio. Then he turns on a television, and another. Then he turns on an electric Casio piano. Eventually he has plugged in or turned on a beehive of competing sounds; the room is a cacophony of random stimulation. He puts on a pair of sunglasses and announces in a soft voice (barely audible above the chaos) "Okay, I'm gonna lay down now." His mother, who had presumably seen it all before, remarks matter-of-factly: "He falls asleep with all that stuff on…it's when I turn it off that he wakes up."

IV. If You Have Ghosts

A few things that the assembled evidence seems to render indisputable: Roky Erickson was, and remains, a sensitive and sweet human being; he was blessed with an extraordinary voice and had an intense interest in music very early on; his upbringing was complicated, even when measured against the understood assumption that some dysfunctional families are more dysfunctional than others.

V. Earthquake

Seminal scene number two: The camera pans down a long, empty hallway with white walls. A voice speaks; it is Roky, taped in a 1975 interview: "I felt like a male Jane Eyre in that place…all I had to look forward to was (being told) 'You're still insane.'" Back-story: June

'68, Roky abruptly returns home from San Francisco. He is filthy, scab-ridden and incoherent. Alarmed, his mother takes him to a doctor, who promptly, if blithely, declares him an incurable schizophrenic. He is subsequently "rescued" by one of his band mates and they hitchhike back to the Bay Area, where Roky eschews LSD for heroin. He begins hearing voices. Upon contracting serum hepatitis from a dirty needle, he returns to Austin, and that fateful marijuana bust. In a matter of months Roky has gone from the center of a psychedelic summertime to bunking up amongst the profoundly disturbed, and violent, residents of Rusk Hospital.

VI. Fire Engine

The similarities between Roky Erickson and Syd Barrett, while obvious, are nevertheless extraordinary. Barrett was more popular, his story more often told, and he was more missed once he was gone. But once Syd was gone, he stayed gone: after 1975, when he shocked his old mates by showing up at the studio as they were putting the finishing touches on the Barrett-inspired *Wish You Were Here,* he retreated to the care of his mother and abandoned all interest in music. Erickson, despite a similar appetite for acid (not to mention the heroin abuse) and regular shock treatments at Rusk, never stopped thinking about music. Unlike Syd, the fire of creating and making music never died inside Roky and was, ultimately, inextinguishable.

VII. Unforced Peace

Seminal scene number three: Bob Priest, Rusk's resident psychologist, recalls how Roky played in a makeshift band that included a rapist, and two murderers. "Most of the time he'd have a yellow legal pad, sitting in the hallway writing music…he was a real nice little guy, he didn't have a whole lot to say; he wanted to write his music, he wanted to play his music — and that's all."

VIII. I Walked With A Zombie

It's 1972: finally released from Rusk, Rocky begins making music, but is plagued by paranoia and the aftereffects of what was, to say the least, his not exactly salubrious recent environment. Increasingly, he is convinced that he's an alien and conniving humans are "zapping" his mind. His attorney takes him to the dime store several times to buy toy laser guns so he can zap them back. It does not work. Finally, she hits upon the idea of preparing a document declaring that Roky is, in fact, an alien, with the hope that whoever is sending telepathic shocks to his head will stop. It works.

IX. Starry Eyes

Seminal scene number four: A man out of time, he looks like it's 1969, he sounds like it's 1969, but it's actually 1983. The same year synth-heavy pop was lip-synched around the clock on MTV; the man who may have invented psychedelic rock is in his mother's house, being videotaped as he strums a song he wrote for her. He is disheveled and most of his teeth are now gone. It is poignant, but also more than a little painful to watch. And yet. That voice, those eyes, the honesty. As Melville wrote "You cannot hide the soul."

X. She Lives in a Time of Her Own

At this point you are thinking: his mother is a saint. She took him in when no one else would, and every indication suggests that she accepts him and genuinely loves him, without reservation. If her rigid distrust of doctors and medication is unfortunate, it is also understandable, considering how she has seen her eldest son suffer. Certainly, she is eccentric; she could easily be the focus of a captivating documentary herself, recalling how Robert Crumb's brothers occasionally, if chillingly, stole the spotlight in Terry Zwigoff's justly celebrated film (speaking of controversial, odd artists). When Roky is interviewed at one point he confesses, sounding not only vulnerable and guileless, but childlike, "I wish I could be somewhere else." The door of domestic unease creaks open and one wonders: how much of a good thing is this arrangement, after all?

XI. Don't Slander Me

While the documentary keeps the focus firmly on Roky, the broiling undercurrent of familial tension (past and present) moves to the forefront when Erickson's younger brother, Sumner (who plays tuba with the Pittsburgh Symphony Orchestra) asserts that years of therapy have helped him understand how domineering their mother has always been. At first his sentiments seem more driven by an obsession to exorcise painful childhood demons, Sumner's intentions to assist Roky are made touchingly clear when he offers to let his brother come live with him.

Eventually, it is up to a judge to determine who is best able to help Roky: his mother correctly claims to have helped him out when nobody else was able or interested; his brother insists that Roky now deserves the opportunity to help himself. The judge ultimately concurs with Sumner's assessment that his mother, by refusing to let Roky take any medication, is effectively suppressing any possibility of improvement and, intentionally or not, keeping him in a state of dependence. The documentary, at this point, has portrayed enough candid incidents and interviews that the viewer will likely endorse the judge's decision, but it is still an uneasy resolution.

XII. I Have Always Been Here Before

Seminal scene number five: After the court rules that Sumner can take his brother back with him to Pittsburgh, their mother silently leaves the courthouse. She stops by Roky's apartment and, one by one, turns off the machines he'd left on when he left home, leaving her behind.

XIII. Splash I (Now I'm Home)

One year later, Roky is preparing to return home to visit his mother for the first time. Sumner, who seems wary whenever her name is mentioned, acknowledges that she probably did the best that she could to provide for her son. Nevertheless, Sumner's influence has been profound, and positive: Roky's teeth are fixed, he has been prescribed (and is taking) modern meds, and he is seeing a therapist, who encourages him to play songs. He seems happy and healthy, sitting outside on a balcony, playing his guitar again. The voice is still not of this earth, but there can no longer be any doubt, if there ever was any, that Roky Erickson is indeed an earthling. The greatest ending of all is that the story has not ended.

(*Postscript*)

Special mention must be made of the extra features, which are generous bordering on mind-boggling. In an era where, unfortunately, one almost expects to get less for more (if there is material for two albums, try and stretch it into three; if there are any leftovers, package them up and push it for the "deluxe" edition), the bonus footage could comprise another full documentary—one of equal value and interest.

Huge kudos to McAlester and company for doing the right thing for the fans, and for Erickson: newcomers who see this footage will almost certainly be inclined to check out some vintage 13th Floor Elevators, as well as the unconscionably overlooked post-Elevators music Erickson made. In addition to an incredible collection of vintage performances from over the years (mostly solo acoustic), there are deleted scenes and readings of original material by Roky and his mother.

Lastly, and perhaps most importantly, at least one more amazing chapter is presented here: the documentary wrapped in 2002, but Roky's astonishing recovery saw him performing live for the first time in almost 20 years at the 2005 Austin City Limits Festival. To watch the reception he gets, to hear how great he sounds, and to behold how fulfilled he appears, it is not possible to be unmoved. "It's a cold night for alligators," he sings. Damn right it is.

August, 2007

UNEASY LIES THE HEAD THAT WEARS A CROWN

Listen: this story has been told so many times it is inextricable from the history of America. F. Scott Fitzgerald infamously (and incorrectly) declared that there are no second acts in American lives, but he was writing his own epitaph at the time. Little did he know that artists, and later, politicians, would perfect the Lazarus routine to the point that it was itself an art form of sorts.

Some great American artists could not handle the hype of their success, or remained paralyzed by the prospect of following up their uncanny grand slam (think Ralph Ellison after *Invisible Man* for the prototype). Some artists famously flamed out in part because of the pressure or else were consumed by their own demons (insert any number of movie stars and rock gods: James Dean and Charlie Parker remain the heavyweight champs of this routine). Some artists never had a choice in the matter: what can we say about the fact that Melville received less than a little acclaim after he wrote *Moby Dick* (even his good friend and contemporary critical darling Nathaniel Hawthorne—to whom Melville's masterpiece was dedicated—thought little of the book, revealing him as either an exceedingly poor judge of genius or else an insecure literary prince who could not brook the very real competition Melville presented), and the man who may be our great American author (at least of the 19th Century) died broke, unknown, and embittered.

But none of these case studies can come close to approximating the one-of-a-kind wunderkind who became the King of Pop. His story is unique and will likely remain the triumphant and ultimately tragic cultural touchstone of our times. He had already lived at least three lives before he died, each one more improbable than the last.

I will leave the career-spanning overviews and detail-oriented obituaries to the myriad individuals who are more qualified (not to mention more interested) than I to properly assess Jackson's short and unhappy existence.

I can offer some opinions and recollections of what it was like, in real time, to witness Jackson's awesome and irresistible trajectory. Any pronouncement, no matter how passionately proposed, is ultimately irrelevant regarding what constituted the ideal demographic for MJ's steady rise and sluggish fall. All I can say is that I was a kid in the '70s and I remember loving the Jackson Five songs and watching their cartoon reruns on TV. In other words, I was the ideal age to experience it, and still remember it. To assert that Michael was the all-American pop icon is both facile and also an indication of how naive and blissfully unaware people my age were to...well, too many things to count. But in MJ's case, young fans were oblivious to the behind the scenes angst that crippled his childhood. That he was abused is undeniable and well-documented. It also scarcely scratches the surface of the pressures and pains that were inflicted upon him. Even a cursory acknowledgment of what he'd been through, before becoming a teenager, should leave the most cynical critic astonished that he was able to create the lasting work he did, as an adult.

Flash forward to 1979: *Off The Wall* was the ubiquitous hit record and every time you turned the radio on you heard "Rock With You" (which, incidentally, sounds every bit as fresh and funky three decades later). MJ was on top of the world. It seems fair to suggest that nobody, including the young superstar, had any idea that he was about to *own* the world.

Thriller, of course, changed everything. It made all that came before it prelude and everything, especially the not-so-good things, which came after an epilogue. People who weren't around then probably can't imagine it, but Jackson was the biggest thing in the universe circa 1983 (and into 1984). It wasn't even close: he was as prevalent as Coca Cola or McDonalds, and it was easy to avoid him as it was to avoid breathing. If you were alive, you were aware. Like it or not.

In fact, if *Thriller* had not happened, people from my generation might be fondly recalling how they skated to "Don't Stop 'Til You Get Enough" at the roller rink. Or how great those Jackson 5 songs still sound. But, of course, *Thriller* happened. And we can (and will) talk about, and remember, all the songs, all the videos and the brand that Michael Jackson became during that span of commercial dominance.

But for now, I'm going to talk about *the moment*. You know what I mean: the performance of "Billie Jean" at the *Motown 25* TV special.

I still get goose bumps every time I watch it. Now that he is gone, I'm sure each subsequent viewing (and there will be many, as I don't expect I'll ever tire of watching it) will be burdened with a melancholy even more profound than the one I would have felt anytime up until June 25, 2009. In other words, even before he passed on, watching a moment like this obliges one to relive one's youth; it's inescapable. So naturally one can't help lamenting that loss of insouciance, of Innocence (with a capital I) and the many things time takes from us.

The previous generation had the moon landing; we had the moonwalk. That is not intended to be overly coy; I actually think I would invoke the moon landing regardless of the obvious word association. In my opinion, the few seconds that Jackson spent introducing that new dance move to the world are *the* defining cultural moments of my generation. In fact, I can't readily think of anything else that enters the discussion. People have spoken about the other MJ (Michael Jordan) having played basketball better than anyone else did anything. I feel we could find other examples (Daniel Barenboim playing Beethoven piano sonatas; Gustave Flaubert writing fiction; Glenn Beck being an asshole), but I would propose that this performance is the apotheosis of what a pop star can achieve. No one, before or since, has been better at being a star, at seizing the moment, at overtaking the world by force of will and talent, quite like Michael Jackson did that evening. What is truly remarkable is not merely how incredible it was, then, but how inimitably cool and untouchable it remains, now. Everyone saw that and everyone reacted to it. It was (and is) impossible to be wholly unaffected or unmoved by what happens during those five minutes.

There are probably people (perhaps lots of them) who still won't see the art or genius (and the many layers of that genius: the song itself—a slice of irrepressible pop perfection, his dancing, and the fact that he is lip-synching it) of this moment, but it's simply not possible to remain indifferent. You can fail to acknowledge this the way you can fail to acknowledge the Grand Canyon, as you are being pushed over the edge, eyes shut and screaming all the way down.

A confession. I was not necessarily a fan. I certainly was able to appreciate that dancing, and that song (and any male my age who attempts to deny that he desperately wanted to perfect the moonwalk is lying through the acne-glazed haze of adolescent recollection). It was a bizarre time to be a teenager: all the girls in school *loved* Michael Jackson and all the guys loved Jim Morrison. Oh wait, that was just me? Well, as corny as I would have considered it for any dude to have a poster of MJ, I am not particularly proud to reconsider the prominent spread of leather-clad Lizard King photos on my bedroom wall. I say this only to underscore the impact MJ had at the time: I was well tired of the non-stop hype and ceaseless radio play (*seven* Top 10 singles?!), and it was simply beyond human capability to separate oneself from *Thriller's* impact. You may not have loved it (you may not have *liked* it) but I have never spoken to anyone who actually *hated* it. I'm sure there is someone out there, who also hates the Sistine Chapel and The Lincoln Memorial. Or *Moby Dick* (just kidding, sort of.)

We all know what happened next.

Icarus flew too close to the sun, and none of the bills he earned could ever break his fall.

I am also content to let the historians, the haters and the opportunistic biographers slash and snap at this detritus like piranhas in a feeding frenzy. I don't think it's a stretch to suggest we'll soon have more detail than we'd ever want to imagine about all the things that did (and didn't) happen when the media cameras weren't rolling. By the '90s, it's not a stretch to suggest his music took second billing to his increasingly surreal escapades.

And it's at that point that we'll be unable to resist the analogies. Neverland Ranch? Was Jackson the real life apotheosis of *Citizen Kane*? Perhaps he embodied the American tragedy implicit in the eponymous hero of Fitzgerald's *The Great Gatsby?* For me, those two works offer the finest, and final, take on how money and memory trump success and satisfaction. A person with a troubled past can never escape the shadow forever hanging over his present. Add almost unlimited power and all bets are off. And while Michael Jackson epitomizes the eternal child in search of a childhood he never had, his tragedy is both deeper and more disturbing. As such, I believe Jackson existed as a sort of inverse Dorian Gray. Of course that antihero traded his soul for eternal youth, but the evidence of his decay was hidden on the portrait he fastidiously kept from public view. Jackson's metamorphosis (the physical and spiritual) unfolded right in front of our often disbelieving eyes.

Ebony and ivory, anyone? This transformation was somewhat beyond *Dorian Gray* because it was real, and this did not represent the comparatively straightforward (and, of course, fictional) deal with the devil: this was hubris facilitated by money and modern medicine. What Jackson did to himself would have been literally unimaginable a generation earlier, and perhaps been done with a greater degree of proficiency a generation later (that, of course, is an appalling commentary on how we're "evolving" as human beings and what we can accomplish in the name of vanity). It was unseemly, it was embarrassing, and above all, it was unfortunate that it served to nourish the insatiable tabloid zombies who live to profit from the pain of others.

But more than a little of Michael's anguish was self-inflicted. True, he engaged in an often futile effort to find things he could not have, but he *did* look for them, using the muscle his money provided to plow through the world, a fragile bull in a not-so-delicate China shop. Ultimately, the only thing he broke was himself. And even at his most irresponsible (or despicable, if only a handful of the charges he successfully settled out of court were legitimate), it was difficult not to feel intense pity for this child crammed inside a King's body. Let the myopic arbiters of taste and the more prurient amongst us declare him a fool or a freak. Let the smug quoters of scripture remind everyone that it does not profit a man to gain the world and forfeit his soul. They should be reminded that the world got to him first. I feel nothing but sorrow for his poor, fractured soul and pray that his heart, at long last, is at peace.

June, 2009

GOD IS NOT DEAD: LET US ALL GIVE THANKS AND PRAISE FOR JIMI HENDRIX

What more can possibly be said, at this point, about Jimi Hendrix?

It is exceedingly refreshing to see that Sony's Legacy Recordings is making the most of this opportunity and reissuing the official Hendrix catalog, with bonus (DVD) material at incredibly—bordering on unbelievably—reasonable price points. Ten bucks for remastered sound and a mini-documentary DVD? This is no brainer, redefined. Which brings us to the crucial question: what more can possibly be said, at this point, about Jimi Hendrix? Actually, it is entirely fair to propose that we have not yet said *enough* about him. As it has long since been established that he is the Alpha and the Omega of electric guitar, conversation tends to stop there: what more *needs* to be said, we say, when we don't say anything more. As a result, the actual scope of his virtuosity tends to, however unintentionally, get reduced to stock phrases (see above) and the sorts of encomiums that preempt elaboration. So how do we explain the truly singular genius that is Jimi Hendrix? Aside from the innovation (he did it first), apart from the obvious (he did it best), what sets him apart?

When it comes to Hendrix, there is really no conjecture. The growth he displayed in only a couple of years is unlike anything we've witnessed from just about any other musician or composer, ever. We're talking *light* years, the universe expanding; real quantum type shit. Put it this way: Miles Davis, who didn't have many good things to say about even the best *jazz* musicians, made no bones about his desire to get Hendrix in the studio to collaborate. That's like Michael Jordan saying he'd like to play some pick-up, or Sugar Ray Robinson asking you to spar with him.

1967: there are the immutable opening salvos, those hit singles that remain radio-friendly four decades on ("Purple Haze", "Hey Joe", "Fire", "Foxey Lady") and the moodier harbingers of what lay ahead ("Manic Depression", "I Don't Live Today", "Love or Confusion") and then there are the outright masterpieces. Consider "The Wind Cries Mary": written the night before, brought to the studio the next day and captured in one take. An example like this underscores the seismic shift that blasted an unsuspecting world when *Are You Experienced* hit the streets, the unambiguous arrival of a major, *scary* talent. But (as the companion DVD details in a series of interviews with engineer—and unsung hero—Eddie Kramer) it is the subsequent embellishment, courtesy of five overdubbed guitar parts, that move this track from mere classic to one-of-a-kind epic: the mood and *feeling* of melancholy Hendrix conveys calls to mind Poe's edict about the totality of effect.

Then there's the psychedelic space jazz of "Third Stone From the Sun": the ways Hendrix navigates an almost surf-rock elegance with proto-thrash distortion and makes it sound not just natural but *inevitable*, is part of why the first album continues to merit consideration as the most fully realized debut album in rock history. Finally there is the title track, which truly is one of those instances that defy time and description on so many levels. This song could only have been released in '67, but it still sounds unsettling and slightly ungraspable in 2010. Perhaps more than any of the other tracks, this one signified the summation of Hendrix's strategy at that stage: backwards solos, restless feedback and subtly effective piano plinks build up the tension like the song was programmed to detonate. And by the time anybody knew what had hit them; Hendrix was already back in the studio.

Axis: Bold As Love did not have as many instantly accessible singles, but in spite (or because) of that, the second album is unquestionably a major step forward in several regards. This is the disc to slip into any discussion regarding Hendrix's indisputable, but underappreciated compositional acumen. The guitar is consistently front and center (while Redding and especially Mitchell remain impeccable, as always, in the pocket), but the emphasis on Jimi's vocals turns purposeful attention on some of the best lyrics he ever penned. While *Are You Experienced* remains the sonic boom that cleared away all competition, even the best moments on that effort could never in a thousand years have anticipated songs like "Little Wing", "Castles Made of Sand", "One Rainy Wish" and "Bold As Love". (Even an ostensibly throwaway tune like "She's So Fine" is instructive: Jimi's lightning leads and delectable falsetto choruses shine, but then there's Mitch Fucking Mitchell. Only one drummer in rock was this fast and furious circa 1967 and his name was Keith Moon.)

The songs on *Axis: Bold As Love*, for the most part, are concise and unencumbered (the clarity of sound on these remasters more than justifies their acquisition), and this is in no small part due to producer (and then manager) Chas Chandler, who brought a strictly-business professionalism to the proceedings all through '67. He explains his old school M.O. on the companion DVD: "If a band can't get it in two or three takes they shouldn't be in the studio." How can you not love this guy? And watching Eddie Kramer at the console, isolating guitar tracks and vocals while recalling how the songs came together is a treat true Hendrix fans will lap up like voodoo soup. Indeed, the only gripe about the bonus DVDs is their brevity; I could easily listen to Kramer and Chandler tell war stories for hours on end without getting bored, and I'm certain I'm not alone.

There is also an air of adventure and daring that augments the sometimes disorienting edge of the debut. Hendrix is clearly pushing himself, each day coming up with new ideas and electrified with the air of possibility. That vision is convincingly and definitively realized, and we can only lament the comparatively primitive technology that prevented alternate takes from surviving the sessions. Imagine, for instance, where "Little Wing" continued to go after the tapes fade out. If there is one particular moment on any of these tracks that best illuminates Hendrix's insatiable creativity and unerring instincts, it comes toward the end of the incendiary "If 6 Was 9". After declaring, in one of the all-time great rock and roll F-offs ("I'm gonna' wave my freak flag high!"), a sort of whinnying, high-pitched noise slips into the maelstrom. Kramer explains that there happened to be a recorder lying around the studio, and Hendrix simply picked it up and started wailing. Kramer then applied the appropriate effects and echo, and the rest is history. In the final analysis, there is no way to improve upon practically any part of *Axis: Bold As Love*: this is as good as music is capable of being.

By 1968 Hendrix has relocated from London to New York City and it was during the open-ended and generally unrestrained *Electric Ladyland* sessions that Chandler, ever the taskmaster, famously fled the scene. "Gypsy Eyes" alone allegedly required forty different takes before Hendrix was satisfied, an intensity surpassing obsession that literally drove Chandler out of the studio. This circumstance was inevitable, and frankly necessary. Hendrix absolutely needed and benefited from Chandler's mentoring, but now he had more than come into his own and nobody could keep up with him (he could scarcely keep up with himself). The results scream for themselves and to say that *Electric Ladyland* is yet another major advancement (how do you improve upon perfection?) is of course a pallid understatement.

Just as little from *Are You Experienced* hinted at the next installment, *Axis: Bold As Love* seems almost pedestrian and conservative compared to the staggering triumph of style and sound that is *Electric Ladyland.*

This is Hendrix's masterpiece, and it is on this double album that practically every trick in his oversized bag is employed to its fullest extent. The storytelling skills are displayed on tracks like "Crosstown Traffic", "Long Hot Summer Night" and "House Burning Down". The compositional prowess is evident in every note, most especially on the song suite that covers side three and spills over to side four. What Hendrix was able to achieve, despite the contemporary limitations of old-fashioned recording equipment is, on a song like "1983… (A Merman I Should Turn To Be)", heroic. It also offers the best evidence we have of what he saw and heard inside his always-teeming imagination.

What remains vital, and compelling, all these years later is the way Hendrix appropriates blues music, creating a template that copycats are still trying, in vain, to emulate. "Voodoo Child (Slight Return)" and the live-in-the-studio riot of "Voodoo Chile" are rock music touchstones, and nothing anyone has attempted has come particularly close to them. Hendrix himself puts it best when he boasts "Well I stand up next to a mountain/And chop it down with the edge of my hand." That is exactly what he did, and he remains king of the mountain he scaled, and then razed.

From "Purple Haze" to "Rainy Day, Dream Away" in less than two years still seems inconceivable, even impossible. But it happened.

And, of course, Hendrix continued to broaden his scope and incorporate more styles and sonic experiments (check out the full, funky brass accompaniment on the title track from *South Saturn Delta*), pushing past the boundaries he had already blown away. The material collected on *First Rays of the New Rising Sun* represent many of the songs Hendrix was assembling for another double album in the summer over 1970, just before his death. Noel Redding is gone and Billy Cox, having already worked with Mitchell and Hendrix during the *Valley of Neptune* sessions, is a liberating presence that allows the band to spread out and chase the guitarist as he soars above, around and beneath them. With all due respect to Noel Redding—and nevermind the rumors that Hendrix simply played all the bass parts himself—one of the tantalizing prospects remains what avenues would have continued to open with Cox freeing Mitchell to incorporate his jazz stylings into the mix.

Back to the genius thing and how to wrap our minds around the extent of Hendrix's gifts: Eddie Kramer analyzes "Dolly Dagger" and uses the console to demonstrate the fastidious attention Hendrix devoted to every second of every song, down to his ability to multi-track his own vocals, knowing in advance exactly where each note and inflection was meant to go. When Kramer isolates the guitar tracks on "Night Bird Flying", it's not just a matter of how great each one sounds and the ways they complement each other; it's more the uncanny way each one could easily and convincingly stand alone as a fully formed statement. Many of the songs, like "Izzabella", "Stepping Stone", "My Friend", "Straight Ahead" and "Astro Man" are loose and as light as Hendrix had been since some of the tracks on *Axis: Bold As Love*. Then there are irrepressible gems like "Ezy Ryder", "Dolly Dagger" and "Belly Button Window" that bring the band directly into a new decade. Most of the material has a fresh and unfettered sound: much less overdubbing and Hendrix's infatuation with "phasing"—which he took to its logical limits on *Electric Ladyland* (think "Moon, Turn the Tides…Gently Gently Away")—is now discarded in favor of a more straightforward assault. This direction is nicely encapsulated in the instrumental "Beginnings" where there are no frills or tricks, only a scorching a workout that showcases Hendrix's ability to create fire without any smoke.

Of course, there are also a handful of tracks that elevate themselves above the rest and go to that *other* place. "Freedom", the perfect album opener, is just a clinic of where rock and roll had gone, and where it might have continued to go; "Room Full of Mirrors" is a tour de force of multi-tracked guitar bliss (including cowbell!) and "Hey Baby (New Rising Sun)" is, or will have to be, as suitable a farewell statement ("May I come along?") as we could hope for. And finally, the one-two punch of "Drifting" and "Angel", that, not that it's necessary to quantify, might represent the most beautiful work Hendrix ever recorded. Inevitably, some measure of outright hyperbole is unavoidable: if there is such a thing as beyond perfection, it's achieved on "Angel" and "Drifting".

And then he was gone. The magnitude of his loss remains unfathomable. There is no question, absolutely no doubt whatsoever, that he had years and years of untapped magic to explore and nourish. On the other hand, perhaps Hendrix *did* live and record for four decades; he just crammed it into four years. Hendrix and the gift of his music are subjects that can never be exhausted: the songs hold up, they must be studied and dissected, and above all they should be savored. They are, like the man who made them, incapable of ever being forgotten.

March, 2010

THEY'LL NEVER PUT ME IN THEIR BAG: THE CONTINUING STORY OF SYD BARRETT

When he died in 2006, after decades of cult-figure status and willful anonymity, Syd Barrett was arguably better known as the person who inspired one of Pink Floyd's best albums, and not the man who once led and named them. Certainly, the fact that he put out two albums, even after (and/or during the continuation of) his epic—and archetypal—drug-induced disintegration has always seemed more of an afterthought than fans in the know find acceptable.

Perhaps the release of *An Introduction to Syd Barrett*, a generous sampler of selections from those two albums, along with highlights from Pink Floyd's debut, *The Piper at the Gates of Dawn*, and a handful of singles from 1967, will signal a long overdue reappraisal. When it comes to Barrett, it's not so much a matter of whether the time is right. Syd was infamously unfashionable by 1970 (when both of his solo albums were released), and that music has always been difficult to attach to a particular time or place. While this fact ensured that the albums were marginalized and misunderstood then, they remain, as much as any pop music made four decades ago, timeless.

This collection begins, appropriately, with the single "Arnold Layne", a song sufficiently original and compelling to land Pink Floyd (then called "The" Pink Floyd, and named by Barrett after semi-obscure blues musicians Pink Anderson and Floyd Council) an offer from EMI. The single—which hit number 20 in the UK—concerning a cross-dressing clothesline thief, still astonishes with its wit, poetry ("doors bang / chain gang") and brazen finger in the eye of buttoned-down British sensibilities ("takes two to know"). It signaled the arrival of a significant and utterly unique talent. That promise was realized on the follow-up single "See Emily Play", which, with its shifting tempos, sped-up pianos, backward taping, and Technicolor trippiness, provides an authentic English counterpoint to the hippier and dippier Flower Power singles being cranked out across the sea in 1967.

With considerable confidence, Pink Floyd entered Abbey Road studios to record the debut. Across the hall, the Beatles were busy tinkering with the album that remains the most talked about work from the Summer of Love, *Sgt. Pepper's Lonely Hearts Club Band*. The results, remarkable in and of themselves, assume an added layer of relevance when considered as primarily the result of one man's singular vision (as opposed to the Four Fabs, or five if you count George Martin—and you should). The three selections, "Chapter 24", "Bike", and a remix of "Matilda Mother" (an early version with different lyrics) are an adequate overview, but anyone who wants to more fully understand Pink Floyd, 1967, psychedelic rock, and one of the more consistently satisfying debut albums ever is obliged to acquire *The Piper at the Gates of Dawn*.

Oh, by the way, *this* one's Pink. With due respect to Waters, Wright, and Mason, the band's first effort was Barrett's baby. His lyrics, ranging from the obligatory astral imagery of the era ("Astronomy Domine") to the obligatory shout-out to *I Ching* ("Chapter 24") to the brain salad surgery of "Bike", reveal an erudite and eccentric wordsmith, more light than dark, more ebullient than enigmatic. *Piper*, in short, is a happy explosion of creative potential, producing fruit that flourishes more than 40 years on. And intriguing as Barrett's words and voice are throughout, the real revelation is his songwriting. The compositions, with the notable exception of the extended space-rock jam "Interstellar Overdrive", are exercises in precision, packing maximal sound and feeling into bite-sized bits. Barrett's clever if unconventional use of a Zippo lighter as a makeshift slide gave him the ability to play fast while conjuring a shrill metallic shriek from his guitar. Those glistening cries are in full effect on the single "Apples and Oranges", adding just enough quirky edge to give it the signature Floyd sound (that, and the "quack quack" after the line "feeding ducks in the afternoon tide"—a classic Barrett embellishment).

Considering *Piper* and the handful of singles and outtakes, one could make a reasonable case that Barrett's diamond shined as bright as any artist's in 1967. (And beyond: Although not included in this set, consider the fey, teasing vocal performance on "Candy and a Currant Bun"—formerly "Let's Roll Another One", a title the band was obliged to change for obvious reasons—which is worth noting for the template it provided the young David Bowie.) The world had every reason to think that Pink Floyd was going to make game-changing music and be around for a long, long time. As we know, they did, and were; albeit without their front man, who was asked to leave the band less than a year after *Piper* was released. It was unbelievable then, and remains difficult to completely comprehend now.

So what happened? Theories and stories abound, but all you need to do is look at the pictures. Before, during, and just after the release of their debut, Syd is, quite simply, a specimen. Even if you never heard him play or sing, he had charisma and beauty to burn, and it is easy to understand why so many people attached themselves to him. By the time David Gilmour—whom the frantic bandmates recruited to at first fill in for, and later replace, their increasingly erratic leader—begins turning up in group photos, Barrett has dark trenches under his eyes and is already perfecting the thousand-yard stare Roger Waters would later immortalize ("Now there's a look in your eyes / Like black holes in the sky"). Was it drugs? Schizophrenia? Probably both, possibly neither, but everyone who was there attests that Barrett went from experimenting to ingesting, and that his intake of LSD went from awe-inspiring to alarming in a matter of months. Certainly the rapid (too rapid?) ascent from paisley underground to Top of the Pops would potentially prove dodgy for any sensitive soul who may have happened to be a genius. Add those drugs and the likelihood of a preexisting condition, and the resulting damage was best, if most starkly, described by Syd himself: "I tattooed my brain all the way…"

The next part is where it gets intriguing, if still unresolved. That Barrett saw his shot at superstardom dissipate into the darkening circles of his bruised brain is more than a little tragic. That we have a soundtrack to some of that dissolution, as both an artistic and *human* document, is more than a little miraculous. Whatever one thinks of the work he recorded post-Pink Floyd (and opinions, predictably, are all over the place), arguably not since Vincent Van Gogh and Edgar Allan Poe have we seen, for posterity, such poignant creative evidence of an aggravated, altered psyche pushed well past endurable limits.

With this in mind, listening to "Jugband Blues" (the only Barrett track to make it onto Floyd's second album, *A Saucerful of Secrets*) and the way the song shifts from buoyant to desolate could almost be considered a case study of psychosis *as it was happening*. But it is, of course, more than that: It is also a tape recorder running while a brilliant, fragile musician screamed his last scream. And even in *those* moments the case for Barrett's madcap acumen is powerful. On "Jugband Blues", he made the puzzling decision to bring a Salvation Army band into the studio. What ensues is at once hilarious and harrowing, and by the time the din dies down and it's just an acoustic guitar and Syd's somber voice ("And what exactly is a dream? / And what exactly is a joke?"), you wonder how he made it work even as your heart breaks.

Considering he was the one who benefited most (artistically and financially) from Barrett's exodus, it's both fitting and touching that David Gilmour probably did the most to help his old Cambridge mate. After his songs "Vegetable Man" and "Scream Thy Last Scream" (both widely bootlegged, but never available for official release, and presumably unavailable—due to legal or copyright issues—for this collection, though they would both be welcome and essential additions) were rejected by the band during the *A Saucerful of Secrets* sessions, Syd was mostly absent from recording studios and the public eye for the better part of a year. After some aborted sessions in '68, Barrett resumed work on a collection of songs that eventually became *The Madcap Laughs* (released in January, 1970). Jerry Shirley (drummer from Humble Pie) was recruited, along with members of the Soft Machine. Toward the end, with the proceedings in danger of falling apart, Waters and Gilmour stepped in to help finish (playing bass, producing, and, one imagines, prodding).

It's unlikely that anyone hearing these songs (or the songs from the follow-up, *Barrett*, released later in 1970) for the first time will know what to make of them, particularly with *Piper* as the presumable point of reference. Obviously, that was the comparison listeners would have made, by necessity, when these albums arrived, and the differences between what Barrett achieved in '67 and what he created in 1970 are universes apart. That said, this is, for a variety of obvious reasons, challenging, unusual music that requires an investment of time and patience. Once it is received on its own terms (and this simply may not be possible for some people), a flow reveals itself and most of the material makes quite a bit of sense in its own uncanny way. The songs range from the gorgeous and hypnotic "Terrapin", which features only an acoustic guitar and Syd's inimitable croon, to the almost unbearably raw "If It's in You" (the latter likely to be either majestic or nails on a chalkboard, with little chance of middle ground). The upbeat "Love You" comes close to capturing the '67 whimsy, and "She Took a Long Cool Look" picks up where "Jugband Blues" left off, the plaintive yearning replaced by a frosty resignation.

The two highlights remain "Dark Globe" and "Octopus", and both warrant further scrutiny. The latter might be described as a deceptively sanguine jaunt into the mouth (or mind?) of madness. Non sequiturs and stream of consciousness combine with the upbeat music to take the listener on a guided tour of Barrett's tattooed brain, where "the madcap laughed at the man on the border". Two couplets in particular leave little to the imagination, and one realizes that, at least when he wanted to or could be, Syd was in complete control of his fac, his f-a-c-u-l-t-i-e-s:

Isn't it good to be lost in the wood
Isn't it bad so quiet there, in the wood meant even less to me than I thought…
The winds they blew and the leaves did wag
They'll never put me in their bag.

"Dark Globe" is like a man singing an epitaph for the person he'd been and who he had become. It is a remarkable achievement and remains unbearably poignant: "Please lift a hand / I'm only a person" and "Wouldn't you miss me at all?" As difficult as it is to hear those words today, one wonders what it was like for Waters and Gilmour that day in the studio.

On balance, the songs from *The Madcap Laughs* are neither as formless nor disconsolate as one might expect. Likewise, the collection of songs on *Barrett* contain some head-scratchers and a few moments that are as sublime as anything he—or anyone—ever did. Exhibit A, "Baby Lemonade": featuring brilliant imagery ("In the sad town / Cold iron hands clap the party of clowns outside"), the welcome presence of Rick Wright's organ, and a cleaner overall sound (the drums are clear and Gilmour's bass gives the sound a palpable bottom), this song actually could be said to transcend even Barrett's best previous work. Two of Syd's most well-known songs, "Gigolo Aunt" and "Effervescing Elephant", indicate that the wordplay and humor were still intact and affective. Consider the hilarious "Bob Dylan Blues", wherein Barrett takes the piss out of Dylan by (gently?) mocking his too-easy-by-half rhyme schemes and streak of self-righteousness: "Cuz I'm a poet, don't you know it? / And the wind, you can blow it!"). Finally, there is "Dominoes" (check out David Gilmour's hear-it-to-believe-it story of how Barrett envisioned and pulled off his guitar solo). If "Dark Globe" told us where Syd had been and where he was, "Dominoes" previews where he may have been headed, if the subsequent silence and unwillingness to engage with his past or the world is any indication:

It's an idea, someday
In my tears, my dreams
Don't you want to see her proof?
Life that comes of no harm
You and I, you and I and dominoes, the day goes by…

And here's the rub: *real* Pink Floyd fans have little choice but to thank the heavens for this complicated chain of events. Put plainly (if coldly), no Barrett breakdown, no Gilmour. The sound Floyd subsequently perfected was a combination of accident and inevitability, while the collection of increasingly confident transitional albums is a prog-rock treasure trove. Which brings us to *Dark Side of the Moon*, the first album to directly invoke Barrett ("Brain Damage/Eclipse"). And of course, we literally wouldn't have *Wish You Were Here*, Waters' meditation on madness and mourning inspired by and dedicated to his old friend. Finally, the story, which *has* to be apocryphal except for the fact that it isn't, and is enough to make you concede that forces greater than us may indeed have the controls set for the heart of the sun. The band, busy completing the final mix of the album (allegedly working on "Shine On You Crazy Diamond"), did not notice the bigger, bald stranger who had wandered into the room; only after several moments did anyone recognize their former leader. At one moment jumping up and down to brush his teeth with his fingers (a pitiful sight that reduced Waters to tears), the next Barrett was offering to add his guitar parts to completed work. Upon having his services politely declined, he walked out of the studio and no one in the band ever saw him again.

There was so much more for Syd to achieve… or was there? Do we dare ask for or expect more from any artist who gave so much? Is it both selfish and short-sighted to wonder what he may have achieved in the '70s and beyond when we consider what he'd already done? Did Syd pay the ultimate price for fame and artistic immortality? Or did he contentedly turn his back on the machine that once welcomed him? By most accounts, his final decades (spent mostly with his mother at the house he grew up in) were without turmoil. Certainly, the strain he put on his system had permanent psychological effects, and perhaps we'll never know if his voracious consumption of chemicals accelerated the onset of a profound condition. In the end, the most pertinent, if unanswerable question is, does it matter?

November, 2010

ROBERT JOHNSON: THE CENTENNIAL OF AN AMERICAN GENIUS

Does any single figure loom as large over an art form as Robert Johnson?

Bach and Shakespeare come to mind, but classical music, like literature, took centuries and multiple cultures in order to unfold and evolve.

The history of American popular music came to be dominated by rock and roll, which initially flowered as a (mostly white) appropriation of the blues. The blues was the common language and unifying force of all rock's earliest practitioners, many of whom were obsessed with the music made in the first part of the 20th century. It's well documented that most of the artists from what came to be called the British Invasion were inspired and driven by the example of blues legends like Muddy Waters and Howlin' Wolf. Put simply, the one individual who even *those* masters must be measured against, in terms of influence and innovation, is Robert Johnson.

Perhaps the most effective way of getting a handle on Johnson's unshakable impact is to consider the number of his songs covered by other musicians. Even a listener more than casually acquainted with rock (and blues) history is likely to underestimate how many compositions—popularized by other rock (and blues) musicians spanning several decades—were originally written and recorded by Johnson over the course of a mere seven months in 1936 and 1937.

That he died so young, under sketchy circumstances (allegedly poisoned by the jealous husband of one of his many lovers), leaving behind less than two total hours of recorded music, and being in possession of impossible-sounding guitar skills and a voice no one has ever equaled naturally, perhaps inevitably, led folks to conclude larger forces were at work. Larger in this case meaning *evil.* As spurious, even silly as that sounds to modern ears, this was an era where anything other than music sung in church might be referred to as "Devil's music". In fact, the aforementioned Howlin' Wolf is only one of myriad geniuses whose decision (as if men like Wolf had any choice) to pursue a musical calling alienated—or ended—close personal and familial relations; in Wolf's case, his mother, who never spoke to him again.

Of course, there are more than a handful of sociological elements at play in this particular legend. Not unlike Shakespeare, whom many reputable scholars refuse to believe composed all the works he's credited with creating, there were undoubtedly some folks who refused to fathom that a man in his mid-20s could possibly accomplish what Johnson did, in fact, achieve. That there are racial (and racist) elements in play scarcely warrants elaboration. Mostly, humans have been creating legends to explain the inexplicable, whether it involves cave drawings or gods on top of mountains or Faustian deals made with the prince of darkness.

Back in those days, spinning records backwards was neither possible nor necessary. It didn't require silly stratagems to try and decipher the hidden codes because the lyrics themselves came right out and acknowledged—or alluded to—what certain people suspected. These song titles alone serve as signposts for anyone ready to believe, or instigate, some controversy: "Hell Hound on My Trail", "Me and the Devil Blues", "Last Fair Deal Gone Down" and, of course, "Cross Road Blues". That Robert Johnson met and made a deal with the devil, being granted immortality in exchange for his soul, is one of the enduring, if clichéd folk tales in American musical history.

Here are the facts. Robert Johnson was born May 8, 1911 in Hazlehurt, Mississippi. He worked diligently to develop his skills and cultivate a style, initially emulating (and imitating) fellow legends Son House, Charlie Patton and Willie Brown (who gets a shout out in "Cross Road Blues"). In short order (too short for comfort, according to the conspiracy-minded) Johnson began to attract enough attention to become a fixture throughout his home state and into Tennessee. At the same time he steadily gained a (bad) reputation as the most incorrigible of ladies men. In 1936 he entered a studio in San Antonio and laid down the tracks that continue to cast a shadow over everything else everyone else has ever done. In 1938, he was served a drink that was poisoned, probably by an angry husband, and he died at 27. His beatification was neither immediate nor overwhelming: it took decades of highly regarded players performing and name-checking his material for consensus to inexorably emerge. Robert Johnson belongs in a category unto himself.

And so Johnson remains a figure who almost everyone knows even if not that many people *really* know him. Sales of his various compilations have certainly sold well enough, but one suspects many people come by his work the same way they encounter Shakespeare: through other artists' interpretations. This is okay; indeed it speaks volumes about the persistence of his legacy. Nevertheless, considering how incendiary—and consistently satisfying—the source material is, now is as good a time as any to encourage anyone and everyone to get intimately acquainted with the man Eric Clapton insists is "the most important blues singer that ever lived". In fact, Keith Richards and Jimmy Page (making this three guitarists who have collectively influenced more aspiring musicians than could be counted) all concur that Robert Johnson is the Alpha and the Omega, and who would argue with them?

In preparation for his centennial, Sony/Legacy has produced an attractive, affordable and *essential* two-CD set compiling the original San Antonio ('36) and Dallas ('37) recordings, along with more than a dozen alternate takes. The package is near-perfect, with extensive liner notes, photos and most crucially, radically improved sound. For anyone, like this writer, who has the old *Complete Recordings* edition (the original Holy Grail), the sound on these discs is revelatory. Certainly, there is no disguising the fact that these are *old* recordings, produced by antiquated means, and that dusty authenticity is impossible to disguise (thank goodness). On the other hand, many of the hisses, shifts in volume and other distracting elements from previous incarnations have been lovingly minimized. This is worth picking up even if you are completely satisfied with whatever recording you currently own; in fact you owe it to yourself to hear the difference.

Is there anything else that needs to be said? It's always enlightening to hear the unfiltered first takes on masterpieces like

"Sweet Home Chicago", "From Four Until Late", "Traveling Riverside Blues" and "Love in Vain Blues". As anyone who knows can attest, this is not remotely music for a museum, relics to acknowledge before moving on. It is exciting, joyful noise, brimming with purpose and ingenuity, fun and frightening, enigmatic and awe-inspiring. And once again, it is remarkable to consider the diversity of artists who have been drawn to these touchstones, and our musical heritage is incalculably richer for all of the faithful and unconventional "cover songs" Johnson unknowingly commissioned.

One more thing needs to be said. T.S. Eliot wrote that "humankind cannot bear very much reality". The reality is this: there was no deal with the devil; there was no devil. There was one man, one guitar and one abiding legend. That legend grows in direct proportion to our capacity to come fully to grips with how influential—and unbelievable—Robert Johnson remains.

May, 2011

AMY WINEHOUSE: LACK OF LOVE IS A LOSING GAME

Last year, when I was making the list of what I considered the 50 best (rock) albums of the decade, I had this to say about Amy Winehouse's *Back To Black*:

Between the pre-release hype and the post-release meltdown, it's almost difficult to remember how many naysayers this album humbled. Trust me, I was one of them. I recall reading a rapturous review a month or two before the CD dropped (and seeing her for the first time in the accompanying photos and thinking, Hey she's kind of hot in a coke binge, bar-crawling, tat- sporting, wig-wearing, hot bowl of mess kind of way) and acknowledging that serious marketing money had her pegged as the story of the year.

And then I *heard* the thing. Yeah, the rehab song was okay, I guess. And this album definitely isn't a masterpiece, because there are some serious clunkers on there. But my God there are some flat out stunners as well. It got overplayed (through no fault of its own) but there's no denying "You Know I'm No Good" (holy shit what a songwriter! Are you kidding me with those lyrics? That is some sardonic self-loathing that gives even Morrissey a run for his money) and the title track and especially the most hilarious song of the decade "Me & Mr. Jones":

What kind of fuckery are you? Aside from Sammy you're my best black Jew!

Quite frankly, nobody in the world could ever in a million words write a line like this and actually pull it off. And then there's straight-up one of the best songs of this decade, or any decade, "Love Is A Losing Game". I remember reading that Prince had begun covering this in his live shows. Repeat: Prince. Yes, *that* Prince. Just to be clear, people cover Prince's songs; Prince does not cover other people's songs. Get the picture? It's one thing to emulate and imitate the old

Phil Spector girl group vibe, but to craft a tune that can easily stand alongside any of them? Wow. And, astonishingly, Winehouse saves the best for last, literally. “He Can Only Hold Her” is an out-and-out masterpiece, a perfect song. Every second, every syllable, every sound: utter perfection. Check out those lyrics: can you say “less is more”? That’s not just a short story, that’s a fucking novel in three minutes. If you know anything about anything, you simply shut up and marvel at genius (yes, genius) like that.

Look, Winehouse was already at Defcon-4 by the time this album broke big; to a certain extent she earned her excess and the sadly predictable tabloid soap opera her life became. Let’s hope, for her sake and ours, that she gets her act together and makes an attempt to do the unthinkable: making another album half as great as *Back To Black*.

7/26/11:

Well, we'll never get the chance now, will we?

Whenever an artist dies too young, particularly when it’s a self-inflicted surrender, there is an inevitable (irresistible?) tendency to romanticize or lionize. That Winehouse joins the infamous "27 club" (Jimi, Jim, Janis, Cobain, etc.) only ups the ante and ensures that the same folks who salivated at her death-spiral will now weep reptilian tears.

I'm disappointed, as a fan, that we won't get a chance to hear her mature and evolve from the precocious chanteuse whose destructive and self-loathing tendencies overpowered the better (and prettier) angels sulking deep inside. I'm sad, as a fellow human being, that a woman with so much talent and potential was not able to love her life—and herself—enough to see how much discovery and excitement lay ahead of her. I sincerely wish she could have listened to her own music and felt the same thrill and astonishment so many millions of people felt. It may not have been enough to save her, but it might have been enough to help. And sometimes help is the first step to salvation.

I hope, and trust, she is sleeping well. And if there is any karmic justice she is able to feel some measure of peace and fulfillment that in some small way approximates the pleasure she was able to provide so many of us, despite the pain she was so obviously in for so long.

July, 2011

R.E.M.: THE GREATEST AMERICAN BAND. EVER.

Almost exactly three years ago I tried to settle a question many people had asked me (and that I had asked myself): what is the all-time great American band?

The only way to tackle a project like that is to have fun with it. I did manage to have fun, but it was also—as anyone who cares too much about music can appreciate—exhausting and at times, excruciating.

Here is the strategy I came up with:

In the spirit of two quintessentially American inventions (obsessions, really), baseball and rock and roll, it seemed like a swell idea to merge the two in a lighthearted exercise designed to celebrate the World Series. If one were to imagine fielding the ultimate all-star team comprised of the greatest "players" from the roster of rock music history, how would one begin? Well, for starters, this project could best be understood as falling somewhere in the spectrum of compulsive list making, a passionate engagement with rock music, and the increasingly ubiquitous phenomenon of fantasy teams that exist in the shadow universe of sports freaks. This discussion might begin with the innocent posing of an impossible question: who is the all-time MVP of rock and roll? Or, who are the chosen ones who would find their way onto the roster of any respectable short list? Most people, once the considerable pool of candidates was properly examined, could quickly reach consensus, right? Keep dreaming. The only thing more inimically American than sports and music is our unquenchable compulsion to compete, to choose a side and see what happens.

Picking the most important (greatest? best? all of the above?) band, I actually had little difficulty. There are tons of worthy contenders to make a claim for the number two spot, but to me, pound for pound, no American band can touch R.E.M. Here is my quick and uncomplicated summation:

The clean-up hitter and arguably most impressive player on the squad is that most American of bands, R.E.M. Not only the ultimate run producer and homeruns leader (from their rookie season in '83 through at least '96, their prime is one extended batting title). Consistency has always been their hallmark, and only the most versatile, fearless and original band could cover the hot corner (at 3rd base) year in and year out. If they've shown their age in recent years, it does not (cannot) diminish their credentials: a longer heyday than any other American band, hands down.

Now with the news of R.E.M calling it quits blowing up the Internets, I am obliged—and delighted—to put my stake more firmly in the sand and stand by my assessment: REM is the best (and/or greatest, most important) band America has produced. In terms of influence and output, no one else can touch them. And here's the thing: just about everyone knows the hits, and unlike most bands (even some of the better and best-loved bands) R.E.M could easily fit their "greatest hits" on a double-disc set. In terms of influence, is there any debate? R.E.M. has the ultimately winning combination of their sound(s) and the underground aesthetic that helped inspire more American bands than Velvet Underground and The Ramones combined (I can't quantify that assertion but I still feel confident in proclaiming it). Actually, how about this: REM inspired more bands who could actually play their instruments and make worthwhile albums than Velvet Underground and The Ramones combined (throw in the Sex Pistols as well, for bad measure).

Where R.E.M—like any band—really distances themselves and makes their true case for greatness is in the lesser-known and semi-obscure songs. That is where we settle into the real meat and potatoes and start to get a handle on how unbelievably diverse, progressive and brilliant the band was for such a long time. Has any band been that good, that consistently, for that long? To me it's not particularly close: R.E.M is *it.*

September, 2011

THE PAST IS CALLING: RECONSIDERING THE WHO'S *QUADROPHENIA*

Most popular Who album? No.

Most important Who album? No.

Most influential Who album? No.

Best Who album? Definitely.

More: Best album of the '70s? Probably.

More? Best rock album, ever? Possibly.

Let's break it down.

Quadrophenia is an album that has something for everyone and everything for some people. It concerns itself with virtually all the themes that have defined rock music through successive generations: alienation, rebellion, redemption. Sex. Drugs. And rock 'n' roll, as well as Mods, Rockers, punks, godfathers, bell boys, drunken mothers, distant fathers and fallen heroes. The sea, sand, surf and suicide. Rain, uppers, downers and drowning. Zoot suits, scooters, school and schizophrenia. Dirty jobs, helpless dancers, pills and gin. Stars falling, heat rising and, above all, love. Love of music, love of life and the love of possibility. Faith and the attempt to make a cohesive—not to mention coherent—statement on the meaning of all these things. And more.

Is that too much? More like it's not enough.

Quadrophenia is, in no particular order, The Who album that has best defied time and fashion (one crucial criterion for measuring the ultimate impact of a successful work of art is how it fares over time), a guitar-playing tour de force, and Pete Townshend's most realized conceptual effort. This is it: he was never this energized or inspired again; this is career-defining music. A double LP that is not as immediately approachable as *Tommy*, it takes a while but once you get it, it gets inside you—and never leaves.

A beach is a place where a man can feel he's the only soul in the world that's real…

The Who's masterwork could almost be described as accidental beach music. Most of the narrative details the mercurial urgencies of young Jimmy, the disenchanted Mod who also could represent just about any teenager who has ever lived. As such, the words and sounds and feelings are alternately frantic ("Can You See The Real Me?") and claustrophobic ("Cut My Hair"): the story of a sensitive, chemically altered kid uncomfortable inside his skin. There are few releases, and even the sex, drugs and rock 'n' roll can't always be counted on.

The one place where he feels safe and free is at the beach. The album opens with crashing waves and ends with the electrified air of a summer storm. In between there are seagull chirps, scooters careening out of the city into open spaces, bass drum thunder and cymbal-splash raindrops. The album, like the protagonist's mind, wrestles with itself, rising and falling like the moods of adolescence. Eventually, inevitably, the fever breaks, the skies open and the air is dark, cool and clear.

The genius of *Quadrophenia* (an album that manages to get name-checked by all the big names and seems universally admired but still not *quite* revered as much as it deserves to be) is certainly the sum of its parts, but also warrants, and welcomes, song-by-song scrutiny. Less flashy than the "rock opera" *Tommy* and less accessible than the FM-friendly *Who's Next* (both masterpieces in their own right), *Quadrophenia* is, nonetheless, significantly more impressive (and indispensable) than both of those excellent albums.

Everything The Who did, in the studio and onstage, up until 1969 set the stage for *Tommy*: it was the consummation of Townshend's obsessions and experimentations; a decade-closing magnum opus that managed to simultaneously celebrate the death and rebirth of the Hippie Dream. Everything Townshend did, in his entire life up until 1973 set the stage for *Quadrophenia.*

It's all in there: the pre-teen angst, the teenage agonies and the post-teen despondency. Politicians and parents are gleefully skewered, prigs and clock punchers are mercilessly unmasked, and those who consider themselves less fortunate than everyone else (this, at times, is all of us) are serenaded with equal measures of empathy and exasperation.

And the songs? It's like being in a shooting gallery, where Townshend picks off hypocrisy after misdeed after miniature tragedy all with a twinkling self-deprecation; this, after all, is a young misfit's story, so the bathos and pathos is milked and articulated in ways that convey the earth-shattering urgency and comical banality that are part and parcel to the typical coming of age *Cri de Coeur*. And the band, certainly no slouch on its previous few efforts, is in top form throughout (isolating Moon and Entwistle on any track is a process that can yield ceaseless wonder and bewilderment, and provides a clinic for how multi-dimensional each player consistently managed to be).

From the extended workouts like the title track and "The Rock" (which sounds a bit like an updated and plugged-in version of *Tommy's* "Underture", to slash and burn mini epics like "Dr. Jimmy" to pre-punk (and post-Mod) anthems like "5:15", the band is flexing rhythmic and textural muscles that are as big as any band's ever got.

The attention to detail is striking and, for the time, remarkably innovative: consider the "found" sounds of the screeching scooters, the rain, the surf, the bus doors clanging open and, on "Bell Boy", the sound of Keith Moon's howl merging into the synthesizer (a technique later used to excellent effect on "Sheep" from Pink Floyd's *Animals*).

There are the subtle yet masterful touches that are still capable of providing added pleasure after all these listens: the winking but ingenious meta of "My Generation" (in "The Punk and The Godfather") and "The Kids are Alright" (in "Helpless Dancer") as well as "I'm The Face" (in "Sea and Sand"). These are not just clever self-references, they are historical notes—from the history of The Who and, by extension and association, rock 'n' roll.

Being a double album (quite possibly the best one, and that is opined knowing that *Electric Ladyland, Physical Graffiti* and *London Calling* are also on the dance card), the combination of sheer quality and precision still manages to astonish, all these years later. Unlike most double albums that tend to drag a bit toward the end, this one gets better as it goes along, and none of the songs feel forced.

Some of the numbers on *Tommy* seem shoehorned to fit the storyline but that's never an issue with *Quadrophenia*; Townshend had a unified vision and the songs tell a cogent and affecting tale. As great as *Who's Next* really is, you can have "Baba O'Riley", "Bargain" and "Behind Blue Eyes"; give me "Helpless Dancer", "Sea and Sand" and "Drowned".

And then there's the song Pete Townshend was *born* to write (and no, it was not "My Generation", although only he could have written that one, and all the other great ones); that would be "The Punk and the Godfather". That song more than adequately advances the tensions of Jimmy's unfolding story, but more than that, it also serves as an epitaph—for Townshend, and every rock legend that had the audacity to *not* die young—to the decidedly anti-rock notion of growing old, selling out and achieving some manner of satisfaction:

We tried to speak between lines of oration
You could only repeat what we told you,
Your axe belongs to a dying nation
They don't know that we own you…
We're the slaves to a phony leader
Breathe the air we have blown you!

Although the well-known "Love Reign O'er Me" is the ultimate coda for this, or any, album and a showcase for one of Daltrey's most deliriously intense vocal performances, it's the song that closes Side Three that still functions as the pinnacle of what this band achieved on their finest outing. If "A Quick One (While He's Away)" is a mini rock opera that's heavy on the humor and light on the pretense, while *Tommy* is a serious and (at times overly) ambitious Rock Opera, "Bell Boy" takes the best elements of both works and distills them into a rollicking epic that clocks in at just under five minutes(!).

The devastation of a younger kid bumping into his one-time hero who is now kissing ass for tips and working for "the man" is undercut by the inspired decision to let Keith Moon "sing" the forsaken idol's version of events: "I got a good job and I'm newly born / You should see me dressed up in my uniform". It's not a confession, really; it functions for the listener as mordant commentary, delivered with a wink and a pint.

The Who were rightly regarded as one of the top live acts of their time: their patented perfection of "Maximum R&B" is rock music's own barbaric yawp and no one did it better. What they don't get enough attention or credit for is what remarkable technicians they could be. From the canny and prescient incorporation of radio jingles on *The Who Sell Out* to the early and innovative use of synthesized sounds on *Who's Next* and Townshend's ability to seamlessly build songs using acoustic and electric flourishes in multi-tracked glory, The Who were not only some of the best musicians, instrument for instrument; they took full advantage of technology and Townshend's edgy vision to create work that *mattered.* They combined their best material, most inspired playing and urgent sense of purpose to craft an album that challenges and convinces like few others in rock. Lyrically, sonically and emotionally, *Quadrophenia* endures as an uncanny exploration of the anguish and ecstasy of being alive and bearing witness.

One might wonder, with 2013 being the 40th anniversary of this album, why we are getting this latest reissue in late 2011. Simplest answer: Why not? Actually, according to the press materials, Townshend and Daltrey are planning on hitting the road in 2012 with a show based around *Quadrophenia* (something they last did in 1996/1997).

Further, we have a double-disc "Deluxe Edition" and a multi-disc "Director's Cut" hitting the streets just in time for holiday wish lists. Both releases boast remastered sound and previously unreleased material (the two-disc set has 11 extra songs; the multi-disc set has 25, plus a 5.1 surround-sound mix of eight tracks). The sound is definitely top-notch, though not dramatically different from the mid-'90s reissue.

Hardcore fans, like this writer, may be disconcerted to realize that the original mixes were not utilized (long story short: the most recent remaster has several minor but glaring "edits", notably adding some sound effects to certain songs and removing them from others, such as the barnyard noises toward the end of "The Dirty Jobs"…meaning this does not sound like the original album. The quibbles might be minor, but Townshend has bragged about creating the "definitive" experience and while he's within his rights to tweak the original mixes, that should be advertised up front.)

On a happier note, the demos and various works-in-progress are crucial additions to a fuller understanding of how this tour de force evolved from concept to completed product. As usual, Townshend had sketched out rough cuts of virtually all the final songs, and he handles the initial vocals. These provide not only an interesting contrast to the definitive versions, but also reveal how much depth, grit and balls Daltrey brings to the table. Of course on the final product Townshend's vocal embellishments function as honey undercutting Daltrey's rum punches.

Also, on the songs where Townshend handles lead vocals (such as "I'm One"), he acquits himself brilliantly, as always; even on the songs where Daltrey is up front, Townshend is yelling, crooning and cooing in the background. These demos, in sum, illustrate once again how even the most inspired creative minds need to hash out their ideas and let the elements sufficiently coalesce before they get their final take(s).

If, for whatever reason, you've never added *Quadrophenia* to your music collection, it simply can't be recommended more unreservedly. Even after four decades the music is so urgent and *alive* that listening to it remains an exhilarating experience. Combining the band's best playing and capitalizing, fully, on Townshend's encompassing aesthetic that fuses raw punk energy and refined compositional prowess, this album is an essential cornerstone of the rock 'n' roll canon.

There is sound and fury, signifying *everything*: it's incredibly smart, but fairly oozing with soul; it's nostalgic and, almost impossibly, prognostic. It's the material Townshend was placed on this planet to make. Let the tide in and set you free.

November, 2011

THE ONCE AND FUTURE KING: *SMILE* AND BRIAN WILSON'S VERY AMERICAN DREAM

What if I were to tell you the 21st Century has already produced its great American novel? And what if I told you it was actually written almost five decades ago? And then I mentioned that it's not a book, it's an album? And then, this: no one has ever heard it and no one ever will, because it remains unfinished. And yet: *everyone* has listened to the opening chapter, a prologue to the most infamous what-could-have-been in musical history. The song: "Good Vibrations". The band: The Beach Boys.

Stop me if you've heard this one before. Icarus soars too close to the sun. Othello, vulnerable and halfway crazy, mistakenly trusts the evil Iago. The product of a celebrated cultural era sets out to fictionalize some of the forces that made his ascent—and disintegration—possible (hint: he is the same author who opined there are no second acts in American lives). The captain of a sinking ship, obsessed unto madness by a malevolent mammal, takes his crew with him under the water into oblivion. A small man, armed only with a sling-shot, takes aim and slays the giant. The underdog gets off the mat to dethrone the champion, the nerd flies out of a phone booth, the orphan slides a magic slipper on her foot, a kid who would be king pulls the sword from the stone…

Get the picture? All of these elements are, to varying extents, contained within this epic Tragedy that detours into Comedy and ends up as Romance. And the rest is History: the construction, dissolution and redemption of one man's very American Dream.

Speaking of America and dreams, there's one overriding rule. We want our artists to earn it, to *mean* it, and sometimes the world sees to it that they suffer. If any single artist left it all, every scrap of his ambition and energy, on the table, it's Brian Wilson. He didn't pay the ultimate price; he didn't die. But for an unconscionable number of years—and years that got broken into months into weeks into hours into minutes into seconds like all the grains in a sandbox—Wilson had to reconcile himself to what must have seemed an irreconcilable verdict: a senseless world declared that he was insane. And then, having to live with a failure only he could be accountable for, even if blame could fairly be laid at the rubber souls of almost everyone that surrounded him.

For anyone new to the story, or unfamiliar with the intricacies therein, it might be useful to summarize what has long been rock and roll's ultimate cautionary tale. There was this band called The Beach Boys and they crafted best-selling pop confections about cars, surfing and girls. Driven by the increasingly determined—and restless—front man, the group dropped *Pet Sounds* on a mostly unprepared world. How influential was it? Paul McCartney who, at that time, brooked competition from no other mortal not named John Lennon, was intimidated, and ultimately inspired by what he heard. In typical Fab Four fashion, he and his mates rose to the challenge and first *Revolver*, then *Sgt. Pepper's Lonely Hearts Club Band* followed. Of course, *Pet Sounds* was not a commercial success, at least compared with previous number-one-with-a-bullet efforts from admittedly less complicated times. This did not sit well with some of Wilson's sidemen, particularly the Kiddie-Pool deep Mike Love.

When "Good Vibrations" dominated the charts in late '66, it was a gauntlet thrown as much as a premonition of greater things to come. The Beatles got there first and *Sgt. Pepper* became the undisputed artistic and cultural event of 1967. *SMiLE*, initially—and tellingly—entitled *Dumb Angel*, was supposed to be the Beach Boys' counterpunch. Impossible as it might be to imagine, Brian Wilson was poised to share the stage with Lennon/McCartney. It doesn't compute to contemporary minds because decades of blank space and unfulfilled promise did what history always does: vindicate the winners. But Wilson, as much as his peers across the pond, was edging the idiom toward the avant-garde, and the arresting results of "Good Vibrations" could be seen as an opening salvo. *SMiLE*, then, was going to be the band's masterpiece, and possibly the crown jewel of the Summer of Love. It very well might have put The Beach Boys, not The Beatles, on the top shelf critically as well as commercially.

But it wasn't meant to be. Wilson lost first the goodwill and support of his brethren and then, his mind. (Not unlike the other sad casualty of '67, Syd Barrett: it was an escalating intake of drugs—especially the LSD he credited with unlocking the doors and assisting the great visions— that accelerated his southward spiral.) And so, the work in progress was mostly scrapped and the shell-shocked group cobbled together the odd, occasionally sublime—if ultimately underwhelming—replacement, *Smiley Smile.* In the ensuing decades those aborted sessions—the strange fruits of Wilson's measureless mind—became rock music's Holy Grail. The material simply could not find the light of day; Wilson was too far gone and the results allegedly too impenetrable for public release.

And now, in a real-life *Deus ex Machina,* rock's scariest horror story has been transformed into pop music's *Dead Sea Scrolls.* Salvaged from oblivion with the blessing—and assistance—of the man who made them, in late 2011 we received the opportunity to hear them, in full (or as full as we can reasonably hope) for the first time. The results must be considered as close to an unvarnished approximation as possible of Wilson's original vision, and they are miraculous. Like a bombed and burned-out cathedral, there is dirt and dust aplenty, and the stained glass is, in places, broken and filled with cobwebs and strange empty spaces. This dirty authenticity only adds layers of meaning to the overall impact.

First reaction: it's difficult, bordering on unreasonable to believe the current incarnation of *SMiLE*—modeled as it is after Wilson's crucial but now less significant *Brian Wilson Presents SMiLE* from 2004—is comprised mostly of uncompleted drafts, bits and pieces. It sounds that great; it feels that complete.

Second reaction: I kept finding myself thinking much less of *Sgt. Pepper* and more of two later Beatles works, *The Beatles (White Album)* and *Abbey Road.* It's all in here, and where *The White Album* is a glorious, murky mess, these *SMiLE* sessions are more like wave after wave crashing onto soft sand. There are moments that conjure the acoustic bliss of "Julia" and "Mother Nature's Son", the surreal parlor music of "Martha My Dear" and "Don't Pass Me By", the baroque touches of "Long, Long, Long" and "Good Night" and the kitchen sink chaos of "Wild Honey Pie" and (of course) "Revolution 9". And where Lennon/McCartney got some wonderfully satirical licks on topical—and enduring—American history via "The

Continuing Story of Bungalow Bill" and "Rocky Raccoon", Wilson was clearly attempting to tackle the whole mythical cycle of westward expansion. As such, *SMiLE* might be best understood, or appreciated as a psychedelic tour of forward motion, incorporating sounds and sights (and smells and tastes) invoking myriad aspects of Americana. We are treated to chanting, cowboy movie theme music, field studies ranging from Indian to Hawaiian, cool-ish jazz, tone poems with classical elements, cartoonish sound effects, Musique concrete and a yodel thrown in for good measure. And most of all, tons and tons of the best harmonizing you've (never) heard, until now.

To me, the high-water mark of harmonizing, with due respect to Simon and Garfunkel, Crosby Stills and Nash and even earlier Beach Boys material, remains *Abbey Road* (and it is still astonishing to consider the trajectory The Beatles took, starting with the glistening sheen of the early hits to the *mano-a-mano* glory of *Rubber Soul* to the all-in, panoramic sweep of their final work). All that notwithstanding, I'm unsure I've heard anything approaching what is happening, on a purely vocal level, throughout *SMiLE*. It is instructive here to note the bonus tracks, particularly the "SMiLE Backing Vocals Montage", which makes it abundantly obvious how these sounds were stacked, shuffled and overlaid to create miniature symphonies of human voice. To hear these efforts come to fruition in songs as radically different as "Wonderful" (the aforementioned yodel, along with harmonies to rival Side Two of *Abbey Road*), "Do You Like Worms" (the previously described faux-Hawaiian chanting) or the pinnacle of harmonies and emotion in "Wind Chimes" (of which more, shortly).

One can—and should—recognize that, beginning with *Revolver*, The Beatles had the inclination, and money, to spend as much time in the studio as they saw fit, tinkering and tailoring until they were satisfied. They also, for understandable and well-documented reasons, had collectively grown weary of touring. Wilson too, had no stomach for the hustle and grind, even in the better days, but of course his band mates did (and still do). For the undeniable advancements of *Revolver* and *Sgt. Pepper*, Lennon and McCartney enjoyed a mutual focus and solidarity, not to mention the quite capable services of Harrison, Starr and the invaluable George Martin. Wilson, by comparison, was trying to hit a grand slam with no one else on base—or on board (and he just about knocked it out of the ballpark before a Tempest blew in and suspended play for almost a half-century). Needless to say, unlike the environment in the Beatles' camp, the *SMiLE* sessions comprised the inevitable tension of a band following the unsteady lead of its eccentric yet brilliant conductor, with one eye on The Road and all this entailed: adoring crowds, fat wallets and the safety of hit singles.

"Don't fuck with the formula," Mike Love supposedly complained as the material grew too complicated—and unconventional—for his liking. Love's words, and the attitude that prompted them, serve not only as a succinct summary of the internal forces Wilson found himself confronting (even in an increasingly fragile state of mind he was still the de-facto leader and resident visionary, something Syd Barrett abruptly ceased to be well before his eventual ouster), but also represents the rapacious imperatives of any commercial enterprise: keep it simple, appeal to as many people as possible and above all, never leave any opportunity for money on the table.

That Wilson lost this battle, ostensibly a victim of his own excesses and weakness, says a great deal about the ugly side of the unbridled '60s. Like Syd Barrett and too many anonymous psychedelic foot soldiers to count, LSD was a major incentive for creativity and expansion, but it carried a cost. By Wilson's own reckoning, acid played an essential role in his stylistic and compositional progression, but it also hastened some of the off-kilter internal mechanisms that preyed on his confidence, if not his ability to cope. The already controversial and clownish Mike Love comes off worse than ever the more one thinks about these circumstances and what was at stake in late '66 and early '67. Shouting not-so-sweet nothings in Wilson's ear would be unfortunate enough coming from a record company executive; coming from a fellow band mate, especially one who had gained a great deal more fame and wealth than he ever could have done on his own, is unforgivable.

What has tended to get lost or forgotten in the shuffle of sensationalistic trivia is that Wilson did not go down without a hell of a fight. He may not even have gone down at all so much as he was forced down, which makes the proceedings Tragic with a capital T. There can be no doubt that a primary instigating factor in Wilson's meltdown was his utter lack of guile. Remember, the Beach Boys were square. Wilson forced them, through a combination of will and his own curious brand of genius, to be successful. They were always more than a little corny, and that formula worked on the clean-cut, if innocuous early singles. *SMiLE* illustrates the struggle of a naïve but proficient artist chasing the white whale inside his own head. He was making it up as he went along and just about nobody was along for the ride. Much of this can be more easily understood by hearing the numerous takes of the eventual tour de force "Heroes and Villains". He knew what he was after, and he convinced, cajoled and begged his compatriots to cross the finish line. The results more than validate his obsessive effort: the song is masterful, complex but accessible, intense but assured, the fully realized vision of a unique talent.

So where does that leave us? Assuming that *SMiLE* is superior, ultimately, to *Pet Sounds,* how profoundly does its belated release shift of perceptions of the '60s; of rock and roll history? First, in what ways does it alter our well-ingrained admiration of *Pet Sounds?* It shouldn't, necessarily. Put simply, just as everyone is, correctly, comfortable with The Beatles having *several* albums represented in what we acknowledge as the upper echelon (think *Revolver, Sgt. Pepper, White Album, Abbey Road*, which typically land in the Top 20, if not Top 10, of critical lists), *SMiLE* must correspondingly assume its overdue but welcome place in the pantheon.

Now, the fun begins. Where does it go? Is it better than *Pet Sounds*? In terms of ambition, scope and execution, this writer has no problem putting it at the top of the heap. And, the unthinkable: is it better than *Sgt. Pepper?* Yes. More influential? Obviously not. More popular? Not even close. More important to the band's development? Hardly, since unlike The Beatles, The Beach Boys retreated, getting back to where they once belonged. But taking it on a song-by-song basis, is it superior? Unquestionably.

Now, the *real* fun: not much can stand alongside "With a Little Help From My Friends" and "A Day in the Life". You can even throw in "She's Leaving Home" and "Lucy in the Sky with Diamonds" if you must. Can even those four stand comfortably alongside "Heroes and Villains", "Surf's Up", "Cabin Essence" and—take your pick—"Do You Like Worms" or "Vega-Tables"? We can leave aside "Good Vibrations" to accompany "Strawberry Fields Forever", both released as singles in '66. It could even be conceded that, based on the above, The Beatles best songs edge out whichever ones we can throw up against them. But, as is the case with most classic albums, it's the odds and sods that make the ultimate case for greatness. Consider the opening salvo of "Our Prayer", and remember Wilson remarked that his desire was to write a "teenage symphony to God". The creepy acid-washed "You Are My Sunshine"; the gorgeous segue of "Look (Song for Children)" into "Child is the Father of the Man"; the quirky, Zappa-esque romp of "Holidays"; the pre-*Abbey Road* majesty of "Wonderful"; the Beatles-meet-Beefheart "The Elements: Fire (Mrs. O'Leary's Cow)"; the presciently prog-rock "Love To Say Dada".

And, above all, the dark gem of the lot, "Wind Chimes". This, more than anything else The Beach Boys did (and only Love and The Doors came close, or tried), seems to provide the until-now unheard and definitive counterpunch to the phoned-in feel-good anthem that *did* dominate the summer of '67, "All You Need is Love". Calculated if not entirely cynical, "All You Need is Love" is LSD-Lite, the calm before the *White Album* aftermath. As a complete and consistent artistic statement, only Love's *Forever Changes (*similarly embellished as it is with horns, strings, and harpsichord, with harmonies and a sense of dread lurking around every other note, occasionally threatening to move in and suffocate everything) presages the ugliness around the corner like "Wind Chimes" does—and it does so with a feeling and lack of self-consciousness that seems all the more remarkable, today. Perhaps Syd Barrett's "Jugband Blues" delineates the harrowing descent, breaking down in real time, better than anything else. "Wind Chimes" splits the difference, and does so with the benefit of Wilson's inimitable combination of innocence, wonder and frailty.

What results is a product that defies anything any hipster or detractor—of any generation—can credibly dismiss. *SMiLE* is earnest, it is honest and it is almost entirely unique. Its arrival explodes, or at least expands, the already rich narrative of 1967. It is at once the story of what was and what could have been. The question could be asked: does it represent what *should* have been? Probably not. Maybe the world would not have been ready for this. Maybe *SMiLE* would have come out and been laughed off the shelves. Maybe music would not have changed (for better, for worse) if this enigmatic masterpiece had been able to go toe-to-toe, a musical rumble in the jungle, with *Sgt. Pepper.* The only answer is that we can never know.

There's undeniably a cognitive dissonance listening to this, trying to make sense of it, all these years later. As awkward, or uncomfortable, or awe-inspiring as it is to hear 1966 with today's ears, it cannot be overlooked—attention must be paid. Assessing *SMiLE* and giving it its deferred due need not detract from everything The Beatles are worshipped for doing. This is, nevertheless, paradigm-shattering stuff, and most welcome to honest and open minds. How often does an artifact come along that radically disrupts, and reconfigures, an established understanding of history? How exceedingly seldom does this happen, if it ever does? It has happened here and everyone has reason to be very happy it did.

In the final analysis, the vision that sustained *SMiLE* was undeniable; delicate yet capable of withstanding an uninterested world—which is pretty much precisely what happened. The music, this beauty, bears witness to a dream—at times dark yet always unadulterated—and it remains Wilson's, and our, triumph.

August, 2012

LOU REED: ROCK AND ROLL'S DARK, BEAUTIFUL HEART

Everyone who joins a rock band wants to be heard.

The good ones want to be unique, while the pretenders tend to imitate what has already been done. The soulless ones regurgitate musical ideas manufactured by others and served up to them on soiled platters. Sadly, this third group tends to enjoy the greatest success.

And what is success? Financial success certainly is the easiest to measure, with an artist's influence ranking a close second. What is not so simple is identifying what will *endure*. In all but the rarest of cases, only the inexorable passage of time can reveal, long after the artist and the initial audience has expired, what has truly mattered to us.

Lou Reed was just such a case. His import and legend were established pretty much from the get-go, and he went wherever he wanted to go: underground, gutter, mainstream, whatever. He was a leather-wearing Whitman for a postmodern America, and his leaves of grass were the kind we used to smoke before, during and after we tuned in. Sweet Lou was inscrutable, elusive and still, somehow, everywhere.

1967 was for rock music what 1959 was for jazz.

Consider both the quantity and quality of '67's seminal releases; obviously *Sgt. Pepper* assumes the spotlight, but those twelve months also yielded a stunning spectrum of halcyon platters from Love's *Forever Changes* to the (then, unreleased) *SMiLE* by Brian Wilson and The Beach Boys. How about the debuts? Pink Floyd and The Grateful Dead went on to become two of the biggest bands on the planet. Yet even including the mind-boggling brilliance of the

Doors/Hendrix/Captain Beefheart holy trinity, it might not be wrong to suggest that The Velvet Underground's shot heard 'round the underground remains the most influential.

Hendrix changed the way the guitar was played, and everyone who has picked up a guitar ever since is, in some way, paying homage to the Temple he raised. But Hendrix was not human; Lou Reed was the New Testament Jesus (or Jesus' son, if you like) compared to the Old Testament God (or at least Moses) of Hendrix. As such, we stand in awe of Hendrix, but we recognize we are not of his kind; no one ever will be. The Velvet Underground on the other hand? Well, since everyone else always invokes the quote, I'll do my obligatory bit and nod to Brian Eno's astute assessment: "The first Velvet Underground album only sold 10,000 copies, but everyone who bought it formed a band."

That may well be true, and in fact, it may even be an understatement. But none of those bands—ranging from R.E.M. to David Bowie to The Pixies, just to name a few—ever released anything as strange and ecstatic as the first Velvet Underground offering. Over four decades later, it continues to confront our innate capacity to understand or to assess; it is simple in the way Dylan is "simple": ostensibly straightforward stories sung by voices that never won any talent shows, which inspires the visceral appeal of the Velvet Underground in general, and Lou Reed, in particular.

Reed was the perfect imperfection rock music needed: neither a naturally brilliant guitarist nor a honey-throated singer, and not always the best lyricist; let's not let his death sanitize the fact that he wrote a lot of ham-fisted stinkers over his long career, although Lou might have been the first—and best—example than anyone could do this. It's an illusion, of course: many people have tried, and most of them have failed. But Reed got there first, a darker version of Dylan who combined punk, glam and the paradoxical one-two punch of apathy and self-aggrandizement. Precious are each generation's artists who can cultivate such a subtle flash of brilliance.

As much as he's both lionized and lambasted for his poetic pomposity, Jim Morrison tapped into something quite a bit darker than *Dionysus For Dummies* circa '67, as songs like "The Crystal Ship" and "The End" evince. Reed was tapping into something even darker and more disturbing (his own veins, for one thing). Setting narcotics, sexual ambiguity and S&M to exotic, surreal soundtracks, like a marching band in Hell, Reed not only wrote like a grown up in what had long been a child-like art form, he wrote—and sang—like no adult anyone had ever known (the same could be said, sort of, for Nico, who functions as an uncertain angel to Reed's imperious demon on the debut). He still sounds that way to today's less sanitized sensibilities, and for decades he took his role as reporter and raconteur as a badge of dishonor. Some of those early tracks still sound surreal and exhilarating half a century later: if you ever want evidence of a wholly unique and inimitable vision, stand in awe of "Venus in Furs".

One way you know you've made not merely an indelible impact—itself enough of an achievement in our fifteen-minutes-of-fame-dumb-world-order, and yes I'm invoking Warhol on purpose— is when the accolades arrive in a deluge. Circa 2013, when hipper-than-thou tributes compete for pathos-per-pound—as they have been with Reed—you're likely to remain relevant. Aside from the musical and cultural import that he carried like a piece of tattered luggage, Reed never stopped mattering because he didn't half-step to anyone else's beat. He was the drummer of his own perplexing parade, and he was both confident and cool enough to keep the interlopers, imitators and especially the music critics at bay. Well-played, indeed.

Speaking of cool. It's easy to attempt when you're young, since that's when it matters the most. Reed dodged all appearances of giving a shit for the entirety of his career, and consequently he only became cooler as he aged. Although it happened to become a big hit, it still seems remarkable to consider what Reed pulled off with his signature song "Walk on the Wild Side" (He was a she? The colored girls? Even when she was giving head?). Or the middle finger to everyone in the world, including possibly himself, with the electric drill in the ear assault of *Metal Machine Music*. Or that he played with musicians ranging from Don Cherry to Metallica and, for lack of a better cliché, did it his way. It didn't always work, but Reed always did it the way he wanted, and anyone who wasn't down could hit the bricks. That, in art as well as life, is how cool happens.

More: he carried the cool as neither a burden nor a status to maintain; he was what he was. He did not just live in and sing about New York City, he was in every regard a living seed in that big dirty apple. Most legends don't live this long or that well when anointed so young. We could all learn a lot from Lou Reed, and our world is a lot less cool, and a great deal colder without the beating of his dark, beautiful heart.

November, 2013

A PORTRAIT OF THE BOSS AS A YOUNG MAN: ON BRUCE SPRINGSTEEN'S FIRST SEVEN ALBUMS

There is one key question that arises whenever a new box set of previously-available material is released: is it necessary?

With Bruce Springsteen's eight-disc *The Album Collection Vol. 1: 1973-1984*, the answer is an unequivocal, "Yes!" For one thing, five of these seven albums have, unbelievably, never been remastered. For those of us who own the original CD pressings, or have not particularly fond memories of how they sounded on vinyl or especially cassette incarnations, this sonic overhaul is not only very worthwhile but quite overdue.

Take it from an old-school Springsteen fan: the clarity on these reissues is game-changing. If it's now obligatory, when talking remasters, to mention sounds never before heard and nuance not previously detectable, all of the usual, positive accolades apply here. The two that needed this treatment most, *Greetings from Asbury Park, N.J.* and *The River*, in some ways sound like new albums. Presumably, Bruce disciples need no cajoling, but anyone on the fence can be reassured that this is not the typical window dressing disguised as an (expensive) upgrade. These suckers needed some TLC, and now they've gotten it.

A (very) few words about the accompanying booklet: it is underwhelming, to put it kindly. No interviews, no essays, no new nuggets of information or detail about the various recording session are included. None of these things are imperative for the box set's success, but considering that such features usually accompany reissues of this sort, and Springsteen has so much history to pore over, these omissions are curious at best. Aforementioned sonic upgrades aside, and taking into account the cost of this set, the bust of a booklet is a bit of an embarrassment. That said, it's all about the music, and this music is more than capable of telling its own story.

Those Romantic Young Boys

Believe it or not, Bruce Springsteen wasn't always the Boss. In fact, he paid persistent and less-than-productive dues for years as a work-in-progress. The breakthrough success of *Born to Run*, which landed him on the covers of *Time* and *Newsweek* in 1975, seems inevitable, even preordained. The reality is that fame and fortune were elusive, and by the time his debut dropped in 1973, he was an exceedingly experienced veteran of tiny clubs up and down the east coast.

Knowing what was to come, his uneven but promising first two albums reveal the work of an audacious if imperfectly formed voice. More than anything else, *Greetings from Asbury Park, N.J.* and *The Wild, the Innocent and the E Street Shuffle* convey the enthusiasm we still associate with Springsteen's legendary live performances. It's a passion for creating, playing, and connecting that could scarcely be contained by hit singles or three-hour concerts.

Critically embraced but unable to catch fire commercially, his debut is really more like a first novel than a first album. The young narrator is trying to cram together everything he's witnessed, everything he's tasted, smelled, imagined and dreamed about. At times the explorations feel ill-suited to the format, shoehorned as they are into three-and-four-minute snippets of song. Of course, there were the unavoidable—and not entirely unwarranted—comparisons to Bob Dylan. For the most part, however, these early songs sound less like an homage to his hero than an experiment to see how many marbles he can fit into his mouth (see: "Blinded by the Light" and "For You").

Interestingly, as it was released during the same year, *Greetings from Asbury Park, N.J.* is rather like a toned-down *Quadrophenia* for the Jersey Shore, with its litany of losers, hustlers, teenage theatrics and the tension between masculinity and creativity and how, if harnessed with sufficient care and talent, it can be translated into sensitive art. Occasionally indulgent ("Mary Queen of Arkansas"), sometimes anthemic ("Growing Up", "It's Hard to Be a Saint in the City"), it's when there is a lack of self-consciousness that Springsteen hints at perfection ("Does This Bus Stop at 82nd Street?").

The one-two punch of "Spirit in the Night" and "Lost in the Flood" combines many of the obsessions Springsteen would spend the rest of his albums investigating: haunted veterans of real or imagined wars, along with hoodrats and wannabe heroes with goofy nicknames (Wild Billy, Hazy Davy). In an album full of fantastic lines ("I said 'I'm Hurt' she said 'Honey, let me heal it'" and "Tainted women in VistaVision perform for out-of-state kids at the late show"), the young boss delivers an opening salvo that would become his aesthetic Holy Grail: "And I swear I found the key to the universe in the engine of an old parked car."

For his follow-up, *The Wild, the Innocent and the E Street Shuffle*, it's a double-down of sorts, more Van Morrison than Bob Dylan, more funk than folk, more sounds than words. In most regards, this is all for the best; with hindsight, we see how things were moving irresistibly to the bigger and more brazen enterprise of *Born to Run.* We get another program full of characters (Sandy, Kitty, Rosalita, Spanish Johnny, Puerto Rican Jane, etc.) looking for love, or each other, or themselves, etc. A little of this goes a long way, and since there's a lot of it, we can see how and why Springsteen struggled with ways to harness and hone his indefatigable determination.

On *The Wild, the Innocent and the E Street Shuffle*, there is more attention to detail, and the musicians, especially the brilliant keyboardist David Sancious, get plenty of space to stretch and assert themselves. Bruce, who gets less credit than he deserves as a lead guitarist, does some tasteful shredding on "Kitty's Back", and the use of strings ("New York City Serenade") and both tuba and accordion ("Wild Billy's Circus Story") give the proceedings a panoramic sweep. If the debut at times sounds like a cherry bomb inside a soda can, the follow-up is the soundtrack of summer evenings on a fire escape after the rain stops.

If it wasn't for the masterworks that followed, certain songs on this album would likely be more highly regarded. Certainly we have the concert-friendly "Rosalita" and "Kitty's Back", as well as the ebullient and odd obscurities of the title track and "Wild Billy's Circus Story". "New York City Serenade" strains for profundity and, with the aforementioned finesse of Sancious, it nearly succeeds.

"Incident on 57th Street", on the other hand, is an abundantly-realized mini opera. This is the first instance where one can imagine even Van the Man and Dylan perking up an eyebrow and thinking "Who the hell is *this* kid?" Likewise, "4th of July, Asbury Park (Sandy)" is at once a summation of what Bruce was trying to do to that point and a preview of the muscle-ballads to come. (The song also has arguably best line of the album: "Did you hear the cops finally busted Madam Marie for tellin' fortunes better than they do?") Even though neither album was enough to put him over the top, it's hard to claim anyone had a more productive, enduring year than Springsteen did in 1973.

The Promised Land

In a rather counterintuitive turn of events, the fact that the first two albums didn't make as much noise as they could (or should) have ended up being the best possible thing that could have happened for Springsteen as an artist and us as an audience. Instead of packing it in, Springsteen quadrupled down and spent many subsequent months agonizing over every second of every new song, making the recording that ensured nobody would ever forget his name.

As has been amply documented, it was the lack of big-time success that ultimately convinced Bruce he had to put not only his oversized heart, but his mind, his soul and bone marrow into a tour de force no 25 year old had any business making. It could be said that the go-for-broke inspiration the Boss became legendary for providing in his songs initially sprang from the most authentic source: himself. As he grappled with how to translate the music he heard in his head, he gradually attained the ideal balance of more-is-more lyrics and epic scope with rawest and most honest emotion. The resultant material revolves around a theme that is basic as it is elusive: everyone wants to be fulfilled.

Every element comes together in the creation of rock's mid-decade and post-Watergate response to the American Dream. Unlike his first two albums, where the narrators and heroes are kids in the midst of chasing shadows, making mistakes, or trying to escape their environment, on *Born to Run*, many of the protagonists have already seen and done enough to know that, for them, drastic action is required. There is an air of regret mixed with a not-yet extinguished defiance: the dream, whatever it may entail, is not quite dead. Thus the Romeo in "Thunder Road" declaring "it's a town full of losers and I'm pulling out of here to win" and the defiance of the title track "we can live with sadness / I'll love you with all the madness in my soul" and the affirmations of dudes and/or bandleaders knowing they got what they wanted in "She's the One" and "Tenth Avenue Freeze-Out".

There are also those unlikely to get away or win, those who already have the deck stacked against them and are either unable or unwilling to acknowledge it. Despite the driving pulse of "Night", where the everyman escapes the daily boil of his dead-end job and irksome commute to simply feel alive by driving off to nowhere at night with the yellow lines racing by beneath him, we know these flights are fleeting.

While the restrained bordering on elegiac musical backdrop (just piano, bass, and a killer trumpet cameo by Randy Brecker) on "Meeting Across the River" strains in its solemn way to make a hero out of this nobody, the tension of the song is that while he stands to score two grand, there is just as good a chance that he is about to get whacked. The track is neither ironic nor patronizing; the action (the song's working title was "The Heist") is relayed from this guy's point of view ("Tonight's gonna be everything that I said"), and there is little doubt what's at stake: "We got ourselves out on that line". We don't get to find out what happens, and whether the setting is 1975, 1875, or 2025, we don't really need to.

What else? Not much, except this masterpiece arguably has the best opening and closing songs of any album, ever. With "Thunder Road", Springsteen condenses a full record (a full movie, really) into just under five minutes. Getting a proper handle on "Jungleland" would require more than a paragraph or even a full review, really. And there it is: after a couple of tentative years as an apprentice, this is when Bruce became the Boss, and regardless of how you feel about everything that followed, the work here sufficiently secures his status for all time.

Streets of Fire

We have an understandable tendency to regard our biggest and best artists (and athletes) as fully-formed entities, miracles of evolution that, by their example and very existence, necessarily set them apart from us mere mortals. The reality is that while many of these icons are endowed with extraordinary gifts, the ones who make sustained and durable contributions invariably put in the work, and the work does not always, if ever, come easily. Put another way, our most successful innovators figure out what works by experimenting to determine what doesn't work. When we consider artists like Michael Jordan or John Coltrane, it's easy to assume it was destiny, and not discipline, that placed them in the pantheon.

Springsteen had done all any rock musician could reasonably ask or even hope for all by the time he set out to make his fourth album. For that reason, and certain other ones that have also been well documented, he took his time trying to follow *Born to Run*. Springsteen is now so huge and so ubiquitous that it almost seems disingenuous to mention, but the fact that he was even willing, much less able; to step into the studio again warrants a measure of admiration.

With *Darkness on the Edge of Town*, Bruce cemented his legacy as his hero for some, while crossing over into unforgivable pretension and posturing, for others. In this author's view, the folks in the latter category miss the mark—but more on that later.

Here's the deal: Springsteen found fame, fortune, and acclaim. Then he made his darkest album yet, one that put him solidly on the side of society that didn't inherit money or get blessed with good luck. The haters will say this was rich dude's guilt or, worse, blatant slumming to earn solidarity and record sales from a blue collar audience. Once again, it would seem apparent to anyone who's read the lyrics or followed the man's career of putting his time and energy where his mouth is, that these are risible notions.

Some critics and many fans think *Darkness on the Edge of Town* is Springsteen's best album; this critic and fan does not agree. If it signals the beginning of a new era where a more mature artist addresses more adult, real-world crises, it's also the advent of too many songs that are overproduced and too slick by half, featuring music that does not always match the often somber material. Perhaps a starker soundscape would have made the album intolerably bleak, but the carnivalesque elements, prominent drums (consider me possibly the only person who has wondered how much better things would have been had the Boss retained the services of Vini "Mad Dog" Lopez), and bombast make it occasionally difficult to savor. This formula would reach its intolerable fruition on "Born in the

U.S.A.", which proved that the team's commercial instincts were astute, even at the expense of making what should have been one of Springsteen's most harrowing tunes an arena-ready anthem.

This is serious music, and there is definitely darkness here. There is also resilience bordering on optimism, notably in "The Promised Land", "Prove It All Night" as well as the scorching title track, a song that deftly combines individuality and defiance. There is the righteous fury of "Adam Raised a Cain" (taking us from Asbury Park to the Old Testament), the straightforward rock triumph of "Candy's Room", the weary stoicism of "Streets of Fire" and the aforementioned tribute to the lunch pail crew in "Factory". And then there's the ballad "Racing in the Street", one of Springsteen's best, which could be considered a stripped-down continuation of pint-size epics like "Lost in the Flood" and "New York City Serenade", or perhaps an apotheosis of the emotional heft achieved in "Incident on 57th Street" and "Jungleland".

The River is, in some regards, a bigger but ultimately slighter continuation of the moods and themes from the previous album. Indeed, several of the songs were outtakes from the *Darkness on the Edge of Town* sessions. Like so many double LPs, debate can rage regarding whether a better set would result from it being pared down to a single album, as Bruce initially intended. And like all great and debated double LPs, it's the messier and (debatably) less successful bits that bestow an extra staying power, not unlike the way that fat makes for a well-marbled slab of steak.

Perhaps to lighten the tension or, heaven forbid, indulge in some good, old fashioned feel-good rock, the material shifts from ebullient to the intense. Revealingly, some of the softer material provides a template for his chart-crushing *Born in the U.S.A.*, while a few of the heavier numbers sound like blueprints for *Nebraska*. For evidence of the former, consider the disarmingly upbeat "Hungry Heart": like "Badlands", only less so, the buoyant music undercuts the cynicism ("We fell in love I knew it had to end"), the desperation ("We took what we had and we ripped it apart") and the immutability ("Don't make no difference what nobody says/Ain't nobody like to be alone") pumping that hungry, restless heart. For evidence of the latter, consider "Stolen Car" or the title track.

It would be too easy to characterize this as "Jungleland" writ small, but if anything, it cuts deeper and has that universal resonance, because this is a story everyone has seen, heard or experienced. And that is the essential import of Springsteen: he became Superman by singing, compellingly, about the most average, unremarkable people and problems. If American rock music has a poet laureate, it's Springsteen.

Now those memories come back to haunt me
They haunt me like a curse
Is a dream a lie if it don't come true
Or is it something worse
That sends me down to the river
Though I know the river is dry...

Game, set, match. After this Bruce was, for all time, the Boss. He had nothing left to prove. Nevertheless, he would go on to make his most personal and possibly important album, after which he became a decade-dominating supernova.

Deliver Me From Nowhere

Perhaps because of what followed—the next album, the acclaim—Springsteen's decision to make the ultimate lo-fi album seems even more prescient, appropriate, and perfect. If *Darkness on the Edge of Town* was a, well, darker departure from *Born To Run*, then *Nebraska*, after the mostly genial proceedings on *The River*, was like a belly flop into the abyss.

Nebraska carries with it death, despair and the electric chair—and that's just on the opening song. If Springsteen had carved out an affirmative niche, cataloging the difficult paths traveled and infrequent respites rewarded to our working stiffs, he now turned his sights on the dispossessed, the down-and-outs, the embittered outcasts and the irredeemable hard-cases. On *Nebraska*, he's not simply telling their stories (often without apology or unease); he is also using their seemingly preordained fates as a commentary on the things that don't get mentioned when we talk about the American Dream. *Nebraska* is not a dark album so much as an album filled with voices calling out, sometimes whispering, sometimes shouting, from a vast, inescapable darkness.

After more than 30 years of declining middle class wages and a major recession that saw taxpayers bailing out the cretins that caused it, much of what Springsteen sings about seems familiar, quaint, and perhaps even a bit naïve. That is why *Nebraska* is still important now, and why it was radical in its time. Springsteen might not have been the first major artist to call out the Reagan Revolution as the farce it was, but he certainly had the biggest bullhorn. *Nebraska* could only be called a political album by those who consider an examination of cause and effect a political act.

This is, in so many ways, Springsteen's most human album, not just because of its stripped-down aesthetic, but because each song deals directly with the themes he's made a career stalking like a stenographer: the would-be criminals, the convicted, the could-be champions, and the ones born beneath the underdog, to quote Charles Mingus. *Nebraska* joins the ranks of essential but demanding albums, like Sly and the Family Stone's *There's a Riot Goin' On* and Neil Young's *Tonight's the Night.* This record is not one you return to for pleasure, though the pleasures are manifold; instead, it's one you return to in appreciation, to savor and pay witness. Like all great art that tells us what we need to know and don't necessarily want to know, we must be thankful that someone else, using fiction, has created a kind of reportage that is truer than newspaper truth.

Nebraska remains a work that insists on being absorbed in a single setting, each song anticipating and in some cases commenting upon the next. The immortal line "I got debts no honest man could pay" turns up twice and the notion of inevitability, be it debt or death, is a running leitmotif throughout all ten songs.

Still, the single line that unifies the whole is another that surfaces in two separate songs: "Deliver me from nowhere". The narrator of the title track, recalling The Misfit from Flannery O'Connor, is resigned to his fate ("I guess there's just a meanness in this world"). The man staring down life in prison in "Johnny 99" has an indictment for those indicting him ("It was more than all this that put that gun in my hand"). The aimless driver who may or may not be describing a felony-in-progress (again recalling the Misfit) offers the ultimate *J'accuse!* to an indifferent universe ("The only thing that I got's been botherin' me my whole life"). Yet after the various encounters and carnage have unfolded, the Boss—both judge and jury—offers up a refrain that defines his very American sensibility: "At the end of every hard-earned day people find some reason to believe."

Glory Days

As anyone who drew breath between 1984 and 1986 recalls, Springsteen was ubiquitous in the mid-'80s. For numerous reasons, *Born in the U.S.A.* was the right album at the right time. For many understandable reasons, it's the single album that appealed to the largest group of people. Being indifferent to it, then, and having no stomach for it now, is not a cantankerous badge of honor, or mean-spirited attempt to seem old school. The fact of the matter is that much of this material made many fans extremely happy. More power and props to all involved.

For this fan and, presumably, at least a handful of folks who knew who the Boss was before "Dancing in the Dark", there is very little of lasting value on this absurdly radio-friendly monstrosity. To be certain, *Nebraska* was (intentionally) unsophisticated, but its heart is off the charts. On this, we have the most simplistic formula on repeat cycle: unsophisticated songs on the lyrical and musical front, and a production gloss that will give your ears cavities. The hyper-amplified and overplaying Max Weinberg alone is a deal breaker, but the synthesizers suck the life out of everything. (Yeah, okay, it was the '80s).

Worst of all, for once, the "working man" motif actually does feel like shtick. To take but one example, "Working on the Highway": listening to it 30 years on—like Alex from *A Clockwork Orange* with ears pried open—one wants to like it, and can almost appreciate how it invokes Eddie Cochran… but then the cheesy synth comes in and it becomes half-assed rockabilly filtered through a cotton candy machine. Only "I'm on Fire", "I'm Goin' Down", "Downbound Train" and, barely, "My Hometown" salvage this from the über-commercial scrap heap.

Mileage varies, obviously, but for me, *Born in the U.S.A.* takes the softer sheen of *The River* and the sporadic gloss of *Darkness on the Edge of Town*, puts the mess on a cycle of steroids with a cocaine chaser, and the result is MTV Eden.

And then there's the whole issue with the title track, easily the most misunderstood song of all time. Any defense of Springsteen's intentions can and should point to the lyrics, but there is simply no excusing the chest-thumping, insipid sing-along music, which predictably led simpletons (like George Will) to try and appropriate this as a "Go America!" theme song.

No Surrender

Here's the thing about Bruce Springsteen looking back over 30 years after his biggest album dropped: he seems content, and he has every reason to be content. He is no longer a young man, but he's kept after the same issues and injustices that inspired his best work. That alone absolves him from the cynics, skeptics, and all-purpose haters.

Some final words should be said to the self-satisfied conservative sorts who love pointing out how an opportunistic Springsteen has gotten wealthy by offering up feel-good platitude. (Kind of like Ronald Reagan, an irony entirely lost on these True Believers). Springsteen puts his time and money where his heart is, and he has done more for this country, as an artist and an advocate than just about any politician. He remains a man amongst boys, and if some of his work has not aged well or his later work at times inevitably disappoints, he himself presents a model for how to advance through life with dignity and integrity. He is and always will be the Boss, and America has produced very few artists who have depicted and appraised their country with more passion and purpose.

February, 2015

ORRIN KEEPNEWS: HERO FOR AMERICA'S MUSIC

Orrin Keepnews frequently talked about jazz the way war veterans will talk about experiences on the front lines. There were at least two reasons for this. One, it was never strictly business with him; it was *always* personal. More importantly, it was necessary.

See, Keepnews didn't gravitate toward a career in jazz—as producer, writer and battle-scarred raconteur—because it was fashionable or profitable. He immersed himself in the idiom for the same reasons any of us who make the music and those who become enchanted, then obsessed by it do: because there is no choice in the matter. Once you get in, as a fan but especially as an artist or producer, you don't get out easily. You don't want to. In Keepnews's case, he didn't know how to.

To get a handle on the debt we owe him, it must be adequately understood that Keepnews didn't *merely* oversee some of the seminal sessions in jazz history (e.g., American history); he did not *just* encourage some of jazz music's (e.g., American music's) most significant players; he was hands on, sleeves rolled up and directly involved in ensuring the tunes came out the way they did.

Exhibit A, and it's one for all-time: the perfectly titled composition by Thelonious Monk, one of music's most sublime iconoclasts, "Brilliant Corners". This masterwork, the recording of which confounded two of the most adept and astute men who ever walked into a studio, Max Roach and Sonny Rollins, was ultimately spliced together from multiple takes by Keepnews.

That Keepnews was one of the foremost ambassadors for jazz is common knowledge to anyone who knows anything. His street cred dates back to the great old days when giants roamed the earth, when he produced and championed geniuses like Monk, Bill Evans, Sonny

Rollins, and Wes Montgomery. He was properly lauded by people who had a handle on jazz, history and—most importantly—propriety. That he wasn't remunerated or revered in a fashion commensurate with his achievements underscores a truth almost frivolous in its familiarity: like the artists he advocated, the riches attained were rare, obscurity was all but inevitable and disappointment often the reward for a lifetime dedicated to stalking an increasingly unappreciated sort of brilliance.

As such, Keepnews could talk about racism. He could comment on an industry where banality flourishes and genius is ill-understood, if it's recognized at all. He could tell stories from a very unique period in American history where, when it came to the intersection of art and culture, it was at once the best and worst of times. What Keepnews eventually grasped, and what historians will confirm, is that as challenging and confrontational as the scene could be in the '50s and '60s, it was as good as it would ever get, and jazz will never have that type of audience again.

Almost a decade before the Summer of Love, Keepnews produced, and wrote the epic liner notes, for Sonny Rollins's tour-de-force *The Freedom Suite.* In other words, Keepnews was literally on the front line of the struggles inherent in everything that came to the fore during America's Civil Rights movement. This was music as statement, and it was not fashionable or facile; it was in almost every sense, a matter of life and death, as livelihood and a way of living. Jazz was music with a social conscience before it was cool.

Keepnews took the arrival of rock 'n' roll personally. More than once he correctly claimed that the Beatles and everything that came after changed things, forever. When I had the opportunity to chat with him, we agreed to disagree that music changed, for the worse. Yes, the rise of rock certainly didn't bolster the prospects for jazz (music or musicians), but the artistic and societal shifts were, in many ways, attributable to the doors of perception that rock and the attitude it embraced blew open.

While I was young and more foolish than I apprehended, I realize now, more than I did in my mid-'20s, that Keepnews wasn't just lamenting a cultural revolution that dumbed down the discourse, even as it elevated consciousness in many non-clichéd ways. Rock, and the eruption of talent, including both listeners and players who may otherwise have gravitated toward jazz, inexorably sucked oxygen out of an already tiny space. Jazz could not compete, which meant the music didn't get to flourish at the same rate, for the same-sized audience. As a result, many of these men and women would have a harder time making a living. It wasn't just business; it was personal for all involved.

Keepnews never retired and he never went away. Active, interested and engaged until the end, he continued doing what all great producers do: discovering new talent and celebrating the old masters. What Keepnews did for jazz music was a form of dedication that bordered on the heroic, but it's a mistake to view his life's work through this narrow if elemental lens. Rather, we should acknowledge the ways he held himself to a relentless standard of excellence. He accepted the challenges, embraced the lack of easy solutions and, in the process, advanced the music. He is a rare example of what we hope to emulate when we invoke the best American tradition of invention, discovery and improvement. He is a model for how to follow one's purpose, with a lack of fear and passion that only death can extinguish.

He lives on, of course, in our memories and always, forever, in the miraculous sounds that, without his guidance and collaboration, we may otherwise never have heard.

March, 2015

THREE: FILM

THE DAVID LYNCH DILEMMA

There are some movies that require a certain commitment of time to figure out what's going on. David Lynch's movies, I've become convinced, are *about* trying to figure out what's going on. And that's fine, as far as it goes. In its art-for-art's sake, uber-pretentious, anti-commercial, anti-audience sensibility, Lynch hoists a freak flag that is, upon closer inspection, a fuck you flag. The question, as it is with all challenging art, ultimately must be: is it worth it? His films are odd and unsettling, and they are often unlike anything you've ever seen before. And yet: is that enough?

Well…take any of his films, then take away the attractive female characters, their inexorable (contractual?) nudity, and the handful of very brief—but very brilliant—scenes, and Lynch's work seems to be a series of somethings that seek to defy being identified for what they look and smell like. You are left with an oeuvre that seems to separate viewers into three camps: the good (those who claim to "get it"), the bad (those who don't, or can't), and the ugly (or, the angry; those who tried to get it, failed, and then, upon repeat viewings, determine that they are unworthy and, most importantly, uninterested).

Consider me ugly. Not angry, but certainly perplexed at the consistent, and reflexive, critical accolades. And let's acknowledge the fact that Lynch does not merely have fans, he has advocates. Defenders of the faith. Crusaders. As a proponent of acquired taste anomalies running the gamut of high and low culture and all points in between (especially the points in between), I appreciate the allure, and I don't begrudge it. What I am curious about is, who are these people, and what is it they actually see in these films?

First—and this may well elucidate my dilemma—the only Lynch film that has spoken to me, post *Elephant Man*, is *Wild at Heart,* which generally seems to be ranked amongst his weaker efforts. For my money, this one could practically be validated by Willem Dafoe alone: Bobby Peru is not only indelibly sinister, sick and hilariously oleaginous, he represents what is best about David Lynch: extreme weirdness in adept (and mercifully brief) quantities. But the movie abounds with minor tour de force performances by all involved, with Nicolas Cage and Laura Dern doing some career-best work, even when their clothes are on. Wonderful supporting work is delivered by a wickedly over-the-top Diane Ladd and a typically sullen (here bordering on docile) Harry Dean Stanton.

But, of course, *Blue Velvet* is the one that, in order to assert one's pointy-headed credibility, you have to sanction. I call bullshit. To be sure, I don't fall in with the camp who loves it, but I also don't loathe it; I just think it's...okay. More bad than good, but containing enough intriguing scenes ("Heineken? Fuck that shit! Pabst Blue Ribbon!") to make it memorable. But still. I saw it in the '80s, saw it in the '90s and have seen it during this decade, and it's simply impossible to look past the (typically) improbable—bordering on intelligence-insulting—story line, the (typically) maudlin, fifth-rate dialogue, and the ostensibly bold assessment of American sadomasochism that quickly unravels like so much stylized soft porn. Granted, an authentic sense of surreal tension is nailed—then hammered into submission, and Dennis Hopper's (overboard, over-praised) Frank Booth is scary enough, kind of the like the boogeyman is frightening, despite being fake. In terms of peeling back the layers of plastic conformity of an older (or even contemporary) America, captured in the notable but not revelatory opening scene, it works. That it's considered one of the seminal films of the '80s strikes me as disconcerting, akin to the way I'd concede that New Kids on the Block were one of the most successful bands of that decade. Mobs are mobs, even when they are different sizes.

But the mystery train truly goes off the tracks with *Lost Highway,* the ultimate "you're with us or against us" entry in the Lynch catalog. For me, it really boils down to two pretty straightforward questions. One, can anyone claim to know what the movie is about? Two, can anyone claim to have actually enjoyed it? Hearing ten different people offer ten different interpretations of a movie is, in one regard, evidence of a successfully engaging work of art. But that sure seems to be setting the bar embarrassingly low for a director with Lynch's obvious talent. (My personal favorite bent-over-backwards attempt to put lipstick on this pig is the claim that Lost Highway is a highly illusory homage of Ambrose Bierce's masterful short story "An Occurrence at Owl Creek Bridge". Even making the exceedingly generous indulgence that this is the case, an adaptation of any classic work of literature should actually be good, shouldn't it?)

Weirdness for the sake of weirdness is fine, and in shrewdly doled out doses, it can be instructive and enjoyable—like eating fish eyes, for instance. And I don't begrudge Lynch one bit for being that one-in-a-billion artist whom remarkable numbers of critics and fans have designated as their go-to guy. My issue lies with the same fans and critics who lazily defend his work by asserting that anyone who doesn't like it simply doesn't get it. Remember Gary Larson's *The Far Side* cartoons? It was true that if you had to explain one to someone, it was hopeless. However, if you had to explain it, you could; it would lose most of its humor and punch, but virtually every one of them was explicable. In other words, it's a much more impressive—and worthwhile—piece of entertainment if it provokes or even befuddles, but is still, on some level, intelligible.

Granted, all willfully difficult artists will attract ardent (I won't say fanatical) proponents—to a certain extent, that's the point of their excessively abstruse vision. Too often, a self-indulgent, or unpersuasive (I won't say incapable) effort is credited for being authentic because it is impenetrable, and that is where the fans and critics come into play with Lynch. Analysis is unnecessary, it's already understood that the work is brilliant, and it's a given that, with Lynch, you are about to see something that confronts your puny, preconceived notions of reality. The less sense it makes, the more adeptly he is revealing how ensnared you are in the linear charade of conventional storytelling. Or the system. Or something. Where this becomes insufferable is when esoteric artistes inherit a priori acquiescence in a fashion too similar to the ideological blank slate politicians count on from their compliant bases. We know how this works: an already-accepted conclusion is invoked, or promoted, and the appraisal (of the product, of the candidate) is liberated from subjective analysis, it's already understood. Discourse is discarded for absolution in ways that say more about how the viewers view themselves than the film. And perhaps that is, if unconsciously, the entire point?

In the final analysis, I'll admit that David Lynch is very much like God. I watch his movies the way I look at the creation of the world: most of the time I can't claim to discern what's going on, but someone seems to have gone to a great deal of trouble. Beauty, not to mention intelligent design, is always in the brain of the beholder. The question remains: is that enough?

May, 2008

CHINATOWN: THE ONLY PERFECT AMERICAN FILM EVER MADE

Chinatown does not usually make the short list of best American films. In fairness, it probably shouldn't. It will have to settle for merely being the only perfect American film ever made. Perfect? Well, perfection is in the eye of the beholder, and the definition of perfect might include the notion that there's no such thing as perfection in art. Nevertheless, by any number of criteria, Chinatown continues to satisfy more than thirty years on. In the final analysis it's the magnificent sum of its considerable parts: it's tragic, it's hilarious, it's (at times) scary, it's challenging, it's complicated, and it is unnerving. It is, in short, America. Or at least it does the near impossible: it articulates the symbiotic relationship between greed and power that props up capitalism, a narrative that played an ever-increasing role in 20th century America. Much could—and should—be said along these lines, and how Robert Towne's meticulous screenplay was ideal fodder for Roman Polanski's dark and utterly authentic vision (Polanski also deserves extensive praise for resisting the happier ending Towne wanted).

That's all well and good, but why does *Chinatown* remain compelling, and worthy of repeated viewings? Speaking personally, I've seen the film at least 15 times in the last 20 years, and each viewing has revealed new layers or nuance, and has only confirmed that initial impression: it's perfect. The screenplay, the soundtrack, the casting: all unassailable. Memorable scenes? Really, the entire movie is just a series of memorable scenes. Or, more accurately, a continuous stream of indelible moments: Gittes (Jack Nicholson) in the barber shop, covered in shaving cream, angrily inviting the wiseass banker to step outside and "discuss things"; Gittes sardonically lamenting the loss of his shoe ("Son of a bitch! Goddamn Florsheim shoe!"); Gittes telling the dirty joke unaware of his soon-to-be-client and lover standing behind him; Gittes driving frantically through an orange grove to escape some pissed off farmers whose land he is trespassing upon; Noah Cross (John Huston as the flawlessly named incarnation of evil) persistently, and quite intentionally, mispronouncing Gittes name (Mr. Gits); Gittes calling the officious jerk in the public library a weasel; Gittes imploring Evelyn Mulwray (Faye Dunaway) to let the police intervene against Cross (her father) and her unsettling response: "He *owns* the police!"… the list could go on.

Perhaps most importantly, this is, quite simply a beautifully crafted work, the type of movie that can be savored without the sound on. One example: Gittes sits patiently at the top of a sloping cliff, overlooking the Los Angeles coastline as day slides into evening. He waits, lighting cigarette after cigarette, totally unaware that he has already stumbled into a hornet's nest of corruption. The beauty of what he sees (and we see) perfectly masks the brutal ugliness of what is really going on: unwittingly, Gittes is about to lift up the rock and behold the guts and machinery of what gets sold as the American dream.

Naturally, *Chinatown* passes the ultimate test: is it still meaningful, today? Does it still tell us about something about ourselves? Sadly, it does. Impossible as it may have been for Towne and Polanski to imagine, there would come a time where public trust of those in power deteriorated beyond even the Watergate era nadir of Nixonland. Today, as the fabricated sheen of Wall Street crumbles around us, we might ask the wizards who wrought this mess the same question Gittes asks Cross—and expect the same answer:

"Why are you doing it? How much better can you eat? What could you buy that you can't already afford?" "The future, Mr. Gits! The future!"

There it is: the most accurate and succinct depiction of unfettered greed you're likely to hear. And to see John Huston convey it is to appreciate, and be appalled by, the allure and immorality of depraved power. Jake hears it, and sees it, and for him—and the country—it's too little, too late. As always. "Forget it, Jake, it's Chinatown," his partner admonishes him. But Jake can't forget it, and we know he won't forget it. Neither will we.

October, 2008

THE INSIDER: TEN YEARS LATER

Toward the end of Sydney Lumet's '70s classic *Serpico* there's a scene that encapsulates the conundrum faced by the eponymous cop: already *persona non grata* within the law enforcement fraternity for his refusal to take bribes, Serpico is transferred to the narcotics division, where the beat is the exceedingly dangerous streets way off Broadway. His new colleague grimly explains that, compared to the types of kickbacks Serpico was accustomed to seeing, the haul in narcotics is serious business. "That is big money, *that* you do not fuck around with." In this moment Serpico finally understands that his life is now in greater danger, amongst police officers than at the hands of criminals, because of his insistence on obeying the law.

This scenario, magnified many times over (in terms of the cash, and the stakes) is what Jeffrey Wigand went up against when he made the excruciating decision to defy his former employer, Brown and Williamson, and expose their big, dirty secrets on *60 Minutes.* His reluctance to quietly play ball helped get him fired; his refusal to remain silent made him a target of a very *committed* company with ridiculously deep pockets. Like Serpico, Wigand was obliged to work from within to affect change. He is, in the words of Lowell Bergman (serendipitously portrayed by Al Pacino), the "ultimate insider". So why is this story important? Trying to remember the world when it was still in Big Tobacco's unthreatened sway is sort of like trying to imagine the same world before it was wide and webbed. Yet both of those eras are not impossible to recall: they are still quite clearly in the rear-view mirror; one just needs to see through the smoke.

Even before they started taking down the Marlboro Man billboards, just about everyone agreed cigarettes were bad for you. Macho associations aside, it was more a matter of freewill; not unlike drinking alcohol, certain risks are associated with legal, if unhealthy behavior. That's America. Of course, more than a few people would have been outraged to learn how much chemical manipulation was taking place in order to make those cancer sticks even more habit-forming.

So: some dirty secrets were kept strictly under wraps, as a matter of policy. Big Tobacco counted the money and its executives testified that, to their knowledge, nicotine was not addictive. Considering the money involved, the perjury committed, and the industry's unfettered success with litigation, only the most recalcitrant underling would dare defy its wrath.

Enter Jeffery Wigand, VP of Research and Development at Brown & Williamson in Louisville Kentucky. He is well paid if unfulfilled, but reaches the end of his moral rope once he discovers the company is systematically using toxic chemicals (like ammonia) to enhance the addictive properties of its cigarettes. His refusal to play ball gets him fired; his refusal to remain silent about it invokes the god-like wrath of his former employer. Enter Lowell Bergman, producer for the CBS show *60 Minutes*, who could accurately be called a crusader (as a compliment from his fans and an epithet from his enemies).

Bergman meets Wigand by chance, but quickly realizes the powerful information the scientist is struggling to conceal. The tipping point—for both men—is when they each understand how badly Wigand actually wants to speak out, and it's only the threat of a lawsuit (and loss of severance) that is keeping him quiet. To ensure they have made their position clear, B & W initiates some subtle and not-so-subtle harassment of Wigand's family. Once the death threats begin, he decides to tell his story to Mike Wallace. The rest is history.

The Insider is an unqualified artistic success, and one of the most important movies of the last ten years. It is remarkable drama, compellingly portrayed. It is also director Michael Mann's finest film. It features a gorgeous soundtrack (courtesy of Lisa Gerrard). It boasts some of the finest acting in Al Pacino's legendary career. And Russell Crowe not only delivers his personal best work, he turns in what is possibly the best performance since De Niro in *Raging Bull.* With all respect to Mann's considerable abilities, he wisely manages to stay out of the way and let the scope of this story supply its own abundant energy. His restraint has the opposite effect of the overwrought (and overrated) *Heat*, which attempted to parlay an armed robbery into an opera.

With *The Insider*, he takes grand theater and mostly scales it down to its human elements: the people making the decisions and the people devastated by them. Forget the forever discussed showdown between Pacino and De Niro in *Heat.* The ongoing confrontations (initially contentious, ultimately loving) between Pacino and Crowe are effulgent. Their entire time on the screen is a two-and-a-half hour acting clinic.

Jeffrey Wigand, as a character (and a role) is practically too good to be true: his life is derailed in part by his own hubris and mostly by the ugliest kinds of corporate machinations. Ultimately he recognizes his fate is to accept the circumstances and consequences that are bigger than his privacy or security. Crowe is equal to the task. Beyond the superb script and expert direction, he instinctively grasps that in order to convey the depths of Wigand's turmoil (and, equally important, avoid an easy, almost inevitable descent into bathos—one shudders to think of what the majority of A-List actors would have done to this part, if given the opportunity), he has to present a brilliantly flawed man always at risk of imploding. Wigand is not a saint and neither Crowe nor Mann attempt to portray him as one. There is so much anger, frustration and fear coiled within his super-sized frame, Crowe consistently seems obliged to expel words from his mouth as much as speak them. As Wigand, he's almost unrecognizable with his added weight, bleached hair, glasses and disheveled defensiveness.

As Lowell Bergmann, the irrepressible producer who has the pleasure (and burden) of working with the megalomaniacal Mike Wallace, Pacino conveys the passion and purposeful edge that made Wigand's ultimate triumph possible. Bergmann's quandary is less dangerous but arguably more unwieldy: after gaining Wigand's trust and convincing him to break his confidentiality agreement, he is directed by the brass at CBS to censor the segment. "The greater the truth, the greater the damage," he is told in a sickening sequence that illustrates the ways in which corporate media's cowardice might be even more profound than Big Tobacco's rapacity.

The Insider is a rare artistic achievement that is compelling as it is important. It's a document that recalls the world as it used to be, while depicting the decisions and events that changed it for the better.

March, 2009

THE STRANGE CASE OF DR. DENNIS AND MR. MILLER

At issue is not whether Dennis Miller, after 9/11, lost his mind and starting cheerleading for Bush, Cheney and the Iraq War (he did). It's also not an outrage that, coincidentally or not, he's no longer near as nimble or gratifying as he was in his prime (he isn't). What's important to acknowledge is that, while his newer material is sorely lacking, when he was on his game, he was amongst the baddest—and brightest—stand-up comedians in the country.

For those of us who have pined many moons for his inexplicably unreleased HBO comedy specials from the '90s; it's time to celebrate an overdue victory. *Dennis Miller: The HBO Specials* is exactly what the doctor ordered for fans who remember the days when a thesaurus was a requisite part of the experience. A comic who could make you laugh *and* think is never something to take for granted, as they're always in woefully short supply.

Miller, from his snarky heyday as *Saturday Night Live's* "Weekend Update" anchor in the late '80s and early '90s, was arguably the most consistently entertaining, and intimidating, funnyman on the scene. After admiring him in relatively small doses during the "Weekend Update" segments, it was something of a revelation to see him stretch out and hold court for a full 60-minute set. Starting with *Mr. Miller Goes to Washington* in 1988, Miller has made seven official specials for HBO, all of which are collected in this very reasonably priced and highly recommended set.

When Miller performed in D.C. for his first special it was more than 20 years ago, but somehow seems even longer. Impossible, almost, to recall a time when Reagan was limping out of office and Miller was not yet middle-aged. Indeed, he was young, confident and he had a hell of a head of hair. He knew it, too. At this point in his career Miller took few prisoners and no target was spared from his lacerating sarcasm. Commenting on his recent gigs in the Deep South, he sardonically observes "Talk about Darwin's waiting room…there are guys in Alabama who are their own father."

Later he laments "You spend your whole life stopping at red lights, then at the end there's a cruel irony when you die: they let your funeral procession run the red lights on the way to the cemetery." Regarding born-again Christians who insist he's going to Hell if he's not born *again*; he says "Pardon me for getting it right the first time."

Perhaps tellingly, he has an (admirably) prescient take on terrorists, marveling at the ways horrendous acts can be justified in the name of God/religion. This is the lovably bratty Miller, a smart-ass with a heart of cubic zirconium: he was more intelligent and better-looking than you, and that was all there was to it. Chevy Chase, the first "Weekend Update" anchor, had the corner on this market for a minute, and then Miller ran with the baton for about a decade.

In 1990 he recorded *Black and White* which, for me, is on the short list of all-time post Lenny Bruce stand-up concert recordings: it's an absolute tour de force and easily justifies the purchase of this entire set. Miller begins with a muted bang, claiming "I'd like to start off with an impression…I'd like to, but I'm genetically incapable." For the rest of the special he is at the height of his *more loquacious than thou* phase and it's a delight to watch how unreservedly he revels in his own brilliance.

A few highlights, taken at random: "I view the reunification of Germany in much the same way I view a possible Dean Martin/Jerry Lewis reconciliation: I haven't really enjoyed any of their previous work and I'm not sure I need to see the new shit right now"; "I'm in therapy now, I'm so insecure I get depressed when I find out the people I hate don't like *me*"; "(TV preachers) say they don't favor any particular denomination…but I think we've all seen their eyes light up at tens and twenties."

Of his father, Miller deadpans "My old man made The Great Santini look like Leo Buscaglia," and on the then-new development of interminable automated customer service recordings, "I don't stay on the phone that long with friends contemplating suicide." If you've never seen this, you owe it to yourself.

They Shoot HBO Specials, Don't They?, from 1994, is worthwhile just for its ingenious title, but the show is actually quite satisfactory. Speaking of the post-LA riot tensions, he says "I get pulled over by a cop in LA I don't even fuck around; I just wind the window down and blow the guy."

Politically, he has few kind words for Bush the Elder, and no fondness for Reagan, but he's already dubious at the prospects of Clinton being a successful, or accepted, leader. He actually defends Hillary (!) saying, revealingly, "I think she's a good woman…we need smart people now; maybe she can help." And this is a crucial component of his subsequent devolution as a comic: he was never a *liberal*; he ridiculed pomposity and idiocy which is always abundantly represented on both sides of the political spectrum. Of course, he had a particular penchant for calling out the bullying tactics of media blowhards and the baser instincts (fear, power) that the most cynical politicians prey upon, so it's impossible to ignore the sad irony of seeing him prostrate himself (for a paycheck?) at the fortress of Pomposity and Idiocy at Fox News.

It certainly doesn't make his old material any less funny; it just makes it a tad bittersweet to look at, all these years later. In any event, and for the record, my favorite moment of the entire show is when Miller delivers an impassioned—and quite moving—defense of James Stockdale (remember him?), lacerating the media (and public) that found him lacking for the sole reason that "he committed the one unpardonable sin in our culture: he was bad on television". He ends the show by predicting that the day Dan Quayle (remember him?) successfully runs for president (and he was then threatening to do) "is the day Shelley Winters runs with the bulls at Pamplona." That's good stuff.

By 1996 the also impeccably titled *Citizen Arcane* was in the can, but the first cracks in Miller's fortress are visible. For starters, he seems a tad lethargic; it turns out the Aspen altitude is getting to him and as he reaches for an oxygen mask, a few folks in the crowd scoff at him. "Well fuck you," he retorts. "Get a climate!" To be certain, he's still amusing, and he is still articulate. He offers up perhaps the best summation of Bill Clinton's frustrating legacy I've heard: "The chasm between his potential and his actuality is so vast…and the struggle (to find balance) sets off all his deficiencies." It's pretty hard to quibble with that assessment.

But when he observes "we have too many hung juries and not enough hung defendants", one wonders what his beef is. It turns out, a little bit of everything, as he refers to the US as "one big, violent trailer park." He is (understandably) outraged at the general inanity of the population, which results in easily duped juries. It just seems odd that for a man so obviously intelligent, he doesn't (or doesn't want to) connect the dots between those who are brought to justice and those who have money or influence. In other words, he seems content to scoff at how moronic our talk-show nation has become, but doesn't seem unduly perturbed that it's often his fellow celebrities who waltz away from prison time for very obvious—and odious—reasons.

He spends an insufferable chunk of time lambasting the ACLU and has little to say about politicians or the powerful. At one point he declares "I'm looking to make a little bread, build a wall, take care of my loved ones…and stay out of the crosshairs." Die-hard Dennis Miller fans may have to Windex off their LCD screens after that one.

Miller's HBO feature for the end of the century, 1999's *The Millennium Special: 1,000 Years, 100 Laughs, 10 Really Good Ones* is a terrific idea that is pulled off with aplomb. Miller focuses on the 1900's and breaks the century into 20-odd year chunks. He does "the news" (relaying the popular stories of the times with his trademark "Weekend Update" shtick): it's clever and mostly funny. There is, alas, a trace of a creeping jingoism that would reach its apotheosis in short order.

Miller takes potshots at a few predictable targets: Russia, Germany and (sigh) France; while it's an exercise of shooting fish in a rather boring barrel; it's fair to say that the blood, gore and comedy of the last century provide bountiful material. One of the better moments features the famous picture of Elvis shaking hands with Nixon with Miller remarking "And here we see two of the greatest recording artists of the 20th Century." This one is the last feature likely to prompt repeat viewings.

Flash forward to 2003: we all know what happened in the three years since his last special. *The Raw Feed* starts off promisingly enough. Miller laments that he doesn't masturbate as much these days because his expanding waistline obliges him to slip *himself* the date-rape drug. Later he says "I was raised Catholic: I went to confession the other day and said (to the priest) 'You first'."

He retains some spin on his curveball and it's obvious he still belongs in the big leagues. But then he starts in on the Middle East, and things begin to derail as the stand-up turns into an occasionally ugly right-wing rant. As America was about to deploy forces to Iraq Miller, like many like-minded citizens of the time, is blasé to the point of cockiness. He not only returns to the hackneyed *ad hominem* toward the French, he boasts that once we've "won" in Iraq (quickly and decisively, obviously) the French will be sorry that they blew their chance at the spoils. It's embarrassing.

Then he lays into Sean Penn with the snide pronouncement "Dead Career Walking". Of course, two Academy Awards later, Miller was about as accurate with that assessment as he was about the course of our overseas adventures. Lest any of this sound like piling on, I'm saving the best for last: Miller actually pauses mid-performance to utter the words "I'd like to thank George Bush for allowing me to respect the American presidency again." It is, as they say, to laugh—even if it's for the wrong reasons.

Finally, in 2006 Miller went to Vegas to perform the show recorded as *All In*. It's not terrible; Miller is simply too intelligent, too witty and too observant to flop onstage. But one might think he'd feel obliged (for the sake of his comedy, for the sake of his integrity) to reign in the rhetoric. Then again, not for nothing is the special is called *All In*. It takes less than five minutes for Miller to lay into the cowardice of the French.

The rest of the show teeters between Miller's patented perspicacity and his unfortunate, newly acquired nationalism. Funny bits about being able to access Internet porn anywhere and the plethora of erectile dysfunction commercials give way to longer rants about the dubious science behind global warming, and the benefits of aggressive drilling in Alaska (drill baby drill?). To paraphrase a younger, shrewder Miller, he doesn't favor any particular political affiliation, but I think we've all seen his eyes light up at Dennis Kucinich and Howard Dean.

Bottom line: despite his curious and regrettable turn toward the unfunny, Dennis Miller still looms large as one of the five best stand-up comedians of the past 20 years. This egregiously overdue purging of the HBO vaults should come as a welcome relief to fans who remember watching these specials in real time.

Worst case scenario, the first three (and superior) features are all contained on one disc: if you feel obliged to burn after viewing, retain that first disc and put it in the time capsule. The younger generation might be refreshed to see a less bellicose and more beguiling Dennis Miller, and many decades from now, when Miller's awkward repartee with Bill O'Reilly is a footnote in unintentional comedic history, his greatest work will be remembered, and justly venerated.

March, 2009

IN PRAISE OF PATRICK SWAYZE, OUR ALL-AMERICAN ALPHA MALE

Quick: Visualize *Road House.*

That's our man.

And by *our*, I mean men.

The rest of you can have *this* guy.

(Visualize *Dirty Dancing.)*

And by you, I mean women.

The wonderful thing is, it's the same dude. That is the unprecedented, impossibly perfect Tao of Patrick Swayze. He had something for everyone, and while there are a handful of superstars who have straddled the line between man's man and preening peacock for the ladies, usually the actor in question becomes tougher, or gentler, as he ages. Swayze could incorporate both extremes at the same time, starring in two of the penultimate chick flicks and, quite possibly, the mother of all male bonding films, all in a *three year* window. Guys watch—and cherish—trash like *Point Break* and *Road House* because they are hilarious, and Swayze is both alpha male and court jester, rolled into one.

In the rumble, on the ice or during the cold war apocalypse, this was the bro you wanted to have your back.

Remember *The Outsiders*? (For the full effect, you had to be target audience age when it first came out, which means you were over ten and under twenty). Nobody knew who Patrick Swayze was, then, so that experience is alien to a younger person watching a younger Swayze, now. You could not have shoehorned more pretty young things onto that screen: Dillon, Cruise, Estevez, Lowe, Macchio and C. Thomas Howell (the only one requiring a full name since no one heard from him again, unless you are one of the five people who saw *Soul Man*)and—for the boys— Diane Lane. That was a lot of Gen X eye candy. And then there was this brawny, unknown badass. He was, obviously, the leader of the brat pack; indeed, he was the only one in that group who looked like he actually could (and did) throw down if the situation required it. He was, in short, intimidating. He was perfectly cast, although he *did* seem old enough (even as the "older" brother) to strain credulity. He was also, arguably, the only star on that crowded billing not set to explode into immediate stardom. In fact, it would take Swayze, already 30 years old, another four years to become *the man.*

Everyone remembers how that happened. In the film that shall remain nameless, Swayze made his sweetheart swoon and took half of America with him. He had arrived, and from then on out nobody could put Swayze in the corner. Maybe it's a guy thing, but the movies he starred in alongside Jennifer Grey and Demi Moore are unspeakable. They are sentimental, melodramatic schlock from the fetid heart of Hollywood. In other words, these commercial grand slams were just what the evil doctor ordered. Two things few men will ever understand (or profit from arguing about): Oprah, and those two movies. But Swayze was easily forgiven. After all, he had saved us from the Russians (or at least softened them up for Rocky IV), and helped the Greasers stomp the rich kids. He also dropped the gloves alongside Rob Lowe in what turned out, unbelievably, to be only the *third* most homoerotic flick in his oeuvre. With little left to prove, he dedicated himself to the dangerous task of making wonderfully awful films.

He would redeem himself, not only in the subsequent *Point Break* (clocking in at number two on the homoerichter scale), but in the masterwork that men are genetically incapable of turning off while channel surfing. I'm referring, quite obviously, to *Road House.*

Every man has seen this movie and any man who hasn't is not a man, so that about covers it. I won't insult its integrity by trying to analyze anything; I'll just savor some of the moments that make it so...seminal:

Doc: *Do you always carry your medical records around with you?*

Dalton: *Saves time.*

Dalton: *I want you to be nice until it's time to not be nice.*

Doc: *How's a guy like you end up a bouncer?*

Dalton: *Just lucky I guess.*

Wesley: *Somebody get a drink around here?*

(Everyone): *I thought you'd be bigger!*

Dalton: *Pain don't hurt.*

Jimmy: *I used to fuck guys like you in prison.*

(Repeat: I. Used. To. Fuck. Guys. Like. You. In. Prison.)

He was, for a while there, our contemporary sacred clown. But more than that, he was *real.* As in: it only bolstered his appeal (and considerable street cred) when you realized he did his own stunts, married (and remained married) to his childhood sweetheart and, by any account, was a genuinely good person. One must remain wary about separating art from the artist for all the obvious reasons, but there are the occasional exceptions where the illusion is an extension of the actual.

It was refreshing to hear his family report that he passed away peacefully. Of course he did. It's the least the world could do for him. Besides, death don't hurt.

September, 2009

DENNIS HOPPER: HE MADE OUR WORLD MORE WEIRD AND WONDERFUL

So cancer finally succeeded in cutting short the odd and inimitable life of Dennis Hopper. That's a shame, of course, although we would probably be wise to give thanks that he managed to stick around as long as he did. He danced with the devil so often they were on a first name basis. And if Thoreau was wise to encourage us all to suck the marrow out of life, Hopper sucked, slurped and occasionally mainlined it. I'd like to think you could cut him open and a good chunk of 20th Century DNA would come oozing out. He may have had a few more battles in him, but no one can deny he left it all out on the proverbial field.

To acknowledge his eccentric and very original brand of genius, I'm inclined to leave the biographical nitty gritty (important as it is) to others and celebrate a handful of scenes that helped make our world a more real, and less predictable place.

First up, a one-two punch from one of the more controversial (and, for my money, overrated) films of all time, *Blue Velvet.* Despite its oblique narrative, wooden acting and David Lynch's unparalleled capacity for pretension (which entirely too many suckers wrongly diagnose as audacity), there are still more than a handful of epic scenes to savor. Two that feature Hopper each illustrate what made him so singular and, at times, untouchable. Exhibit A is that *Top of the world, ma!* celebration of perverted depravity, one of the more genuinely scary and disturbing moments in all cinema. Exhibit B is the brief, beautiful shout-out to that most American of beers. No actor but Dennis Hopper could have pulled off either scene with similar success.

Speaking of overrated, take *Easy Rider* (please!).

I'm just kidding. Kind of.

To me, this movie is actually a lot like Bob Dylan: you see it, you *get* it, you appreciate the influence and you can't front on the near-universal endorsement he gets from every artist who came after him. Ditto *Easy Rider*: it was iconic and of its time (boy was it of its time), and like Bob Dylan, laid a foundation that several other writers and directors (and actors) improved upon. Speaking of wooden acting...well, you get the picture. In fairness, it may be that Hopper (and, to a lesser extent, Fonda) were not playing roles so much as projecting themselves. And then, of course, there is Jack Nicholson. Even if this movie served merely as the delivery device to bring Big Jack into the mainstream (and let me be clear, it remains much more than that), it certainly served its humble purpose. Speaking of Jack...let's appreciate him doing that thing he did, arguably without peer, for at least another decade:

It quite possibly says more about me than the movie, but one of the handful of scenes (sans Nicholas) I can stomach happens to be the one where Hopper dies. And no, I'm not saying that the acting is so bad that seeing him get shot is a relief; I'm talking about how effective and unsettling this abrupt ending remains (and I can appreciate how unprecedented it was in 1969). Full credit to Hopper, who directed, and help write, this material. Much like the equally celebrated (and beloved) *The Graduate,* I find the movie almost unwatchable, but there is no denying the impact it had (good, bad and definitely ugly) on film-making in America and America, period.

And then, of course, the unforgettable role in *Apocalypse Now* that begged questions about life imitating art or, more likely, the exact opposite.

And finally, inevitably, his unequalled moment (from *True Romance*, a movie that, pound for pound, features as many sublime scenes as quite possibly any other made in the last two decades).

This scene, notorious for its, shall we say, frank discussion of racial relations, and hilarious for its rather unorthodox delineation of history, is one of the most-quoted from all contemporary films. For good reason, and all praise to Tarantino (who wrote it), Tony Scott (who directed it) and the bravura performances of Hopper and the genuinely incomparable Christopher Walken. It also includes the hulking presence of the then-unknown James Gandolfini.

The scene is certainly problematic (and no politically correct critic would want to touch it with a ten foot soap box), but more than the adults-imitating-schoolchildren one upmanship it sardonically presents, there is *serious* acting going on here. It is to the considerable credit of all involved that this scene never degenerates into (self) parody and is able to be hilarious and horrifying, often at the same time. There probably aren't too many examples of scenes in semi-recent cinema that so successfully skirt the switchblade's edge of tension and release. Hopper goes from scared to crafty, then understands he's screwed and decides to go out with a bang (literally). The moment he realizes he is a dead man, you can almost feel him resignedly saying "fuck it" as he decides to have a cigarette, after all. And when he lets out the mirthful little laugh (a very Hopperesque touch), you get the chance to savor him saying "fuck *you*" to the men who are about to murder him.

The scene is uncomfortable and amusing in equal measure (well, in all honesty, it's probably a hell of a lot funnier than anything else), but mostly a tour de force on every conceivable level. It just might feature Hopper's finest work.

Dennis Hopper came close to death so many times he may have figured he was never going to actually die. But he ultimately found out what all of us will discover sooner or later, and all that proves is that we are human. More importantly, he certainly took more from life than it took from him. And we got more out of this weird, wonderful man than we had any right to expect.

June, 2010

COPPOLA'S *THE CONVERSATION*: A LOVE LETTER TO THE PROCESS OF MAKING ART

In Dostoeyevsky's *Notes From Underground* the self-loathing narrator proposes that every man has secrets he will only reveal to friends and secrets he must keep to himself. And then there are the things he's afraid to admit even to himself, and the more decent the man, the more things he will find himself unable to confront.

In Francis Ford Coppola's *The Conversation* Harry Caul (Gene Hackman) is a man less concerned with the answers to uneasy questions than the questions themselves. He is a well-regarded surveillance specialist; a self-employed spy who builds his own equipment and attracts high profile clients who will pay top dollar for his services. As he explains to his enthusiastic assistant (the always-excellent John Cazale), he's uninterested in the personal lives of his clients or what their motivations might be—he just wants to get the job done as only he can do it.

Caul, who claims not to care about the inner feelings of others, goes to great lengths to keep anyone from gleaning his personal thoughts. And from his old-fashioned eyeglasses, coat and tie attire or the see-through slicker he wears rain or shine, he projects the look of a professor or librarian more than efficient sleuth. This is entirely by design: by making himself as ordinary as possible, Caul believes he can keep others from intruding on his personal space—which we quickly understand is, for him, sacred. As such, he's a human coil of simmering tension, all nervous energy and restraint. He is a quiet man with an urgent dialogue endlessly unspooling in his mind. Or, he has several urgent dialogues simultaneously distracting him. Or, he is ceaselessly trying to suppress these urgent, distracting dialogues. That he is unsuccessful is obvious: his discomfort around others reveals the obsessions and idealizations simmering deeply beneath his austere façade.

Gene Hackman, to be certain, had his work cut out for him here. How to take a character that is so intractable and ultimately *unknowable*, and manage to make him engaging, even sympathetic? Hackman, despite his renowned acting abilities, struggled to fully understand and depict Harry Caul, a role so dissimilar to previous assignments (this is the man who played Popeye Doyle, for God's sake!) and his own personality. Ultimately, Hackman exposes a man who struggles so fervently to avoid telling anyone anything he inexorably shows everyone everything.

As a result, *The Conversation* is a tour de force, but it's a *quiet* tour de force. In fact, it is just about impossible to imagine a movie like this being made today. Few directors could trust—perhaps with good reason—that audiences would embrace the deliberately languid pace and lack of resolution. In fact, while critically successful (then and now), this movie did not fare well commercially at the time of its release.

Of course, the movie is impossible to separate from the early '70s in several important ways. For one, its inescapable political implications (Watergate, wire-tapping) and its art house aesthetic sensibility (*The Conversation* is one of the more durable experiments to come out of the "new wave" of Hollywood bad boys who briefly had—and took—the opportunity to make movies the way they needed—and wanted—to make them). *The Conversation*, perhaps more than any of his celebrated films, makes the purest case for Coppola's genius. The movie's disconsolate message is tempered by its director's lack of cynicism (a refreshing trait early on that ended up marring his later work with excess sentimentality and preciousness). Coppola, who also wrote the screenplay, is perhaps the only director of that era sufficiently unselfconscious to depict a protagonist so self-conscious he is in constant danger of suffocating.

Also worth mentioning is the film's uncanny similarities to *Chinatown* (also released in 1974). In both, an essentially respectable man has seen his best intentions harm others, and vows never to repeat his mistake. In both, a man realizes too late that he has gotten involved (and invested) in something far larger and more dangerous than he imagined. Both films are virtually flawless, from the script to the ingenious structure, the direction, score and acting. Especially the acting. Certainly in the '70s there was plenty of "acting" going on, which is why so few (if any) movies have aged (and seemingly improved) with time as *The Conversation* and *Chinatown*.

"I don't have anything personal, nothing of value," Caul insists at one point, and we know he means it. Or, we understand he thinks he means it. Or we realize, by the end, that he very much *wants* to mean it. Throughout, we see more than his colleagues, his girlfriend (who he considers overly inquisitive when, after many months, she would like to know where he works, where he lives and why he doesn't seem to own a telephone), his priest and—most significantly—he does. But the sum total of these subtle insights (the way he avoids swearing, the time he picks up a cookie and studies it for several seconds before putting it back on the plate, his diversion of playing saxophone alongside an LP recording) ultimately shed insufficient light on what makes him tick. This is actually the secret of the film's success.

In less capable hands we would know everything at the outset: what his back-story was, what he was looking for and what he needed to achieve so we could root for him to "win". There are, of course, no winners here, but the message of the movie is not nihilistic. By the time it concludes, the culmination of events has slyly served to confirm all of Caul's skepticism. He trusts no one and thinks the worst of people, which is his personal tragedy. The larger tragedy is that on the few occasions he lets his guard down, or trusted his own instincts, he is proven spectacularly wrong for having done so.

The comprehension that he is involved in an event that might have appalling consequences unnerves him; the realization that he abetted people he would not knowingly have worked for devastates him. But he's not broken, yet. That dissolution is saved for the last scene, a final indignity wherein Caul's most unimaginable apprehension is realized. After receiving a phone call on his unlisted number, he suffers the humiliation (and terror) of hearing his own apartment being bugged. Panicked, he promptly reduces his apartment to splinters in a fruitless attempt to find the hidden microphone. In what has to be one of the most harrowing scenes in cinema, the camera pans over a desecrated aftermath where Caul plays his saxophone amidst the wreckage. What earlier in the movie might have been construed as a bit of a contrivance (the one-man band playing along with a pre-recorded tune) now symbolizes this man's lonely disintegration: his record player (along with all his other dispensable possessions) destroyed in the rampage, he must finally face the music, while the sound of an unaccompanied horn cries out his sad song.

Even once the crucial twist is understood, the film remains elusive. It is a darkly affecting drama, but what else? Also an allegory for Watergate (not likely, despite the rather facile, if pervasive critical analysis, considering the screenplay was written in the mid-'60s)? A commentary on political chicanery? A love letter to the painstaking process of assembling a work of art, bit by technical bit? Some of all of these, to be certain, and several other things, for sure. It's never quite the same experience once you've seen it the first time, but *The Conversation* warrants repeated viewings. Like the very best films, fresh nuances and details emerge and a deeper understanding and appreciation accrues. Popeye Doyle in *The French Connection* was the role Hackman was born to play, but his embodiment of Harry Caul should be celebrated as the best work he ever did.

September, 2010

ROSENCRANTZ & GUILDENSTERN ARE DEAD: THE PLAY'S THE THING

Spoiler alert: Rosencrantz and Guildenstern die.

They are, in fact, already dead. And they always have been.

But you knew that already, right?

Another spoiler: You, too, shall die one day.

Here's the rub: they didn't know when or why, and neither will you.

But you already knew that, didn't you?

Extended, circular interlocutions about the fragility of life or the meaning of reality or the existence of meaning itself were certainly more fashionable in the late '60s, when this play was first presented, but you need not be obsessed by existential angst to enjoy this slippery mind-screw. *Rosencrantz and Guildenstern Are Dead* is not an instrument used for scratching those metaphysical itches; it is the itch itself. On the page, like so many plays, it is sufficiently delightful, but brought to life (like the best plays) it sparkles. Of course, even the best plays sometimes suffer from casts, however game, that are not worthy of the material they are provided. Fortunately, this one not only made it to the pretty-big screen, it attracted two of the best British thespians of their time: Gary Oldman (who was known mostly for his role in *Sid and Nancy*) and Tim Roth (not really known at all, at least outside the UK, circa 1990). Perhaps most miraculous, it also features Richard Dreyfuss, who manages not to be insufferable, perhaps for the last time in his career.

Anyone familiar with *Hamlet* well recalls that there is a play within a play that takes place: "The play's the thing—wherein I'll catch the conscience of the King." So how about a play *about* a play within a play? That is what Tom Stoppard attempts with *Rosencrantz & Guildenstern Are Dead.* He pulls it off, but also achieves many other extraordinary things in this meditation on life and art, art vs. life, the meaning of life, the meaning of art, the meaning of words, the meaning of...meaning, free will, faith and fate. In other words, he explores the sorts of Big Themes that are usually capitalized.

One of the best scenes occurs when the two protagonists play a game of Questions. This bit qualifies as catnip for the overly literate; for anyone who actually gets excited about art, this is intellectual porn. (Like the play itself, it works well on the page, but is considerably improved by the audio and visual qualities of real people doing real things in the service of artifice. On aesthetic and literal levels, the young Gary Oldman channels intelligence, physical beauty, mental acuity and the fey insouciance of a player being pulled on a playwright's strings, which is precisely what he is. Also, all of the questions inherent in the play—and in the two men's confused existences—are artfully woven into this ingenious little scene.)

A play (and movie) this excellent, if semi-obscure, has been reviewed well (and well-reviewed) enough times that a summary of the plot—such as it is—isn't necessary. Certainly, a passing acquaintance with Shakespeare's greatest work would seem obligatory, although the screen version could arguably be enjoyed on its own terms. For me, Stoppard's true triumph here is not the surreal masterstroke of making marginal characters the main players, or scrutinizing the role of free will (in art, and in life) or in presenting a narrative where the conclusion is telegraphed from the get-go and still making it suspenseful, although those are all remarkable achievements. And, while it is convincingly rendered, he shouldn't receive too much credit for reinforcing the obvious, if facile reality that we are all the stars of our own story, regardless of how inconsequential our thoughts and actions are in the proverbial pages of history ("All the world's a stage", etc.).

The enduring impact of *Rosencrantz and Guildenstern Are Dead* might be the manner in which Stoppard takes on the Big Questions that philosophers, poets, priests and everyone else have agonized over for centuries and arrives at an explanation even The Bard would likely endorse: it's not so much that there aren't any answers (there aren't) but that we ask the questions at all. By asking the questions, we see the silliness, we hear the humor, we observe the awful and we eventually come to understand the most important thing, the only thing that matters: we are alive.

November, 2010

IN MEMORY OF SIDNEY LUMET: CELEBRATING *SERPICO*

It's difficult, and pointless, to try and isolate which film was Lumet's best or most enduring. The fact that he made three of the best movies of the '70s (three out-and-out masterpieces in one decade) is more than enough. There are already several well-written and worthwhile tributes and summaries of his long, amazing career, and they rightly spend time on the many decades he was active (including this last one when, at the age of 83, he directed the disturbing, outstanding *Before The Devil Knows You're Dead*). For me, it was that seminal decade (the '70s) when he did his best work, and that work does the near-impossible: it totally reflects its time and provides indelible commentary on—and for—that era; while managing to anticipate our world, almost forty years later. This is beyond prescient and bordering on prophetic. Of course, it has as much to do with the screenplays as his direction, but it's to Lumet's credit, and indicative of the dilemmas that drove him, that he gravitated toward this material.

In the recent past (2009) I wrote about how *Network* pretty much previewed...everything, focusing on the then-implausible ascension of buffoon Glenn Beck in a piece entitled *A Half-Assed Howard Beale*:

(Right now Paddy Chayefsky is:

a. Rolling over in his grave

b. High-fiving Peter Finch in heaven

c. High-fiving Peter Finch in hell (where it's Happy Hour 24/7)

d. All of the above

There are any number of examples that could be (and probably have been) offered up to illustrate how prescient Chayefsky's screenplay for *Network* really was. Think of phony purveyors of moral outrage ranging from Morton Downey Jr. to Jerry Springer, and the whole concept of *infotainment* to the hastening-of-the-apocalypse proliferation of Reality TV. Stage it and they will come is now the (un)official mantra of media's M.O. And, in the end, it's all pretty much a tempest in a teapot. Or, a tempest in a tea *party*. Which brings us to the unbelievable Glenn Beck. Of course, fabricated indignation has been good business in America since Jonathan Edwards first perfected the formula with *Sinners in the Hands of an Angry God* back in 1741, shortly before the advent of cable television.

Capitalizing on the nervous consciences of the faithful created steady work well into the 20th Century, and Sinclair Lewis codified the archetypal character in *Elmer Gantry* (1926). That pernicious tradition was carried on faithfully by Confidence Men like Pat Roberston, Jerry Falwell, Benny Hinna, and Rick Warren. But of course this act has always been too tempting for politicians not to embrace with every inauthentic bone in their bodies. The only hucksters that can outhustle the pols are the preening simpletons who rile up the credulous citizens who dial in each day for another dose of bad medicine. At the appointed hour, the idiot box transfigures into a burning bush and these rapt minions who otherwise behold Christ in their breakfast food get their Godhead on in the form of a third-rate carnival barker.)

I also wrote about *Serpico* while introducing a piece commemorating the ten-year anniversary (in 2009) of what I consider the best film of the last twenty years, *The Insider:*

(Toward the end of Sydney Lumet's '70s classic *Serpico* there is an unnerving scene that encapsulates the conundrum faced by the eponymous cop: already *persona non grata* within the law enforcement fraternity for his refusal to take bribes, Serpico is transferred to the narcotics division, where the beat is the exceedingly dangerous streets *way* off-Broadway. His new partner grimly explains that, compared to the types of kickbacks Serpico was accustomed to seeing, the haul in narcotics is serious business. "That is big money, *that* you do not fuck around with." In this moment Serpico finally understands that his life is now in greater danger, amongst police officers than at the hands of criminals, because of his insistence on obeying the law.)

I think this one scene, perhaps even more than anything in the embarrassment of riches that is *Network*, tells us all we need to know about how the world really works. Going back to the Watergate story, the reporters were advised to "follow the money". That might be the most disturbingly succinct epitaph of our last century. Every act of violence and venality is prompted by the pursuit of money or the lack thereof, and most of all, the things money can't buy (which, come to think of it, is the central theme of *Before The Devil Knows You're Dead*).

When I ask myself: how is it possible that, despite the will of the people and the painfully obvious cookie crumbs leading to the criminals, Obama has let Wall Street off without so much as a harsh word, or how the Republicans can hold the country hostage for indefinite tax cuts on the wealthiest one percent, or (worse) how so many feckless and supine Democrats can tolerate—and in some cases, abet—this mendacity, or how our military budget is sacrosanct, or how we can continue to fight ill-advised and unwinnable wars (killing countless Americans and "foreigners" in the bargain), when I look at some of my well-educated and otherwise enlightened friends and wonder how they can possibly be immune to this cognitive dissonance, I think of these words: "That is big money, *that* you do not fuck around with."

So in tribute to Lumet's genius, I'd like to revisit a piece I wrote many moons ago, celebrating *Serpico.* I could never (and would never) pick favorites but if I *had* to, I would probably suggest that this movie represented the best work that Pacino and Lumet ever did.

Serpico (1973)

An illuminating moment occurs near the beginning of the film *Saturday Night Fever*—the project that officially launched the trajectory of John Travolta's career, where, with a haircut and white suit, the young hot shot evolved from Vinny Barbarino, Sweat Hog, to Tony Manero, disco icon—a film which, like any formidable piece of art, is as much a reflection of its times as it is the vision of its creator: A lean, mean, and bikini brief-clad Travolta halts in mid-strut and gazes lovingly up at his wall, upon which is a poster of *the man*—a bearded, long-haired, gold hoop earring-wearing undercover cop—and he haughtily, if speciously assures himself "I look like Al Pacino!" The symbolic import of this simple scene is substantial. The act of conferring coolness through establishing, by any means necessary, solidarity with Pacino—particularly a young cat who *knows* he's bad, especially a movie character depicting a young cat who knows he's bad—is about as ringing an endorsement of unequivocal hipness as anyone could reasonably hope to attain. This moment then, signified a passing-of-the-torch of sorts, and an informal promulgation of what most folks already knew: that Al Pacino, in short, *is* the '70s, and along with Nicholson and De Niro, formed the divine triumvirate of American motion-picture ascendency in that decade.

Coming less than a year after the searing intensity of his performance as Michael Corleone—in the role and movie, *The Godfather*, Pacino could not have chosen a more diametric project than the true story of Frank Serpico, the undercover cop who pits himself in a lonely—and costly—war against an entire police force. This film serves as a radical (and realistic) rewriting of the classic—and antiquated—American Dream myth, wherein the best man always wins, and good always prevails over evil. With an escalating irony that could only be culled from real life (otherwise it would be offensively implausible), the more he attempts to distance himself from the wrongdoing around him—which has casually corroded the department like a malignant infirmity—the more scorn he is subjected to. In a word, it doesn't get any more *American* than this: Serpico, the man, and *Serpico*, the movie, are potent amalgams of, and commentaries upon, the country that made them. The idealizing, even naïve young man confronting corruption is arguably an invariable rite of passage for just about every individual who leaves the comforts—and conformity—of home for the bigger, badder realities of the world. When the individual is a police officer, and the subject of his disillusionment is the laissez-faire depravity of his precinct—and, to a larger extent, the backbiting, political *system* as a whole—the stakes are raised rather considerably.

It is sufficient testament of a job well done that it is impossible to imagine any other actor taking on the role of Frank Serpico and delivering such a capable, compelling performance. The tribulations of this alienated underdog provide the opportunity for Pacino to utilize a concentrated fervor in ways he never would (or could) again. It is a tailor-made vehicle for his expressive gifts: this is his superlative performance, his greatest role. He is, in turns, quiet, assertive, tranquil, indignant and incensed. He is a man of intelligence and integrity surrounded by the numbed and indifferent denizens of New York City's police departments, amongst whom he wears out his welcome quickly—and irretrievably.

The crux of his dilemma is an unflinching nonconformity, which obliges the battle-wearied veterans of his precinct to examine not only their own detached compliance, but why *he* won't go along with it. In a development that is perverse as it is ironic, he becomes increasingly regarded with suspicion because he refuses to break the very laws he's sworn (and is paid) to uphold. Because he is honest, he cannot be trusted. If the story, or the actor, wasn't up to the task, this rather unremarkable—indeed scarcely believable—story would seem trite, redundant, or nauseatingly bathetic. Thankfully, this true tale—which, like any worthwhile biography about an extraordinary individual, serves equally as a commentary on society and that evasive and evanescent perception dubbed the *human condition*—is abundantly provocative, discomforting, and ultimately redeeming.

Serpico is one of the rare and wondrous works of art that truly satisfies on all levels: it is, first and foremost, an intriguing and indelible movie experience. It is also an inspirational story that serves to remind us that crime often operates in an unremarkable, but eviscerating fashion. It reminds us that heroes don't wear capes, and seldom wear badges. Often, they wear a look of defiance, and a battered, but not beaten pride—a weary, but unwavering integrity.

Serpico was—and will remain—one of the great things that came out of the much-maligned "me-decade". The bell-bottoms, platform shoes, white suits, pompadours and carefully cultivated obtuseness faded, like the fads that they were. Disco faded; Travolta faded. Just because the cyclical engine of fashion has made some of these things unconscionably, and inconceivably cool again, doesn't mean that they won't once again drift back into the droll depths whence they sprang. The stuff of substance, soulful as it is scarce, will nevertheless continue to stick around—as it always does—especially on the fleet and unfashionable frequencies. And, despite *The Godfather*, despite *Dog Day Afternoon*, despite *Scarface*, despite *Glengarry Glen Ross* and *Heat*—Pacino would never be this cool again. Just ask Tony Manero.

April, 2011

THE ECCENTRIC AND INIMITABLE GENIUS OF WERNER HERZOG

Three Key Films: *Aguirre, the Wrath of God* (1974), *Fitzcarraldo* (1982), *My Best Fiend* (1999)

Underrated: *Stroszek* (1977). A stark, disconcerting and unforgettable experience, *Stroszek* is not a film one returns to for fun. It remains one of the most efficient and ruthless appraisals of the American Dream myth while managing to be amusing, touching and ultimately demoralizing. Using his infallible instincts, Herzog has non-actor Bruno S. embody the unlucky, exploited Stroszek. Fleeing Berlin for what they assume will be the warmer and more prosperous U.S.A., Stroszek and his companions end up in the frigid, desolate landscape of Wisconsin. The final scene, after things have gone predictably off the track, features Stroszek on a ski lift holding a frozen turkey. Beneath him, in coin-operated cages, a duck plays a drum with his beak, a rabbit "rides" a wailing fire truck and a chicken dances while the soundtrack features the ebullient harmonica woops of Sonny Terry. Arguably the most surreal, and satisfying, commentary on the human condition ever filmed: once you've seen it, it stays seen.

Unforgettable: After enabling an entire crew, including his daughter, to die during a doomed expedition to the legendary El Dorado, Aguirre is alone. Having watched his group slowly succumb to disease, drowning and Indian arrows, Aguirre is nonchalant when dozens of monkeys swim aboard his raft. As the creatures scramble and scurry, he snatches one and holds it in front of his face. "I am the Wrath of God," he declares, and the sweeping Amazon suddenly turns claustrophobic. We know Aguirre is near death, and his final disintegration offers an austere commentary on ambition and conquest. The close-up camera angle swirls backward and circles the raft from above, like a silent and definitive judgment from Nature itself. From *Aguirre, The Wrath of God.*

The Legend: Few artists in any genre are as closely associated with the work they do. All of Werner Herzog's films are to a certain extent autobiographical. It's not merely a matter of how much of himself he invests into each project; it's the nature of the projects themselves. Herzog has long combined creative restlessness with spiritual obsession and the results are often compelling, occasionally awe-inspiring and never less than interesting. He was the quintessential critical darling for entirely too long: he made movies that people admired, but he was anything but a household name. Never seeming to care—and certainly not one to covet notoriety—he quietly plugged along, keeping busy and remaining relevant. During the last decade his genius, and superhuman work ethic, have finally been recognized and rewarded.

It was not always thus. Herzog is possibly the ultimate underdog who inevitably got the acclaim and approbation he deserved. Herzog is undeniably a legend based solely on the stunning body of work he has produced. The real legend, of course, is his life and the excitement, misadventure and barely believable anecdotes it has inspired. There are too many to list, but a handful should suffice in order to convey what a unique force of nature Herzog has always been.

He stole his first camera, an act he considered less a matter of theft than necessity. On the set of his 1970 film *Even Dwarfs Started Small* (a wonderfully Herzogian title, and concept), after a few near calamities he promised the crew he would jump into a cactus patch if the rest of the filming was completed without incident (it was and he did). During the filming of his first masterpiece *Aguirre, The Wrath of God* he dealt with the mercurial Klaus Kinski in a fashion that would set the tone for their subsequent collaborations: after Kinski, during one of his typical tantrums, threatened to leave the set, Herzog pulled out a gun and swore he would first shoot Kinski, then himself unless the actor got back to work (it worked). In the mid-'70s, in an attempt to inspire his friend Errol Morris to complete a project, he agreed to eat his shoe (the project was completed, the shoe was cooked and eaten, and the occasion was filmed for posterity). The filming of his film *Fitzcarraldo* (inspired by a true story) involved moving a 320 ton steamship over a mountain—without utilizing a single special effect.

During the filming, one of the Peruvian natives on the shoot, exasperated by Kinski's histrionics, offered to kill him; Herzog was tempted but declined because he needed the actor to finish the movie. In 2006, while being interviewed for the BBC, Herzog was (inadvertently?) shot by an unknown assailant with an air rifle. Naturally, he continued the interview and, after showing the stunned reporter and film crew the wound, calmly remarked "It is not a significant bullet." (This footage, thankfully, survives for posterity.)

It is, of course, the work that endures and it seems likely that Herzog has amassed a filmography that will inspire and be studied so long as people are making moving pictures. It is difficult to isolate, or even describe what aspect(s) of Herzog's style makes him so original and indelible. Certainly his penchant for improvisation can be attributed to a desire for emotion over refinement. His brave, if unorthodox decision to utilize unknown actors (or non-acting natives) speaks to his compulsion for authenticity. His challenging, occasionally unfeasible choice of projects and locations illustrates a recalcitrance that has always translated into integrity. Equal parts Joseph Conrad and Percy Fawcett, Herzog obliterates all clichés and encomiums: he is the Sisyphus who refused to fail, embracing tribulations to prove—to the medium, to himself—that they can be overcome. If Herzog did not exist, he would need to be invented, and then filmed by a director like Herzog.

August, 2011

MAKING THE CASE FOR KUBRICK

Three Key Films: *Dr. Strangelove or: How I Learned To Stop Worrying and Love The Bomb* (1964), *2001: A Space Odyssey* (1968), *A Clockwork Orange* (1971)

Underrated: *Full Metal Jacket* (1987). A naturalistic tour into the dark heart of modern war, preceded by a disquieting tour into the darkness of the hearts that prepare our soldiers to survive there. The second section, on the front lines, a surreal sort of cinéma vérité, is more plodding than cathartic, which is probably the point. The first part of the film, devoted entirely to a group of Marine recruits at Parris Island, is a quicksilver tour de force—at turns riotous and harrowing. It is some of the most assured, affecting work of the decade: not too many movies can take you from hysterical laughter (the initial scenes where drill instructor R. Lee Ermey lambastes the boys is piss-your-pants funny) to disgust and, inevitably, despair. The blanket party scene, where the incompetent "Gomer Pyle" (Vincent D'Onofrio) is savaged by his fellow cadets lingers in the mind as one of the most disturbing scenes in movie history. It manages to illustrate a great deal about conformity, the military, the perceived necessity of truly breaking someone before they can function and what we must kill inside ourselves in order to survive. Most directors would inexorably play this scene for pathos; Kubrick films it matter-of-factly and his shrewd use of subtlety makes it many times more disturbing.

Unforgettable: Kubrick's films are celebrated precisely for their myriad iconic moments, but if obliged to pick the single scene we could call "Kubrickian", it would have to be the unforgettable sequence where "our humble narrator" Alex is given the *Ludovico Technique*. Presented as a revolutionary—and quite controversial—form of behavior modification, the subject is given a daily dose of medicine and obliged to endure scene after scene of depravity and violence. During one of the more intense treatments Alex—eyes forced upon with metal prongs—must watch Nazis marching while Beethoven, his favorite composer, plays on the accompanying soundtrack. He cringes and then screams as he realizes not only is he being "cured", but listening to Ludwig Van (the one civilizing influence from his former life) will henceforth be verboten. The image is at once ironic, amusing and appalling, and speaks volumes about science, sadism and the ill-effects of cynical sociology. From *A Clockwork Orange*.

The Legend: Has any director covered more ground, stylistically and historically, than Stanley Kubrick? From *Lolita* (1962) to *The Shining* (1980) to *Eyes Wide Shut* (1999) he made movies from books few directors could—or would—even consider adapting for the big screen. Incredibly, he made movies that arguably transcended the source material; however much viewers (or the original authors) loved or loathed them, they most definitely were not deferential reproductions of the text.

Kubrick is famous—or infamous—for his meticulous, some might claim obsessive quest for "the perfect shot"; anecdotes abound of actors being forced to produce take after take to the point of exhaustion or distraction. His control freak tendencies may have had a great deal to do with the fact that he "only" made thirteen films over the course of a career that spanned five decades. On the other hand, it's difficult to name many directors who made as many works that are today considered masterpieces, or a director who is cited more frequently for his innovation and influence. Detractors have claimed that his perfectionism resulted in films that were too cold or clinical; some find his work pretentious. Interestingly, if not revealingly, his work has aged well and seems to attract more converts (inside and out of critical circles) than detractors.

Is it even necessary to review the films? There are none that are not worth seeing at least one time; there are several that can be watched anytime, and there are a handful that must be revisited often, for all the right reasons. Is it possible to get tired of a tour de force like *Dr. Strangelove*? Understanding that Kubrick intentionally asked George C. Scott to add one "over the top" take for each scene (knowing full well that those were the takes he planned to use) causes one to further appreciate the perfection. Speaking of irony, how about the use of Rossini during a rape scene, or Purcell post-modernized as early—and eerie—electronica in *A Clockwork Orange*?

Special mention, of course, must be made for *2001: A Space Odyssey*. As time passes and computers make special effects ever easier to produce (and less satisfying to watch), the scope of what Kubrick achieved remains hard to fathom. It's one thing to reassess an older film and marvel at how impressive it was for its time; we can—and should—watch *2001* and still be astonished, today. It's probably not possible, nor is it important to isolate Kubrick's best film. His ultimate achievement, aside from the steady craftsmanship and originality, might be the realization that *Dr. Strangelove* had to be a comedy. The novel he adapted, *Red Alert* was a dead-serious potboiler; Kubrick instinctively understood how poorly that would play on screen (at least in most directors' hands) but also how crucial it was to satirize. The results, equally a tribute to the considerable skills of that remarkable cast, are a testament to Kubrick's intelligence and vision.

Where so many of our most renowned directors cultivate a particular style, Kubrick—perhaps because of his fixations—made movies about so many different people and places it seems impossible (in a good way) that the same man was responsible for them all. Of course, there are the familiar nuances and compulsive touches that connect certain moments as *Kubrickian*. There is the long, disconnected stare (think Alex from *A Clockwork Orange*, Jack from *The Shining* or Leonard from *Full Metal Jacket*). There is the soundtrack music: aside from Scorsese, has any other director made more songs indelibly associated with specific scenes? There is, above all, the irony. Some see pessimism, but attentive viewers understand that Kubrick, for all his precision, always removed himself from the acting and the action. If his films have moments that are more aesthetically perfect than emotionally convincing, Kubrick could never be accused of being cynical. Like our very best directors, he consistently conjures up other times and places while offering profound comment on the here and now.

August, 2011

THEY LIVE: THE MOST BLUNT CRITIQUE OF UNFETTERED CAPITALISM EVER COMMITTED TO CELLULOID

They Live was a postmodern pastiche of old-school science fiction that, for a variety of reasons, was too ahead of its time to be properly appreciated. Actually, that's not quite accurate. It was too *of* its time, in 1988, and it's even *more* of its time, in 2012, and it will not reach its expiration date in 2022, or 3022, if They are still amongst us—or vice versa.

They Live is actually very similar, in many regards, to John Carpenter's other misunderstood and inadequately touted masterpiece, *The Thing. Released in* 1982, *The Thing* did not fare as well as it could—and should—have and like *They Live*, it endures as a cult classic. Where *The Thing* offered an indelible examination of paranoia it was also an eerily prescient, if quite direct and unintentional commentary on the AIDS crisis. *They Live* was an explicit condemnation of the Reagan years, and the fact that its release virtually coincided with the country's decision to effectively give him four more years, with George Bush as the delivery device for an extended "morning in America", suggests some reasons it did not fully connect.

There are other reasons the movie struggled to find a wider audience. It's too dark and truthful to be taken as satire; it's too (intentionally) outrageous, in parts, to satisfy the mainstream critics who take themselves more seriously than the work they do, and it doesn't seek cheap or easy scapegoats. The bad guys, and what incents them, could not be more unmistakable, but the real scorn is reserved for those citizens who will say or do anything to earn admittance into their club. This ethos, of course, was alive and unwell long before and after The Gipper flew Air Force One. As such, *They Live* offers as blunt a critique of unfettered capitalism, taken to its (il)logical extreme, as has ever been committed to celluloid.

For those who don't know or can't remember, the movie's plot is quite simple, but the levels of psychological and sociocultural observation are nuanced and rich. The great reveal (literally) is when the blind suddenly can see (figuratively), a black and white breakdown of epidemic consumerism. The garish billboards decoded to offer simple commands such as "Obey" and "Reproduce" are now legendary, and the use of aliens in our midst is employed as a whacky twist that hits disconcertingly close to home.

Of *course* it takes place in Los Angeles. The city where fantasy is manufactured, for money, every day. The cityscape that we see as the movie begins is the same one shown throughout and the one we ignore, avoid or rationalize: alleys, graffiti-laden bridges, piles of smoldering trash, swarming tenements, a makeshift tent community of anonymous faces, all in various states of distress. There are not enough jobs, there is not enough money, there is less than sufficient trust and next to no expectation except for the worst. Sound familiar? *They Live* was of its time, to be sure, in 1988. It was of its time in 2008, and it will never *not* be of its time, not in America.

For the most part, Carpenter lets this material play out the only way it can be played: surreal, scary and with no shortage of very black humor. In an early scene that might have seemed either throwaway or over the top, we see a young woman on TV baring the soul she'd love to sell: "I stop being myself and I'm the star of a series or I have my own talk show… all I ever have to do is *be famous*." Ridiculous, clichéd, and a pretty perfect depiction of the sordid spectacle of contemporary reality TV (and, to varying if increasing extents, "regular" TV, including the news). Some people look at alien skull masks and see farce; other people see Donald Trump, Ryan Seacrest or Mitt Romney.

A few words about Roddy Piper, the man required to carry the movie on his beefy shoulders. I saw this in the theater and remember thinking at the time: If only they had just cast Kurt Russell (who was, at that time, kind of like John Carpenter's De Niro), what artistic and aesthetic import it might have had. I was mistaken, and a quarter-century has served to reaffirm Carpenter's judgment. The first 30 minutes, perhaps, would be different, even better, with Russell (or another established A-list actor). But once the glasses go on, the film *needs* the levity and authenticity Piper conveys. Of course, as a famous wrestler, "Rowdy" Roddy Piper was quite accustomed to acting, showmanship and spectacle—all of which are called for throughout.

What results is satire, only supersized. Hence, "the scene": that nine minute fight sequence is the movie, the entertainment industry and America itself, in miniature: incredible, hilarious, exaggerated. That we have a wrestler, using wrestling moves in a movie is almost *too* meta. This is probably why it didn't quite play in 1988 and why it could never really work, anytime. It's at once too ludicrous and too real (a couple of blue collar guys, beating each other's brains out, as the world rots around them and a cabal of super-rich, well-insulated freaks goes about the business of doing business).

In the final analysis, *They Live* is like *The Matrix* without the billion dollar ballet routines. And it only needs about 90 minutes to strip the glossy carcass off consumerism, infotainment, political power structures (hint: our elected officials take their orders from corporations, not the other way around), serving it all up in a visionary smart bomb that touches on McLuhan, Chomsky, Goebbels, P.T. Barnum. Carpenter's triumph is the way he somehow distilled the best of George Orwell and Edgar Allan Poe, disguising it as farce turned bloodbath. In the end the good guy wins. Then he dies.

The bonus footage is almost too good to be true, and fans of the film will need this without hesitation. There is an interview with the sagacious, self-deprecating John Carpenter, brief conversations with the perfectly cast co-stars Keith David and Meg Foster, and a brief "making of" feature. The real treat is the audio commentary provided by Carpenter and Piper, which is predictably enlightening and amusing. There is a clear and abiding bond the two men share, Carpenter glad he went out on a limb and Piper eternally grateful he was given the shot.

Two final nuggets. At one point Carpenter is asked if he ever considered shortening the infamous fight scene. "Fuck no!" he replies, defiant as ever. "The '80s never ended," he opines. "*They* are still here, making more money than ever, they are still among us." Meg Foster recounts walking to her car, years after the film was made, and hearing someone shout down to her from a fifth floor window: *They Live!*. "Yes, they do," she says, smiling sadly. That exchange sums up everything that could be said then, and now.

November, 2012

WE'VE SEEN THIS MOVIE BEFORE: TRYING TO MAKE SENSE OF PHILIP SEYMOUR HOFFMAN

This isn't quite in the day John Lennon died territory, but I'll never forget where I was and what I was doing.

Sitting at home, Super Bowl shopping complete, biding my time for the big game. Someone posted something about Philip Seymour Hoffman dying on Facebook. No chance, I thought. No way, I hoped. Then another update, and another. This being 2014, I did what any sensible person would do: I Googled it. Sure enough, the first item that popped up had the wonderful words "hoax". Since this was not the first time a celebrity had prematurely been declared dead, I took solace. But then another update, with a link to an actual news organizations appeared. Then another. And within a few minutes, my entire feed was buzzing with the news. It was true. It had happened.

The man I consider the best actor of his generation (and I'm certainly not alone), dead aged 46. Of a heroin overdose. Needle found sticking in his arm.

No chance. No way.

Method acting taken to its illogical extreme? Nope, he was a once-recovered addict, and as the stories began pouring out, it was revealed that he'd relapsed and had been struggling these last months with this monster that had moved into his life. That's how it happens with addiction: it knocks on the door, or maybe it's a case of breaking and entering. Once it gets inside it's a hell of a lot harder to extricate it than it ever was to seek it. It's an equal opportunity assailant, going after the vital organs (the brain, the heart) and if or when its appetite for death becomes more powerful than the body's ability to tolerate, people are found face-down on beds, curled up in alleys, or sitting in a bathroom with a needle in their arms. They become clichés in the sense that famous people dying of ostensibly self-inflicted wounds are clichés: we've seen this movie before.

And before I talk about his work, and what we've lost, I'd like to personalize this a bit. I don't know about you, but for me Americans have been perfecting a perverse sort of cognitive dissonance that has reached a boiling point. On one hand, we are utterly obsessed with celebrity and, increasingly, the fantasy that we might become famous, if only for a moment. As such, no shame, family secret or personal foible is off limits as we pursue this ridiculous and empty charade. On the other hand, we are able to shrug off another person's misfortune like the most priggish priest, the most sadistic shrink: Americans are experts at judging and lambasting the weakness of others. My Facebook feed has been polluted with asinine comments about "selfishness", "junkies" and "losers". Perhaps you've seen similar, and worse, sentiment.

Here's the logic these folks appear to be following: anyone who is rich and famous, who is well-regarded, and who has a family (!) is acting at the height (or is that the depth?) of self-absorbed evil to piss it all away. Just to get high. As usual, the best retort for such cocksure and half-assed sanctimony is to turn it on its head: how badly must a person be struggling to know they stand to fritter away their fame, security and family (!) in order to inject bad medicine for a sickness that can never cure itself? Similar rationale tends to apply to suicides: no moral person could ever do something that would hurt their loved ones so much. Oh yeah? How about this: no person who was not already drowning in the dark waters of doubt, fear and helplessness could, in their right mind, do something, to themselves, that can never be undone? Hope is not something you purchase with a paycheck or have breathed into your body like a reverse exorcism: if there's one thing folks who consistently hurt themselves have in common, it's a lack of perspective, the absence of hope.

(Incidentally, lest you think I'm content to wax unconvincingly on a topic of which I admittedly—and luckily—have no intimate experience, I'm happy to pass the mic to the incomparable Russell Brand who, last year, wrote eloquently, as usual, about his own struggles.

It is difficult to feel sympathy for these people. It is difficult to regard some bawdy drunk and see them as sick and powerless. It is difficult to suffer the selfishness of a drug addict who will lie to you and steal from you and forgive them and offer them help. Can there be any other disease that renders its victims so unappealing?)

All of which is to say, if there's one thing plaguing our society right now, it's a decided and very soulless lack of empathy. We watch reality TV shows about slick business types (often born on third base) browbeating their inferiors about what it takes to get to the top. And we make these imbeciles even richer; we envy and admire them. And we shrug our shoulders as families on food stamps get their benefits cut, as people out of work are called lazy (or worse) because, obviously if they *wanted* to work, they could find a job. We say ill-informed, offensive things like "minimum wage jobs are not designed for people with families". (Oh really? And: even if that were true, doesn't that make it all the more appalling so many people with families are obliged to work them? Or that the minimum wage has not even come close to keeping pace with the cost of living during decades where we've seen the wealthiest one percent assume an ever-obscene portion of the nation's wealth?)

All of *that* said, I believe it's possible, and acceptable, to wish we devoted more time, energy and media coverage to the anonymous, often impoverished people who succumb to addiction, while also lamenting the untimely loss of a "famous" person. And in this instance, it hurts more than the typical "gone too soon" eulogy because we are collectively being robbed of an artist performing at the height of his considerable powers. We will have no more opportunities to watch him share his gift, effective immediately.

The reason this one hurts so acutely, on a purely artistic level, is because few people could convincingly argue that Hoffman is not among the most gifted, if not *the* most gifted and accomplished actor of his generation. Typically, simple consensus makes me suspicious; a result of groupthink or a media-driven narrative (with big pockets and PR firms doing what they do best: selling product to make money, manufacturing consent by any means necessary). With Hoffman, the verdict came in over a decade—if not longer—ago: he is perhaps the best at what he does, and the range of work coupled with an admirable productivity make a compelling case that is likely to accrue momentum in subsequent years.

Pretty simple, but still unassailable evidence of mastery: an actor who can consistently make you loathe him, pity him or love him—

sometimes in the same movie—is a rare breed. Quick: think of how many excellent, A-list actors are actually capable of making you cheer for them in one role and feel repulsed by them in another? While playing creepy, despicable dudes was, in some ways, Hoffman's calling card, even in the roles where he was unctuous or obsequious (think his early work in *Scent of a Woman* for the former and his unimprovable turn in *The Big Lebowski* for the latter), and being the heavy, in many senses of the word, called for skills he was ideally suited to deploy (think *Punch-Drunk Love* or the blustery Lester Bangs from *Almost Famous),* he was perhaps most convincing as the vulnerable outsider (*Magnolia)* or the disconnected non-content *(The Savages).*

It's one thing to play an outsider; it's easy for a luminous actor to channel alienation or estrangement. But it is considerably more challenging to depict the type of turmoil and inner-anguish that are often best conveyed only in novels. As such, two of his big roles (*Capote* and *Doubt*) were near-perfect vehicles for a man who could realistically portray a person trying to convince others—and himself—that he's someone else.

For me, the ultimate test of what sets the very-good or even the great apart from the greatest, is the *how many* question. If an actor inhabits a role to the extent that not only can't you imagine anyone else playing the part, but can imagine the ways the movie would suffer without their involvement, this would seem a fair and accurate criteria for genius. And while his work in *Boogie Nights* and *The Master* might, and perhaps should, be among the first mentioned (and I'll resist saying more since virtually every other tribute has, understandably, discussed those two roles in some detail), for me it's two lesser-known films that epitomize movies that simply would not have worked without Hoffman's involvement.

First, *Before the Devil Knows You're Dead.* Merits of the actual film aside, is choosing this role too easy by half? Not really. And not because of the facile (although, perhaps not so much) connection with his death; it's not merely (!) that his character is seeking a state of listless oblivion via chemicals, it's the desolation and lack of connection, the slow boiling debasement. His stock in trade was playing men on the run, from themselves. In repeated viewings, I never cease to be struck by the physical intensity and commitment this role required (and/or Hoffman invested in it). It borders on painful at times, and there are moments throughout where it appears Hoffman is about to have a heart attack right on the screen. Yes, that is acting, but it's also…*being.* The character is deeply flawed, mostly despicable; he's a bully, a liar and a coward. And yet, throughout the film (in part because of the excellent script and the direction–Lumet's final film) you not only find yourself feeling pity for him, you aren't conned into it (by the writing, by the acting), you see the sum total of history (his story), the decisions and frailties that make him the beast he has become. Simply put, I can't think of a recent role that was able to show *and* tell, without words, exactly what is driving a character's actions. It seems facile, maybe even trite, but it was during the first time I saw this film when I actually worried a bit about Hoffman's health: how could any actor keep up this type of self-abuse in the service of art?

The other role, which I'd be willing to wager is going to assume added import in the years to come, is his tour-de-force performance in *Synecdoche, New York.* I think the role was so expansive, and he was so comparatively young when he played it, plus the fact that it's more than slightly outside the box, (it tends to make *Being John Malkovich,* another Charlie Kaufman work, appear almost straightforward and commonplace by comparison), damned it to less-than-stellar box office results, as if that ever matters in the long view.

Certainly many fine actors have used skills, make-up and exceptional directing to play characters that age over the course of a film. But I can think of few, if any examples of a role wherein you see the character age physically as well as emotionally, wearing the passage of time like a weight; a weight that is not the addition of flesh so much as the subtraction of vitality, eating itself from the inside-out. By the latter stages of the film Caden Cotard is indeed a bloated, aged wreck, but Hoffman somehow makes it appear that even as he slows down, the agony (physical, metaphysical) within him has accelerated, ravaging him mentally as well as physically. It eventually becomes apparent it has assumed an ever-larger portion of his being, and he carries this burden like Sisyphus with his stone, forever looking up at a hill he can never crest.

This condition is a metaphor for Cotard's life, sure. It manages to be emblematic of what every human struggles with: how to define ourselves, how to understand each other, how to make sense of existence. It also suggests a struggle that Hoffman was unable to win in his own life. It seems safe to assume it was this discontent, this inordinate sensitivity and subsequent commitment to articulating the story he couldn't quite tell that led to the roles we will never forget. It is also, perhaps, the secret to what stalked Philip Seymour Hoffman, the guy with all the money, all the accolades, every reason to live. The silver lining, aesthetically speaking, reaffirms the essence of so much art: his pain is our gain.

We've seen this movie before. But we won't see more movies from this actor and that, above all, is why it hurts so much.

February, 2014

FIVE EASY PIECES: THE AMERICAN DREAM IN STASIS

McMurphy in *One Flew Over the Cuckoo's Nest*; Jake Gittes in *Chinatown*; Jack "Here's Johnny!" Torrance in *The Shining*—these aren't just characters from famous movies, they're permanent fixtures of American culture. Robert Dupea from *Five Easy Pieces* seldom registers on the short list of all-time great acting performances, at least in part because the protagonist, like the movie, is not easy to admire or understand. Indeed, the title is more than a little ironic, as there is nothing "easy" about it: the material, the characters, the closing scene's infamous lack of closure, etc. The type of role tailor-made for an artist who insists upon working without a net, Bobby Dupea is at once emotional, withdrawn, silent, boisterous, persistent and lethargic to the point of apathy.

Five Easy Pieces is, well, easy to recommend, but it's definitely a movie that demands to be appreciated on its own cantankerous terms. The casting is perfect and the performances are stellar, yet special kudos are warranted for Karen Black, the patient yet pathetic girlfriend and Helena Kallianiotes as Palm Apodaca, the furious yet refreshing hitchhiker. And then there is *the scene*, which remains one of the supremely amusing and satisfying in cinema history, when Nicholson clashes with the truck-stop waitress and the system she represents.

In the disquieting climax, when Dupea unsuccessfully attempts to persuade the first woman who seems perfect for him, she poses a rhetorical question that underscores the paradox of his antipathy: "How can a man who has no love of himself ask for love in return?" His inability to answer her, and his unwillingness to change himself, suggest that his self-imposed impasse will remain unresolved.

Five Easy Pieces endures as a study of the restless soul of a gifted individual (who could have been, and still could be, an artist) too smart for his own good, and who has thus far squandered his youth, talent and energy in an ennui-ridden funk where he floats from job to meaningless job, woman to faceless woman, sensation to numbing sensation.

Most us can discern something of ourselves in the insatiable drifter, the citizen who is not content to live a banal existence even as his every action (and lack thereof) further ensnares him in a perpetuation of the life he abhors. In this regard, *Five Easy Pieces* is not only a commentary on the itinerant American rebel, it also examines the suffocating dynamics of a dysfunctional family, and the dilemma of an individual blessed with extraordinary faculties he feels compelled to suppress.

Five Easy Pieces (screenplay by Carole Eastman—as Adrian Joyce—with considerable input from Rafelson and, on set, Nicholson) encapsulates a very particular American phenomenon, circa 1970, and as such, remains a touchstone of its time and a prescient depiction of the cultural rupture that would accelerate during the "me-decade". The film is a character study, of sorts, focused on a very familiar trope: the individual caught between two worlds, and with a remarkable lack of judgment, illustrates the pressures, appeal and conflict inherent in each.

Dupea leads a life of not-so-quiet desperation, equally out of place amongst the working class and the condescending academics. Talented enough to pursue a respectable, possibly even fulfilling career as a concert musician, Dupea is both fallible and free-thinking enough to understand (not happily) that no matter how much this existence is encouraged, if not expected—and is something his father and siblings have done—it's simply not for him.

He's not a malcontent so much as he can't help comprehending that no matter what you're paid or how much you're admired, you're still a trained monkey, in a monkey suit, doing something (however proficiently) that many other people have done before. Dupea is keenly aware that for all his skill, he is still playing songs someone else wrote, and even if he were sufficiently obsessed to dedicate himself to being the best interpreter of, say, Chopin, he's still inauthentic on some level.

Of course, he's certainly not satisfied working on the oil rig, but if a dead-end job has anything going for it, it's something you can walk away from, without notice or regret, at any moment. Too smart and, despite the aloofness he projects, sensitive for his own good, Dupea is the American Dream in stasis, unable to find satisfaction, much less meaning, in the prescribed existence he was born into, or the peripatetic drifting he capitulates to. He is Ahab, but there is no white whale to chase; he is Ishmael, compelled to return to the sea, only he does not know where he's going and the only safe harbor is a family home where he finds no peace.

Dupea, finally, is neither an anti-hero nor an everyman. A product of the first generation ostensibly unburdened by class-consciousness or convention, he's paralyzed by his peculiar autonomy. As the hippie hangover from the '60s begins in earnest, Dupea has neither tuned in nor entirely dropped out: his terminal indifference belies a genuine desire to find something that can't be taught or bought.

Five Easy Pieces is an obvious, if overdue addition to the Criterion Collection. Finally, we have the deluxe treatment, with bonus features and audio commentary (some of this material was already included in the DVD box set *America Lost and Found: The BBS Story* from 2010). The two mini documentaries, *BBS: A Time for Change* and *BBStory* provide wonderful and welcome insights into the DIY ethos that ended up influencing a generation of filmmakers. Nicholson, Rafelson and many familiar faces from the early '70s all offer up interesting anecdotes and some genuine nostalgia for a (much) more progressive, unshackled era.

If you own a previous edition of *Five Easy Pieces* this is a worthwhile upgrade. If you don't own (or have never seen) this masterpiece, it needs to be part of your collection immediately. This is, to be certain, a movie that can be returned to over time: the nuances of the story and the subtle mastery of Rafelson's direction are to be savored, and studied. This might be Nicholson's ultimate performance, and the reverberations from his urgent yet honest portrayal still linger on the lower frequencies of our collective consciousness.

July, 2015

TOP GUN, THREE DECADES AND MANY MILITARY MISADVENTURES LATER

Top Gun remains miraculous, a Nabokovian movie-within-a-movie where the insufficiently endowed, militarded men-children, with minds toupeed like so many half-ass John Wayne wannabes (speaking of movie-within-a-movie), achieve all the things every impotent flag waving closet case fantasizes about. Starring the epitome of style-over-substance insincerity, Tom Cruise, for whom they had to lower the volleyball net to five feet zero, the eternal box office elf wins one for the Gipper (movie-within-a-movie-within-a-cliché) and liberates the Military Industrial Complex forevermore from tax cuts and accountability (the spoils of the Reagan Revolution writ large), providing scared little boys a Big Daddy who'll never disappoint (because, like Santa Claus, he doesn't exist *and* is the gift that keeps giving). Everything awful about the '80s in America, an erectile dysfunction ad disguised as Hollywood fairy tale, a flat-top wrapped in a flag, bleached chicklets smiling to sell the used car soul of an empty empire.

December, 2015

FOUR: LITERATURE

RAGE AGAINST THE (MFA) MACHINE

The people I've known in MFA programs (yesterday, today, and probably twenty years from now) get taught to write.

Or, they get taught to write short stories.

Or, they get programmed to write short stories.

Or, they get programmed to write certain types of short stories.

And?

The language is usually okay, although clichés are dispensed like crutches in an infirmary. The effort, for the most part, is there (no one, after all, would take the time to take a crack at serious writing unless they wanted to do it right; the only exceptions are the ones to whom it comes easily and who write the way most people urinate: often, every day, and it's mostly water, or the other sort: the ones who don't have time to actually write because they're talking about all the books they have planned out in their pointy heads, not only because it's less complicated to discuss one's brilliance at a party or in a bar, but also because there's always an audience, however reluctant). The underlying impulse, the central nervous system of these short stories, always at least approximates technical proficiency.

So?

What we wind up with is a story that avoids everything the young writer has not experienced: love, fear, empathy, and understanding. For starters. Style over substance equals an anaesthetized aesthetic; a soulless solution for a problem the writer created. And the short story, upon inspection, is a shell that reveals its non-essence. Poetic pronouncements of some of the important things the student does not understand.

In other words: short stories that might sell. Short stories that strive to be successful. Short stories for readers with short memories.

And in some cases, a star is born.

April, 2006

MOBY DICK: AMERICAN CHOWDER

If, then, to meanest mariners, and renegades and castaways, I shall hereafter ascribe high qualities, though dark; weave around them tragic graces; if even the most mournful, perchance the most abased, among them all, shall at times lift himself to the exalted mounts; if I shall touch that workman's arm with some ethereal light; if I shall spread a rainbow over his disastrous set of sun; then against all mortal critics bear me out in it, thou just Spirit of Equality, which hast spread one royal mantle of humanity over all my kind! Bear me out in it, thou great democratic God!

— *Moby Dick*, Chapter 26

When it comes to the state of the American novel, there is nothing—or at least, not very much— new under the sun. And this is not entirely a bad thing. Not when most avid lovers of literature reluctantly acknowledge that the prospect of reading all or most of the great works of fiction in one lifetime is an unattainable ambition. Sad, but true, and because of this actuality, a well-intentioned or would-be aficionado must aim to separate the proverbial goats from the sheep, and ensure the books that really matter stand at the top of the list.

For instance, when's the last time you fell in love with an author and spent a month, or a summer, or a decade devoting your attention to their oeuvre? Even when, like in love, you're lucky enough to find that soul mate of an author, how often do you get the chance to indulge yourself? And then there are the authors you should *want* to absorb. Have you read all of Dostoyevsky? (Shame on you). All of Shakespeare? (No? Then get thee to a video store). All of Faulkner? (Don't worry, no one else has either).

The point is, as Tennyson proclaimed, art is long and time is fleeting. And it would seem that because of unexceptional high school and college teachers, the prospect of actually reading a novel is accorded roughly the same anticipatory anxiety as a root canal. This is unfortunate, and the authors of these great books should not be punished simply because most professors are unable to convey the joy that can, and should, accompany the act of reading for pleasure.

Good music and good literature have always seemed to intimidate, or bewilder otherwise open-minded individuals. This is doubtless at least in part due to teachers and critics seeking to justify their own intellectual enterprise by conferring upon art an ivory halo that renders it unreachable by average, simple-minded citizens. Rather than regarding, say, jazz music or 19th Century novels as sacred relics conceived by sullen saints, perhaps it would be beneficial to acknowledge most of these works were produced by individuals whose lives were as conventional as their creative minds were exceptional. Or, reduced to more practical terms, if jazz music is gumbo, the archetypal American novel, with *Moby Dick* as its progenitor and arguably its apotheosis, is a chowder.

Chowder?

Listen: so many novels are meat, or potatoes, or broth, or milk (often watery milk that becomes increasingly rank and repellent as it stands on the counter, or in the bookshelf as the case may be), or a smattering of vegetables. It is the rare and precious novel that's able to (indeed, one that even seeks to) satisfy on multiple levels, aesthetic as well as technical, a work that amuses as well as inspires, a book that informs as well invigorates; a novel that reaffirms one's belief in what the novel, that most indefatigable form of artistic expression, can do.

Can novels do this? Yes.

What type of novel? *Moby Dick.*

It's exceedingly ironic that in an age where cantankerous crusaders of classic literature are defending this increasingly endangered species, the not-so-great white male author, there's a text that actually exists which can satisfy both the hegemony-in-a-haystack-hunters and pugnacious proponents of tradition: *Moby Dick.*

The book's author, Herman Melville, despite getting the unfair (and unjustifiable) tag of boring old white guy, author of the quintessential boring old white guy book about a boring old white whale, not to mention a handful of equally impenetrable short stories (while most high school students are instructed to read *Bartleby The*

Scrivener, most of them, at least partly due to the unfortunate baggage associated with its author, would prefer not to) is, in fact, quite accessible. Really.

But accessibility is often the enemy of integrity. Why not, then, celebrate an all-too-infrequent instance that proves to be the exception to the very rules it rewrites? Like any truly lasting piece of expression, the works of Melville not only have stood the intractable test of time, they remain as viable and valuable to today's dissolute and desperate, but not altogether dissimilar world. Perhaps resulting from the ever-mercurial moods of the left-leaning academic aristocracy, it's become as admissible to dismiss *Moby Dick* as it once was to venerate it. This would be an unexceptionable development but for the fact that this classic American text is also pioneering in its often sardonic assaults on institutions ranging from the patriarchal status quo, to slavery, to the Puritanical thought-police who cast a long, lamentable shadow on early U.S. history. This book celebrates our itinerant American roots and the notion of positive, peaceful diversity not as an apologetic ideology, but imperative axiom. Melville empathized with the underdog and more important, he understood them—he was one—and his real life experiences inform the poetic prose that allows these otherwise unrenowned heroes to sing the songs of themselves, proceeding Walt Whitman's masterpiece by a half-decade.

So: a novel that fulfills on almost every conceivable level, a meditation on our individual essence as well as the push and pull of our similitude as human beings adrift in a turbulent universe that not a little resembles the untamed sea.

If the current, confessional model—a facile forgery not even attempting to entertain, or engage in the possibilities the novel provides—is a bouillon cube: add water (or, the easily-invoked tears of an undiscerning reader) than we might recognize the depth and substance of the real novel. No short cuts, all ingredients carefully chosen, cleaned, cleaved, and combined, simmered slowly over the steady flame of inspiration, seasoned with erudition and integrity, stirred with the passion of purpose (a purpose opposite of navel gazing), and served with the unwavering arm of a confident and direct desire to communicate. It's that simple; that impossible.

And yet, even the richest, most savory bowl of chowder can sustain one for a limited time, one meal per person. This is why art is sustenance for the soul, a benevolent gift that keeps giving. Find a novel and you've found a friend for life, a companion that should lend support and inspiration for any earthly endeavors.

September, 2006

SO IT GOES: REFLECTIONS ON KURT VONNEGUT

Kurt Vonnegut would say in speeches that a plausible mission of artists is to make people appreciate being alive at least a little bit. Often, he was asked: Have any artists successfully accomplished this? "The Beatles did", he replied.

Vonnegut, whom time finally stuck to last week, lived a lot longer than he thought he would. For fans, he lived longer than many of them thought he would, too. Most of his avid readers have been preparing for his death, in earnest, since his suicide attempt in 1984. As it turned out, there were many more Pall Malls left to smoke. Then, in 1997, the author's caliginous assertion that *Timequake* was to be his last novel did seem rather like a settling of accounts.

Fortunately, there was still time to tend to some unfinished business, and for another decade he would clean out the proverbial closets and compile the essays found in *A Man Without a Country*. He managed to remain active, and indignant, right up to the end, most recently sounding off on the idiocy of the Iraq misadventure. That the current administration caused him to consider Nixon in a fonder light speaks volumes of Vonnegut's sensibility, and needs no elaboration. To be certain, Vonnegut made many people appreciate being alive more than a little bit; indeed, his greatest achievement may have been helping some people realize that they *were* alive, with a body of work that at once admonishes us to question reality and, whenever possible, to enjoy the ride.

And yet, Vonnegut was, in critical terms, on borrowed time pretty much for the duration after the unanticipated—and unimaginable—success of *Slaughterhouse Five* in 1969. The good news: maybe about five writers per half-century write defining texts that they can be certain, while still alive, will live on after them. The bad news: having to live with it (and never achieving that height again) while still trying to write new novels. That's to say, it's all but impossible for an author to impress anyone—his readers, the critics paid to write about what he has written, and mostly, himself—after composing a masterpiece in the middle of his life. The only thing more arduous is the incessant hangover of dread and expectation awaiting the novelist who knocks off a tour de force right out of the gate. Suffice it to say, *Slaughterhouse Five* proved to be a line in the literary sand he could never jump across (not many other authors have either, for that matter), although he came as close as anyone should have reasonably hoped with *Breakfast of Champions*, a book that looked forward from World War II and its aftermath to the here and now of a country confronted by new concerns, such as Watergate, and more of the same old problems, like growing old and dying. That book, from 1973, if written by anyone else, could constitute a career. It's not even unreasonable to imagine that, if Vonnegut had never parked himself in front of a typewriter after 1963, *Cat's Cradle* would garner even more attention and receive more accolades than it already does.

(Too often, it seems, we are either celebrating artists too late, or we coronate the unworthy too early. It's not as complicated with our athletes when they retire: that's generally a buoyant affair, with the extended goodwill of a swan song season, complete with gifts, accolades and standing ovations. Sure, there is some sadness in seeing a great performer leave the limelight, but the more famous the athlete is, the easier the transition to sanctified superstar afterlife. They are allowed (and perhaps entitled) to assume membership in an elite fraternity that never expires. Theirs is the glory to unrepentantly live in the past, invoke (even embellish) former flights of fancy, and generally rest on the laurels established in their youth.

With artists—novelists in particular—there are a completely different set of standards and expectations. The only ones at liberty to soar on the effulgent wings of yesterday's triumph are those who have died, which renders them largely unable to appreciate the accolades. Indeed, not only is the living novelist forbidden from basking in the refractory glow of a former conquest, they are often haunted by it, forever in its insatiable shadow. One thinks of Ralph Ellison and the pressure he faced to somehow achieve anything after composing one of the surpassing texts of the 20th century, *Invisible Man*.)

In any event, one could sense a disappointment, even a petty resentment, in the rather tepid reviews and faint praise that *Timequake* generated. It was as if the prospect of an author of Vonnegut's stature declaring, with his faculties intact, that he didn't think he had any more novels in him called unaccustomed attention to the evanescent nature of any life. The fact is, *Timequake* did, in many ways, effectively and gracefully sum up several of the themes and concerns we could clumsily, if accurately call "Vonnegutian".

If, on the other hand, he had just disappeared after writing *Slaughterhouse Five*—pulling a willful J.D. Salinger, or an inadvertent Percy Bysshe Shelley or a tedious, haphazard Malcolm Lowry—we would be in more familiar territory, allowed to write our own stories of what might have been. As socially perceptive literary architect, Vonnegut's body of work simultaneously reflected and defined our times—often with a generous dose of humor, irreverence and buoyant elasticity. Vonnegut often confirmed what we already know (the world is crazy) while finding innovative ways to depict and deconstruct the machinations causing the craziness. He did not hold a mirror up to the world, per se; so much as provide a blurred distinction between the sensible and the insane, the powerful and the unprotected, between justice and charade, reality and simulation. He understood, in short, that for most of us, our better angels are busy drowning in acculturated gray matter.

While never considered one of the more authoritative literary technicians, Vonnegut nonetheless was a model for clean writing that avoided pretense and overly polished prose. He wrote, directly, about concepts and chaos that are anything but simple to understand, and even more challenging to describe in a novel. Always with that grouchy finesse, not quite the wizened grandfather, more the wise uncle. Where Mark Twain, with whom he is often compared, could justifiably be accused of occasional crankiness, Vonnegut came off as a curmudgeon (at times) only in interviews; in his fiction his heart was so large and soft the pages are practically wet.

Autobiographical elements abound in Vonnegut's work, and significantly, he paid the types of dues that were once a bit more obligatory: after the military he labored in a job he detested (working in public relations for General Electric) before managing to support himself, barely, through his writing. Still, his pain was our profit: he had already witnessed enough inanity and atrocity to provide fodder for the obsessions that would inform practically every line he wrote. What Vonnegut made seem effortless is a talent every writer should seek to emulate, and what more writers than you may think do desperately want to imitate: writing books that are embraced by the so-called highbrow and lowbrow readers. Vonnegut established a style that went deep by seeming simple and disarmed by being accessible. Take, for instance, *Breakfast of Champions*, which features actual drawings (by the author) scattered amongst the action: in just about anyone else's hands this impertinence would seem distracting, even self-indulgent. Likewise, there is an authorial intrusion late in the novel that perhaps best evinces the dialogic narrative strategy Vonnegut used—mostly to perfection—throughout his work. His novels remain able to make all the copycats who tried to imitate him seem bromidic and drably predictable.

And yet *Slaughterhouse Five*, like virtually all Vonnegut's novels, concerns itself with one of the oldest—and most perplexingly commonplace—human dilemmas: man's inhumanity to man. But how does one discuss war, violence, insanity, and injustice (for starters) without either preaching or unintentionally trivializing? This was Vonnegut's special gift, and why the concept of Billy Pilgrim coming "unstuck in time" is revelatory: the author was not using science fiction pyrotechnics to mask an inability to express his ideas directly, he'd actually hit upon a means by which he could communicate what our increasingly disjointed world is like to live in. In this way, Billy Pilgrim is everyman even as everything he describes is unlike anything the average reader is likely to have experienced (walking in the snow behind enemy lines, living through the Dresden firebombing, being abducted by aliens, and being taught an entirely different theory of relativity by those aliens, the Tralfamadorians). Vonnegut, of course, was really writing about the ways in which the alienated, often lonely person is affected by the pressure and perversity of life. Never before had hilarity and horror danced on the same page in quite this way. Not surprisingly, people (especially younger people) responded. On the other hand, the fact that Kurt Vonnegut was—and remains—much more popular with college students than adults says more about us than it does about his novels.

Interestingly, the sporadic outer space antics that surface in much of Vonnegut's early work are, in fact, a prescient strategy of grappling with the very real—if inexplicable—horrors of our world after The

Bomb, one of the many ways science fiction was—and remains—well equipped to critique today by projecting where we might be tomorrow. We look to works like *Catch-22* that lampoons the military, books like *Revolutionary Road* or *A Fan's Notes* that peel back the noisome carcass of quiet desperation hidden under the sit-com sensibility of the '50s, or anything from, for instance, Flannery O'Connor and Charles Bukowski that depict the desperate, the seedy, the unredeemed and mostly the inconspicuous citizens whom nobody otherwise acknowledges. But Kurt Vonnegut, as much as any single writer, connected these copious threads, and his collected works comprise a sort of freak flag that flies in the face of complacency, offering an alternative version of the official alibi: he managed to merge the lunacy and the aggression of his time in a broth of brio and vulnerability that could literally make you cackle and weep, all at once. In this regard, his writing is very much connected to the 20th Century, yet it is unlikely to lose its immediacy or relevance since it deals with the same problems that plagued us before he lived and will remain with us, long after we are gone.

So it goes.

June, 2007

MARK TWAIN: THE BIG DADDY OF AMERICAN LETTERS

Mark Twain was the heavyweight champion in a time when giants roamed the earth and our color commentary was written in ink. Twain, along with Melville and Hawthorne, represents the holy trinity of 19th Century American fiction: the great white hope. But Twain was arguably the archetypal American writer; certainly that was William Faulkner's assessment. And if Faulkner says Twain was the "father of American literature" than Twain is the father of American literature, end of discussion. Even still, he was *more* than that. A lecturer, a satirist, critic, commentator; a genuine public figure and ambassador for the well-examined life.

Twain's influence is like history itself: impossible to deny, informing everything that comes later. It's difficult to imagine Upton Sinclair, H.L. Mencken, Paul Theroux and Christopher Hitchens existing without the model laid out by their white-haired progenitor. Has anyone mixed accessible fiction, social commentary (caustic and comic) and travel writing with more élan than the peripatetic Twain? Is anyone, with the possible exception of Oscar Wilde, more deliciously quotable? Mark Twain remains the Big Daddy; distinctly American to be sure, but American in a way that invokes the better practices and habits we used to take for granted. Twain embodies an era when exploration (physical and intellectual), engagement with the world and an insatiable appetite for experience were not rites of passage so much as imperative points of departure.

Of course it was, in many regards, a simpler time: no movie stars or radio-friendly pop singers (no radio, for that matter), no prime time news anchors sensationalizing the story of the day. But to be certain, there were still opportunistic hacks and peddlers of propaganda: as long as art remains a viable avenue of commerce and politics exist, the world will never have a scarcity of these charlatans.

So what? Well, would it be too quaint by half (or whole) to propose that writers in general (and poets in particular, per Shelley's dictum) were indeed the unacknowledged legislators of the world? Expertise earned in the field and conferred via the discipline of expression. The best writers could acquire an old-fashioned kind of authority; the type that conferred upon an individual the honor (and obligation) of expressing truths not beholden to party lines or privilege. The type of sensibility capable of creating *Huckleberry Finn,* for instance. Mark Twain, in short, incorporated many of the aspects we lionize in our leaders: a populist impulse, an instinctive aversion to prejudice, skepticism of power and an unabashed zeal for democracy. This is Twain's legacy: his country did not define him so much as he helped define it. If Hawthorne wrote about what we had been (and, in his despairing eyes, always would be), and Melville wrote about what we could be, then Twain wrote about what we were, and what we *should* be.

April, 2009

OBSESSION, HOPE AND GLORY, PART ONE: PERCY FAWCETT'S EXCELLENT ADVENTURE

They don't make them like that anymore. The thing is, they didn't make them like that *then*, either. Col. Percy Fawcett was *sui generis*, supersized. And if he was the first of his kind, he was the last of a kind: the great old-world explorers. By the time Fawcett died (disappearing in the jungles of the Amazon), the world had become a much smaller place.

New Yorker writer David Grann knew he had an ideal subject when he began researching the Fawcett story; he could not have known he was going to become part of the story. *The Lost City of Z* is the end product of inestimable research and in-the-field reportage, literally.

Like (literally) hundreds before him, Grann cultivated a compulsion that could only be satisfied by experiencing the action himself. Unlike many other reporters, explorers and thrill-seekers who set off to find Fawcett's trail (and, inevitably, subsequent fame and fortune for telling their tale), Grann actually made it out alive. And he also found things even he couldn't have expected or anticipated. (No spoilers here, you'll have to read it to get the scoop.)

What Grann came to understand, before ever setting foot in the jungle, was something that no number of books, movies or documentaries could successfully convey. That is, Percy Fawcett was, in every sense of the cliché, very much a man apart. The mere triumph of entering and exiting the Amazon alive was, as many hearty fellows found out by paying the ultimate price, not an inconsiderable achievement. At a time when the North and South Poles were all the rage, one could be forgiven for assuming that the warmer weather, bustling foliage and diverse plant and animal life all afforded a preferable venue for discovery. On the contrary, the ostensibly bountiful tropical haven was in actuality a death trap. Grann quotes Candice Millard from *The River Of Doubt,* her study of Theodore Roosevelt's harrowing Amazonian adventure:

The rain forest was not a garden of easy abundance, but precisely the opposite. Its quiet, shaded halls of leafy opulence were not a sanctuary, but rather the greatest natural battlefield anywhere on the planet, hosting an unremitting and remorseless fight for survival that occupied every single one of its inhabitants, every minute of every day.

A few words about those inhabitants. Never mind the jaguars, anacondas, electric eels, and piranhas. Those things can kill you quickly, if that's how it goes down. The insects, on the other hand, epitomize death by a billion bites. To be certain, they are quite capable of killing you as well, but it's never quick and it's always painful. Ever heard of a bug that bites you on the lip, unleashing a parasite that eventually assails your brain two decades later, causing an agonizing breakdown of the body? Neither had I. How about maggots that get hatched inside the skin and crawl around in your arm? (If you kill them they rot and cause infection; you actually have to let them *live* even as you see—and feel—them coursing through your limbs.) And then there are just the plain old pests that cover your face all hours of the day and night: biting, scratching, burrowing. And all of these agents of pain pale in comparison to the candiru (look that up, or if you are a male, let's just put it this way: these things are enough to make you believe there is a God and that He has a sick, unacceptable sense of humor). Oh, and then there are the natives who may kill you with a poisoned arrow, or maybe bury you in a hole and cover you with honey so that the bees or ants will turn you into a living lollipop. Or maybe they'll keep you alive long enough to *eat* you. In short, these conditions all, to some degree, exist today; to think what it was like to endure any of these obstacles one hundred years ago is...unsettling.

These were the conditions Percy Fawcett not only embraced, but yearned for. This was a man who, at the top of his game, was called away to fight in The Great War. He hunkered down in the muddy trenches and watched the privation and despair and the staggering death count, and still, having survived, longed to return to the jungle. Granted, after World War I it would be understandable to seek distraction or escape virtually anywhere, but for Fawcett, he was miserable after a while if he couldn't continue his mission. His mission became an obsession, and the difference between Fawcett and almost everyone else is that he had the wherewithal to persevere. Most monomaniacs flame out sooner or later (usually sooner) and even if they don't get themselves killed, the mental toll from being so singularly focused slows them down. Fawcett courted death, but he lived for that adventure: this was his essential nature and he didn't shun it. Indeed, he understood that being unable to live life on his terms would have killed him in ways more cruel than anything the Amazon was capable of inflicting.

Fawcett was, around the turn of the 20th Century, as close to a rock star as it came in those days. Had he cared about money or the shallow spiritual payoff of established notoriety, he likely would have lived a long life (he may, in fact, have lived forever). But where people all around the world were fascinated with him, *he* was fascinated by the unknown and unconquered. And by unconquered, it's crucial to point out that he had no designs on human conquest (and even the pirates who would have claimed they were *only* after treasure could not deny obtaining that bounty necessarily involved eradicating the Indians who possessed it). Fawcett was uninterested in subjugating the "savage" natives, and the practices of complicated Christian conversion or simple slaughter so common at that time repulsed him. Indeed, one of the many secrets of his almost inexplicable success over the years was an instinctive awareness that respect and humility were more powerful weapons than the ones favored (and utilized) by almost every other white man who stepped foot in the jungle.

Certainly, Fawcett knew that if he was able to successfully confirm the existence of "the city of Z", it would make his fortune and his career. On the other hand, Grann's reportage makes it abundantly clear that the only magnet pulling him into the dark heart of the Amazon was his desire to see what others couldn't find, to *know* that his intuition was on target. By his own account, he was miserable if unable to continue his work. And if the work was exhilarating and dangerous in equal measure, it was also solitary: Fawcett was blessed with an inhuman constitution, and cursed by having to hire mere mortals to assist him. These unfortunate souls, no matter how ambitious and game, quickly found themselves out of their depth, and the target of Fawcett's ire when he realized that they couldn't keep up. In this sense, Fawcett is a truly tragic figure: he was better equipped than anyone else to stalk the improbable; what kept him alive ended up killing him.

And still, one wonders who had a tougher time (it seems a safe bet the unflappable Fawcett would have recoiled at the reading list and research materials Grann required to tell his tale). Fawcett only had to *do* it; describing his various escapades from the myriad sources must have been its own brand of torture. The bibliography alone has enough texts to overcrowd an empty warehouse. The painstaking process of getting the story straight obliged Grann to employ many more assistants than Fawcett ever used. And Fawcett was the one who *lived* the tale being told. Conclusion: Fawcett explored so people unlike him didn't have to. Grann puts all the pieces together so people like us don't have to. Paying a few bucks for this book seems an almost offensively safe and unencumbered option, albeit one that is enthusiastically recommended.

September, 2009

SUI GENERIS ON THE ROCKS: CHRISTOPHER HITCHENS, R.I.P.

The best way to compliment a writer, as a reader, is to recommend their work to others. That I wholeheartedly do, and have done.

The best way to compliment a writer, as a writer, is to recognize, with neither regret nor resignation, that on your best day you will always stand in awe of what they achieved.

Reading and responding to The Hitch is ceaselessly inspiring and seldom less than exhilarating. More, it is an instigatory experience: it compels you to get involved more deeply with the world around and inside you. Reading any worthwhile writer is an act of celebration, a shared reaction to the act of creation. More, it is an exercise in how to write, read, think and live.

The best tribute I can offer to Hitch is that even when he infuriated me (something he did often when he wrote about politics after 9/11), he excited me. I've never read a writer who *thrilled* me as consistently and thoroughly as Hitchens did. He is one of the very few writers who could write about virtually anything and I'd want to read his take. Even, or perhaps especially, when I disagreed with him I came away a more informed and better equipped. In this sense, Hitchens—who at different times could accurately be described as a Marxist, a contrarian, a reactionary and an iconoclast—provided lessons for how to engage intellectually and spiritually (yes, spiritually) with the world. And think about those four words (and there are many others I could use): how many public figures could conceivably, much less convincingly, be described thusly? If Hitchens had sold out, his ostensibly contradictory stances might seem like a case of cognitive dissonance. In actuality, it was the evidence of his ongoing evolution, as a thinker, writer and human being. Evolution is never static, and Hitchens was always moving forward: ravenous, curious, ornery, and insatiable. Above all, he burrowed into the world with the glee and intensity of a converted soul. His salvation was not religion; it was the simple and profound act of existing: *I think, therefore I am.*

Hitchens combined the range of Twain, the erudition of Mencken and the irreverence of Hunter S. Thompson. Of course he also had the political courage of Orwell, the acerbic wit of Cyril Connolly and the adroit literary acumen as his great friend Martin Amis. Of all the writers whose work I've worshipped, Hitchens was the most fully-formed summation of his influences; as a result of his addiction to knowledge, he produced an insight that is at once all-encompassing and wholly unique. At his best, Hitchens could remind you of any number of geniuses; at the same time, nobody else is like Hitchens. The Hitch is *sui generis,* on the rocks.

Here's the deal: even as I felt intense discomfort for how cozy he became with the architects of our recently-concluded (?) quagmire, it was difficult to write him off. For one thing, he never stood to profit in any sense of the word, and I believe he was inexorably affected by what his mate Salman Rushdie endured (when he was notably one of the few artists willing to stand up and defend Rushdie). Over time he came to—wrongly in my view—perceive a very gray (and shady) situation as black and white. It wasn't like he ever turned tail and apologized for being a liberal (like some of his erstwhile allies did); he certainly did not embrace his new "friends" on the Right in any meaningful way. He was cocksure, inscrutable and resolute to the end; if he was a bit pig-headed at times, in my estimation he was never opportunistic or craven. How many legit famous people can we say that about?

The best way to compliment a person for the life they lived is how they choose to die.

That seems too cute by half, but I can't think of a better way to put it. Of course, few of us have the opportunity to *choose* how, or when, we die. For the unfortunate folks who contend with cancer, the choice is made for us. The true measure of the courage of one's convictions is how those convictions hold up under duress. Hitchens promised he would never "find" religion once he was diagnosed with what turned out to be the ailment that took him out. True to his word, as usual, as ever, he was unflinching to the end, even as the hideous disease made him emaciated, weak and fried inside-out. True to his nature, he not only refused to give quarter, he took every opportunity to reiterate the feelings he had about all-things religious.

People who live the right way are living lessons on how to exist, aspire and inevitably, to perish. Hitchens, through his example, will remain a vivid and unquenchable exhibit for how to suck the marrow out of this life, as Thoreau admonished us to do. The mind-boggling body of work he leaves behind will ensure that this world is never without him. Which, in the final analysis is a relief, because the world is already a poorer place without further input from this unbowed, inimitable piece of work.

December, 2011

THE GREATNESS OF THE GATSBY

Kathryn Schulz has seized the occasion of the newest—and probably not the last—screen adaptation of *The Great Gatsby* to take the great American novel down several pegs. Indeed, she is not content to critique it; the title of her provocative piece is "Why I Despise *The Great Gatsby*" (*Vulture.com*, 6 May 2013). Naturally, any critic, any reader, is more than entitled to his or her opinion; art is useless unless it's capable of inspiring. At its best it can inspire pleasure and awe, sympathy and thoughtfulness, but it can and must also inspire criticism, and art that lasts is able to sustain both our scrutiny and the passage of time.

As such, I have no particular qualms with Schulz, or anyone else, expressing disenchantment with a novel so many others worship. In fact, the world needs more, not less people willing or able to interrogate our literary sacred cows and offer views contrary to received and/or inculcated opinion. On the other hand, any analysis that disputes near-universal approbation must do the necessary work on its own behalf. Thus, as a statement of personal preference, I celebrate Schulz's decision—however opportunistic—to declare her disdain; it's where she attempts to engage with the novel as a critic that I have reservations, and comments. More, she claims a conspiracy of sorts where we are "not free to dislike this book". Of course we are. But if we're going to put pen to paper in the service of condemning it, we'd better have insights that are compelling and not clichéd.

First of all, I can usually tell where people are coming from when they assail *The Great Gatsby*. They are invariably similar to folks who, striking a rebellious or recalcitrant pose, dismiss Shakespeare as overrated or impossible to appreciate. Of course, all too often it becomes disappointingly obvious that many of these people have failed to read many (or any) of the works in question. Of course this scenario applies to many canonical works, whether we're talking about Mozart, Miles Davis or (sigh) Herman Melville. The reason I associate naysayers of *The Great Gatsby* with Shakespeare deniers is because they frequently make the facile and irritating mistake of approaching older works from a current perspective.

To be certain, one of the reasons an eminent work (like *The Great Gatsby*) appeals to successive generations is its ability to depict truths that cut across time and trends. Ironically, it's precisely the ways F. Scott Fitzgerald's masterpiece remains relevant—and revelatory—that offer its best account for posterity. The fact that the action occurs in definite times and places which, at least on superficial levels, seem obsolete, only augments the novel's import and prescience.

Whenever someone complains about the obviousness or unoriginality of either Shakespeare or Fitzgerald, I feel obliged to remind them that the reason their words and symbols seem so readymade is because so many lesser authors have imitated or copied them. Aside from the fact that virtually any of Shakespeare's mature works and *The Great Gatsby* can be savored on a line-by-line basis solely for the richness of their language, it's almost impossible to imagine contemporary writing outside the large shadow they cast. Anytime a symbol from an older work (like, say, *Hamlet* or *Moby Dick*) seems hackneyed there's a good chance it's because the symbol in question has become such an inextricable part of our culture. Sound pretentious? Think about what the expression "white whale" signifies, or the ways "to be or not to be—that is the question" has been quoted or placed in diverse contexts. Put another way, it's not the fault of the author if their words have become ubiquitous, and it's both unfair and inaccurate to damn the work by comparison with the unoriginal or overused ways it is exploited—or abused—by its acolytes.

I'm accustomed to hearing people protest (too much) about the symbolism in *The Great Gatsby*, but Schulz levels two complaints that I'm not sure I've heard associated with this particular book, and I think, as is normally the case, they reveal more about the writer than the writing. The first is that the characters are unlikable, a quibble I'd expect from a college sophomore or someone who reads books about reality TV stars. Now, to be clear, some of our better scribes have been able to render terrible people as both amusing and endearing. This is something Martin Amis has practically made a career out of, nowhere more successfully than in his masterpiece *Money*. But who needs or wants to *like* all the characters in a work of fiction?

Complaining about the novel she wished Fitzgerald had written, Schulz laments "Indeed, *The Great Gatsby* is less involved with human emotion than any book of comparable fame I can think of. None of its characters are likable. None of them are even dislikable, though nearly all of them are despicable." It is, presumably, a given that both Tom and Daisy are supposed to be unsympathetic (for my money they are, to Fitzgerald's considerable credit, portrayed as two of the most despicable characters in all literature). But let's take a look at the primary players for whom Schulz can summon neither love nor hate. In a book (*the* book) delineating shallow, misguided and spiritually hollow people, Schulz can't fathom why Fitzgerald would create such…shallow, misguided and spiritually hollow people! One scarcely knows where to begin, but I'll take a shot.

As narrator (and what should we take from the fact that he's writing this, years and miles from the events being depicted, safe, chastened, dissatisfied, maybe a tad sentimental, still, for the things that *might* have been had Gatsby been just a little bit greater?), Nick is not supposed to be especially likable. In fact, he's supposed to be exactly what he is: a passive, voyeuristic coward; the guy who silently goes along with everyone and everything even though he—as the less-than-reliable narration would have us believe—knew better. Here is Schulz's assessment: "At no point are we given cause, or room, to feel complicit. Our position throughout is that of an innocent bystander. That's also Nick's role, so the perspective of the book becomes one of passive observation…Yet he never admits to collusion with or seduction by all the fabulous depravity around him. After it's all over, he retreats to the Midwest and, figuratively and literally, tells his story from the safe remove of America's imaginary moral high ground." Does it occur to Schulz that part of Nick's unspoken story is the possibility that, had Gatsby not been killed, he would have contentedly continued to lick his rich benefactor's boot heels? Perhaps Schulz also suspects that in Poe's tale Montresor is the bad guy, or that Marlow is just as culpable as Mr. Kurtz, because he kind of sat around and watched the evil unfold?

Along these lines, Schulz commits the most egregious, and embarrassingly shallow of sins: conflating Nick as narrator with Fitzgerald as actual person. Granted, this type of insouciant psychoanalysis is practically *de rigueur* in today's literary scene (including most college English departments), but it not only undermines the point(s) Schulz attempts to make, it leaves them difficult to take seriously. Worse, she hones in on what she believes exposes Fitzgerald's ultimate character flaw: the fact that he struggled with his contempt for the wealthy and his ambition to be well-off. Gee, sound like anyone *you* know?

Perhaps, just to take one glaring example, a certain demographic in our country that consistently votes against its best interest, enabling taxes on the wealthiest fraction to shrivel because of the infinitesimal chance they, too, might one day be flush? As F. Scott Fitzgerald puts it, knocking it out of the park better than anyone not named H.L. Mencken: "Americans, while occasionally willing to be serfs, have always been obstinate about being peasantry." It's what the novel says about those who are *not* wealthy that comprises the dark heart of its wonder—and acumen—and anyone failing to see the flappers and fools providing their gin are so much expensive scenery misses the entire point.

Schulz also laments that she can't find sufficient reason to believe in Gatsby's love for Daisy (indeed, she can't believe in Gatsby and Daisy, period). I find this incredible: how can anyone read this novel and not understand Gatsby's love for Daisy *is* unbelievable, in part because it is unfeasible; it is, in fact, impossible—an illusion. Like so many could-have-been-a-contender parables, he snatched at his brass ring (erected his Xanadu, etc.), and found, to his chagrin, it was not sustainable. And all that business about "You can't repeat the past?" Hint: Nick (and/or Fitzgerald) is not just talking about Gatsby there; he's talking about all of us, and understanding this puts the entire narrative in sharp, devastating focus. The tragedy of the novel is, ultimately, not a bunch of incurious, brutal people behaving badly; it's that everyone, affluent or indigent, has a human desire to get more than they'll receive, and an instinctive awareness they get less attractive, healthy and proficient after exceeding a certain age.

Once again, Schulz bemoans Fitzgerald's inability to write the book she would have felt more comfortable reading, underscoring how grievously she's missing the mark: "On the page, Fitzgerald's moralizing instinct comes off as cold; the chill that settles around *The Great Gatsby* is an absence of empathy." On the contrary; what Fitzgerald does, with these ostensibly soulless and unpleasant people, is interrogate cause and effect, motive and aftermath, and all aspects of that myth sold to us as the American Dream. He takes this construction and places it on the operating table, dissecting what causes it to breathe, thrive and rot from the inside out. In this single regard, Fitzgerald was more prophetic than his critics can comprehend: he predicted how the roaring '20s would end and be remembered *before* they expired. If the people (like Nick) who wind up on the outside looking in see nothing but emptiness, it's because all vanity, in the end, returns to the ashes whence it sprang. Fitzgerald is not describing anything Ecclesiastes did not say first, if less poetically.

In addition, he depicted the way Americans would react to every calamity of the 20th Century: after each debacle, the architects of said crisis waltz away, licking their wounds and counting their cash. No amount of dour intuition could have prepared Fitzgerald to imagine that, in the 21st century, they also get paid to scold the complicit masses (receiving book deals, going into politics or appearing on TV—the lucky ones doing all three). Think about the cowards in Congress today, who lustily passed legislation (and deregulation) that hastened the latest crash, now pushing austerity (but not higher taxes!). It isn't that their methods or strategies are predictable (they are), it's the narrative they employ that is so quintessentially American: cynicism covered in money, preaching solidarity.

In one of the most quoted passages of the book, Tom and Daisy are described as "careless people…they smashed up things and creatures and then retreated back into their money or their vast carelessness or whatever it was that kept them together, and let other people clean up the mess they had made." One need look no further than Wall Street, or Iraq, or the budgetary realities of a small town under sequestration to see, even with eyes wide shut, the ways everything Fitzgerald held his mirror up to are reflecting back at us, bigger, uglier and more shameless than they ever were a century ago. In America it is not only romance and nostalgia that ensure we are borne, ceaselessly to the past.

May, 2013

WHAT WE TALK ABOUT WHEN WE TALK ABOUT SEX (IN FICTION)

Writing about sex is like engaging in sex: it's hard.

Or, it should be.

It's that time of year again, where we can count on three things: shopping-related stress during Thanksgiving, family-related stress during Christmas, and in between the two, the Bad Sex in Fiction Award conducted by London's *Literary Review*. The 22nd annual honor was awarded last week and Ben Okri takes top prize for the suitably horrific scene in his novel *The Age of Magic*.

This event is not a lark, or limited to third-tier writers. Some legit semi-heavyweights have taken this crown, including Tom Wolfe, David Guterson and (shocker) Norman Mailer. Amusingly—and appropriately—John Updike won a Lifetime Achievement Award in 2008; astonishingly, Philip Roth has never reaped what he's blown, though it's undeniably not for lack of trying. Take this passage (please) from *The Dying Animal:* "...with my knees planted to either side of her and my ass centered over her, I leaned into her face and rhythmically, without letup, I fucked her mouth." (This and other of Roth's overly penetrating portrayals were wonderfully cataloged by Christopher Hitchens in an epic, scathing 2007 piece for *The Atlantic*.)

Here's the, um, climax of this year's best worst passage, according to the intrepid readers and judgers at *Literary Review*: "The universe was in her and with each movement it unfolded to her. Somewhere in the night a stray rocket went off." Okay, that's pretty terrible. Or awe-inspiring in its awfulness. How about an incriminating précis of reigning champs from recent years? Here's a portion of 2012's winning bit, by Nancy Houston (from *Infrared*): "oh the sheer ecstasy of lips and tongues on genitals, either simultaneously or in alteration, never will I tire of that silver fluidity, my sex swimming in joy like a fish in water." That's impossible to outdo. No it isn't. Check this, from 2010, courtesy of Rowan Somerville (from *The Shape of Her*): "Like a lepidopterist mounting a tough-skinned insect with a too blunt pin he screwed himself into her." It can't credibly get worse than that, right? Wrong. Rachel Johnson raised the lowest of bars in 2008 with this (from *Shire Hell*): "he holds both my arms down, and puts his tongue to my core, like a cat lapping up a dish of cream so as to not miss a single drop."

A pattern emphatically emerges, even with this, er, small sample size. They are all aesthetically offensive, cliché-ridden, and suffer from self-consciousness—either too much or a total lack thereof. Regardless of taste or tact, few readers—or few folks with a modicum of experience either fornicating or writing fiction about it—would quibble with how excruciating these excerpts are.

Yet in 2010, Laura Miller at *Salon* took exception to the glee with which these dishonors are doled out, the entire affair a combination of prurience and the puritanical impulse that has ever afflicted our upper classes. She posits that we are a bunch of snobs when it comes to the Reese's Peanut Butter Cup proposition of combining sex and literature. I think she (wisely? cynically?) uses the occasion of the Bad Sex Award to make a larger point about what we talk about when we talk about sex (in fiction): she's all for it. She does, however, utilize a bit of a Straw Man to complain about the *Literary Review's* annual endeavor, suggesting that more self-aware readers have—or should have—no qualms about moments of ardor (and the moments those moments lead to) artistically rendered.

I think the issue is not so much that these scenes exist, but that they're invariably so uninspired or unintentionally ridiculous. Or, readers aren't saying *not* to include sex in novels, but that writers should do everyone a favor and 86 the 69, or any scenes that make a mockery of the function so many people hold sacred—at least in theory. After all, the mostly unspoken calculus that occurs under cover of intimacy compels relationships and builds or destroys marriages, even families. In other words, it's noteworthy. Indeed, for more members of our species than we may care to admit, the deed (the thought of it, the desire for it, and the lack of it) influences almost every waking moment. So, perhaps this award offers a welcome—and by the abundance of material to choose from each year, often unheeded—admonishment for those who would kiss and tell: proceed warily if you must.

Is this too much to ask?

Let's face it: convincing sex scenes happen seldom enough in real life. How—or why—do we expect them to occur in literature? Especially when most writers (the honest ones would admit) are not exactly Lotharios, unless you count the hackneyed rite of passage so frequently painted, involving the professorial seduction of the over-achieving undergrad. And these scenes, even though the authors don't realize it, are less erotic than confessional—and more than a little embarrassing for all involved. I've unfailingly seen the most accomplished authors flummoxed while attempting a basic depiction of consensual love. Or lust.

So how do you do it?

Sex scenes, that is.

Anyone who has a passing acquaintance with the act, much less the art, of seduction and surrender understands that successful sex is like almost any human enterprise: you don't need to talk about it if you can do it—whatever *it* is. Or, the people who speak (and write) the loudest are probably not the people you want beneath you or on top of you, and they certainly are not the ones you should be paying to be your creative tour guide.

A personal favorite comes from the immortal Richard Burton writing about the immortal Liz Taylor. "Apocalyptic," was how he described her breasts. "They would topple empires before they withered." That's not even a sex scene, and Burton was, of course, an actor, but there are novelists whose collected works don't contain a line that perfect.

I'm not sure when, or if, *The Canterbury Tales* started to make sense, but I know things got interesting when I realized everyone apparently was shagging one another, albeit in a difficult-to-understand language. In hindsight, I suspect my professor was hoping to make the material a bit more uh, titillating to easily-distracted students, but I came away with the notion that Chaucer was a bit of a Player. "The Miller's Tale" alone is practically a medieval sex manual.

Exhibit A: "When Nicholas had doon thus everydeel/He thakked hire about the lendes weel/He kiste hire swete, and taketh his sautrye/And pleyeth faste, and maketh melodye."

Exhibit B: "And prively he caughte hire by the queynte/And seyde 'Y-wis, but if ich have my wille/For derne love of thee, lemman, I spille." (Google *queynte.)*

Of course an entire essay could be devoted to virtually any play by Shakespeare, who arguably combined passion, humor and lasciviousness with more élan than any writer, in any language.

Show, don't tell. That's the sacrosanct tenet we're taught in English class around the same time we are(n't) being taught Sex Ed. And except for the masters (in art; in life) who actually *did* it and are speaking from experience, the rule should always apply. The exception can—and should—be made for the ones who are able to put it plainly because their prose is essentially a declaration: I did it, this is how I did it, and if you hope to do it you might imitate my expertise. Put another way, I learned more from Milan Kundera and his understated field notes during my formative years than I ever did from any of the more cocky and forthcoming Locker Room Don-Juan wannabes. And the less said about our more celebrated purveyors of purple-prosed nerd porn like Updike and Roth the better.

Everyone knows most writers are long on word and short on action, with the exception of Ernest Hemingway. He allegedly got plenty of action and instigated lots of excitement, but a contrived—and increasingly pathetic—code of masculinity was the white whale he chased, in his fiction and in his life, until he got too old to make it *or* fake it. (A Freudian could have a field day with what his minimalism actually signifies.) Perhaps our best semi-contemporary practitioner of doing in print what he did—or wanted to do—in the bedroom, is Charles Bukowski. A dirty old man and making no bones about it, he nevertheless expresses so many thoughts and emotions sex imbues with the requisite comic, tragic and prosaic elements it merits, in reality.

And when all else fails, experts have informed me that's what the Internet is for. Nevermind books and even movies. If music, or conversation—that old fashioned and unforced chemistry called charm—or a competently cooked meal can't get you to the Promised Land, you may as well cast a line into the weird, wild web. And, if you are irretrievably old school, seek salvation in one of those books with Fabio on the cover. If you want the genuine article, suitable for a certain type of reading, why settle for half-assed posturing when you can get your Harlequin on?

In the final analysis, the wisest way to handle any conquest, real or imagined, is to imitate the great ones and act—or at least pretend—like you've been there before. And for us literary types, it's worth recalling the words of wisdom offered by the (fictional) intercourse aficionado Jackie Treehorn: *People forget that the brain is the biggest erogenous zone.*

Again, writing about sex is hard. Except when it's not hard enough. And therein, as The Bard reminds us, lies the rub.

December, 2014

IN DEFENSE OF STEPHEN KING

Fact: Stephen King, the most successful author of our time, arguably toils more diligently than any other writer. For this alone he deserves recognition and respect.

To the haters: Yes, it's unlikely any of his works will ever be dissected in graduate seminars. But ask any writer, in whatever genre, about their ultimate goal and the honest, simple answer is to be read. On this score, King has achieved what few authors, of any time, will. For this, too, recognition and respect—however grudging—is warranted.

To the savvy social media hipsters: *How* many likes did you get on that pithy post? You have *how* many Twitter followers? Keep channeling that energy into tweets, cultivate your online presence to evanescent perfection. King just wrote another novel while you refreshed your screen.

Here's the Thing about King: he is so incredibly, so *preposterously* productive it's not unreasonable to imagine the thousands (millions?) of trees that would still be standing if he'd at any time decided to take his foot off the throttle. Then again, how can we do anything but admire an artist for shutting out the very distractions we love to lament? How much reality TV time do you think King is racking up? How many hours is he wasting on Facebook? Sure, he's afforded himself the luxury of not needing to pay the bills, so he gets up every day and punches a different kind of clock, and his time seems regulated not by machines but the engine inside him. This drive—it can't be for money, it's unlikely he craves more fame—keeps him engaged and, if it gives him no rest in the superficial sense, it's provided him peace.

If he won't be accused of being a craftsman, he should be celebrated for putting on his boots every day, without exception or excuse, and killing more trees. Stephen King is the Paul Bunyan of fiction, America's literary lumberjack.

***

It's actually not *that* difficult to imagine some of King's novels getting the grad school treatment; at the very least they may be ripe for undergraduate-level exegesis: "English 301: Stephen King and the Pop-Culture Apotheosis". Here, let's give it a shot.

Salem's Lot can be interpreted as an extended metaphor about the increasing cycle of parasitic capitalism, forcing blue collar folks to feed off the blood of the upper classes, until egalitarianism is achieved, at last, through eternal predation. (But no, it's just a book about vampires rampaging through a small New England town.)

Cujo was written, so the author claims, while he was putting more blow up his nose than Tony Montana in *Scarface*. Perhaps we can reconsider the mucus-coated muzzle of the St. Bernard as an extended allegory regarding the danger and disempowering potential of hard drugs. Or greed, or power, or any vice. (But no, it's just a book about a big rabid dog rampaging through a small New England town.)

Christine: a car possessed by the soul of its original owner, or a car that possessed the soul of its original owner, who now possesses the car that possesses the soul of its new owner: a Borgesian labyrinth deconstructing the self-abnegation and reincarnation inherent in the act of creation? (No, it's just a book about a car rampaging through a small New England town.)

Is it exhausting reading this? It's exhausting just writing it. Plus, the uninitiated could simply watch the movies. Though, in fairness, even the better movies are worse than the most mediocre books (yes, for my money that includes the overly saccharine and sentimental crowd favorites *Stand By Me* and *The Shawshank Redemption*). Again, one thinks of the recurring theme of carnage and the inestimable tonnage of trees…

***

Stephen King has been more defiant in recent years, and he's earned the right to be a tad truculent about his influence. Selling more than 350 million books and making multiple generations of readers into fanatics is undoubtedly gratifying and something a fraction of writers will ever experience. And he can boast penning at least three novels that anticipated colossal cultural trends: he made vampires cool again (a few decades ahead of schedule), he conjured up a delusional sociopath jump-starting a nuclear apocalypse *before* Reagan took office, and envisioned a devastating pandemic before AIDS became front-page news (*'Salem's Lot, The Dead Zone*, and *The Stand*, respectively). This trifecta alone earns him street cred that should extend beyond literary circles. Yet clearly, the critical backlash accumulated over the years sticks in King's craw. As an éminence grise who, it might also be pointed out, paid his dues for many years before his "overnight" success, he is aware he'll always be a tough sell for the lit-crit crowd.

In his recent, extended interview in *Rolling Stone*, King is candid, calm, and not above throwing a few haymakers at some usual—and a couple of unusual—suspects. He gets his licks in on the insufferable Harold Bloom (who went out of his way to savage King when the latter won the National Book Award in 2003), whom he describes as taking "(his) ignorance about popular culture as a badge of intellectual prowess". Fair enough. If King's ghastliest work injures the eyes, it doesn't quite deaden the senses the way Bloom's sacred cow shenanigans often do. And if King is, at times, a one-trick pony, at least there's a horse in his stall. As such, King's bitter tea tastes pretty sweet on the page, and he is justified for calling out people who dismiss him out of hand.

King correctly connects the dots between Nathaniel Hawthorne and Jim Thompson; he rightly invokes Twain and delivers some welcome insights on the ways we are conditioned to receive and respond to different mediums. And his commentary begs necessary—or at least worthwhile—questions regarding labels and poles, high-brow and third-rate, and whether the twain shall meet (they always do, of course, as Mark Twain himself proves). His observations, for instance, on *Jaws*—and how movies are capable of attaining a credibility seldom afforded to popular fiction—offer a refreshing alternative analysis regarding what his work is, who it serves, where it appeals, and why it will endure, in its way.

And then, with a chip on his shoulder as Big as the Ritz, he takes a curious swipe at Fitzgerald, who probably spent more time polishing a paragraph than King takes to write a rough draft. He also sets his sights on Hemingway, and his remarks underscore how simultaneously disarming and exasperating King can be. "Hemingway sucks, basically. If people like that, terrific," he shrugs, gauntlet thrown.

These comments are not as sacrilegious as they may seem, at first. It's difficult to deny that Hemingway—and much of what he epitomized—continues to age poorly, and some of his novels are as overrated as some of King's are unfairly maligned. On the other hand, *The Sun Also Rises* establishes sufficient evidence of Hemingway's brilliance, and many of his short stories are more indispensable than anything King has written (particularly his own short stories). For all the hype and possibly deleterious influence of Papa's minimalism, it does serve as an aesthetic antidote for King, a writer who edits his tomes the way weeds regulate their growth.

King asserts that he has elevated the horror genre, and few would disagree, even if some might say: "So?" He compares himself to Raymond Chandler whom he credits with elevating the detective genre. It's clear that what King covets is more respect. His disdain for the Literary Industrial Complex is understandable, but—unfortunately for him—the people he loves to loathe are typically the arbiters of these matters. On one hand, he can point to his sales stats and declare victory (that's what Hemingway might do; it's also what Tom Clancy—whom King hopes to distance himself from—did). On the other hand, all the clever arguments and eyebrow-raising one-liners can't accomplish what his work must do on its own accord. If sales and celebrity are what distinguish hacks from legends, in the end it's always the writing itself that must outlast or endure the hype.

***

Let me tell you a story.

Stephen King has been very good to me. If I haven't read anything he's written since the late '80s, I sure as shit read everything up to that point. I first encountered him in grade school: I saw *'Salem's Lot*, then I read it. Ditto *Carrie*. From then on, he was always there for me, a new book every time I needed one. By the time I caught up with the back catalog, he was on his early-to-mid decade roll, cranking out *Cujo, Christine, Different Seasons,* etc. It was also when every King effort was made into a movie, so in many regards it was all King all the time for a while there.

It was the *Ulysses* of my adolescence; that novel contained the universe (known, unknown) to me, circa 1987. And if it transfixed me, then, I can still admire the adrenaline and drive, the ambition and sheer *endurance* it takes to attempt—much less pull off—such a project. When we found out, in 1985, that he was also pumping out product as Richard Bachman the scope of his capabilities became apparent. He was Beethoven: inhuman, unreal, too prolific to adequately measure in logical terms, teenager-wise.

It was my Holy Grail; even as a sixteen year old I suspected nothing could ever be the same, I stoically anticipated the inexorable comedown: *How can he follow this? How can I?* Coincidentally or not, soon thereafter I went to college, girls became more than a yearning concept (where they had heretofore been mostly unimaginable, even dangerous, if not quite able to start fires with their minds able to confound and incinerate my own illusions). An undergraduate no longer requires whimsical nightmares via fiction; he is too busy instigating them in real life. Above all, I read authors like F. Scott Fitzgerald for the first time. Hemingway, too, of whom it can succinctly be stated: "A Clean, Well-Lighted Place" has more heft than the best 100 pages King's ever typed. In sum, I grew up. That's not to suggest King is more suited for children, it's to relate that the more widely I read, the more acutely I realized ten lifetimes would scarcely present an opportunity to cover the menu I was compiling.

And yet. King made me want to write. He made me want to be a *writer*. He was the one who consistently made the magic happen. He cracked the furtive code of storytelling: creating memorable, occasionally indelible characters, and, through the use of words and imagination, making our world more vital, more *real*. (And, importantly, he has never taken himself too seriously, as his wonderful cameo in *Creepshow* makes sufficiently clear.)

Stephen King remains as relevant as ever, as a concept if nothing else. While we behold the ongoing implosion of the traditional (and often dysfunctional, elitist, undemocratic) book publishing industry, we should commend a multi-millionaire who is still, somehow, an underdog. King is an unacknowledged legislator of sorts, the man of the people most politicians pretend to be. Accuse him of anything, but no one can say King does not care—about his characters, his readers, his craft. Quick: how many artists of any kind, regardless of rank or reputation, roll out of bed and get busy every day, including weekends? He's the rare individual who can invoke the American Dream and not inspire scorn, or nausea for that matter.

Even if the quality is forever debatable, King's picture could hang on any aspiring writer's desk. Not enticed by (more) money or accolades, King goes about his business without distraction or depletion: he puts pen to paper and does the work. That King is still driven by those demons and finds his faith (in writing, in himself) intact after all this time makes him a hero of sorts. Toward the end of the *Rolling Stone* interview he describes his vocation as only the luckiest and most blessed amongst us ever will: "It fulfills me," he says. "There are two things I like about it: It makes me happy, and it makes other people happy." There is a peace there, something that combines Zen and the certainty of a difficult job, dutifully done. It is, in the final analysis, good to be The King.

March, 2015

MY FIRST TIME

Let's talk about the first.

There's the first story I wrote. (Original story: fifth grade; vaguely plagiarized ones where, looking back and with apologies to Edgar Allan Poe, imitation was the sincerest form of flattery: third and fourth grades.)

There's the first "adult" book I read. (Mary Shelley's *Frankenstein*, fourth grade. Huge mistake. Having seen the movies and read some comic book treatments, I thought I was ready for the real thing. It took me more than halfway through to understand Frankenstein was not, in fact, the monster.)

There's the first success. (Being asked to compose and recite an original poem for an eighth-grade student assembly.)

There's the first readership. (A series of features I wrote for my high school newspaper. For a teenager, a printed byline is as close to the big-time as it got, at least in the old-school era before social media and blogs.)

There's the first publication. (A poem in my college literary magazine.)

There's the first "important" publication. (A short story in another, better-known literary magazine.)

There's the first in a series of unfortunate events. (Also known as writing workshops, wherein the cocky writer's work gets, well, workshopped. Hilarity does not often ensue.)

There's the first in a longer series of ceaseless rejection. (No comment necessary.)

There's the first short story I knew would make me famous. (It's still unpublished.)

There's the first attempt at a novel. (Also unpublished. Fortunately, for all involved.)

There's the subsequent, earnest attempt at a first novel. (Still a work-in-progress. Sort of.)

Nothing especially unique or noteworthy, right? All of these events or experiences were stepping stones most, if not all, writers will recognize and relate to. There is an evolution comprised of myriad firsts (and lasts), but what separates all but the most successful and/or lucky authors is what happens after the familiar epiphanies of the apprentice have occurred and it gets to the eventual, inevitable matter of *perseverance*.

The "first" that was, if not unique, for me the most formative and indelible, involved rejection and resolve.

Let me tell you a story: a famous writer saw a first chapter of this aforementioned novel. Famous writer picks up phone (people still used phones in those days) and tells unknown writer that he loves the material and wants his agent to look at it. Agent receives chapter, loves it too, and asks to see entire manuscript on an exclusive basis. Unknown writer thinks: this is it, the big break, the moment of truth, among other daydreams. An entire summer passes, which is unfortunate. It happens to be the same summer unknown writer's mother—who has been battling cancer for five years—begins to lose her final battle. By the time unknown writer's mother passes away, the novel, the agent and the famous writer are about the farthest things from his mind. On the day of mother's funeral, unknown writer makes the ill-advised decision to check his email before leaving the house. He sees the overdue email from agent. Something tells him not to open it, but of course he has to; according to logic and everything right in the world, not to mention the imperative of Cliché, *this* is the perfect time to see he's about to be represented and eventually published, and this is the miracle he'll employ to overcome his grief, and he'll dedicate this book to his mother, without whom he could never have written it, or written anything.

Naturally, the email is, in fact, a rather terse (but apologetic) rejection.

And this unknown writer, in spite of himself, looks past the computer, looks beyond his disbelief, and looks out to whomever or whatever may be listening (or orchestrating this test of faith) and can't quite believe hearing the words, in a voice that sounds a lot like his: "Is *that* all you got?"

No, this is not going to be the final, unkindest cut, the sign that failure is inevitable, the signal that it's better to move on to other things, the message that it's not meant to be. I'm not doing this, he thinks, because I want to, or that I hope to prove anything, or become famous (he has put away childish things). I'm doing this, he knows, because he doesn't know what else he could possibly do with himself. He does it, he finally understands, because there's nothing else he could imagine himself doing. And that the only failure is to stop. To be afraid, to give up.

It wasn't the first rejection, obviously, and while it may be the biggest, it wasn't the last. In addition to death and taxes, writers recognize at some point, however resignedly, that rejection will always be on offer, for free, forever.

And ultimately it mattered only in the sense that it didn't matter. Or, it mattered a great deal in the sense that it was not enough to dissuade or discourage him from stumbling down a path he made up as he went along; that revealed itself only when he looked back on another piece of writing and thought: Good thing I didn't stop.

This was the most important first, the first day of the rest of my life.

June, 2015

STOP ME IF YOU'VE HEARD THIS ONE BEFORE

i. The Ugly Truth and the Beautiful Lie

When I published my memoir *Please Talk about Me When I'm Gone* in 2013, I certainly was cognizant of the fact that I was, essentially, inviting strangers (as well as friends and family) to review intimate, occasionally embarrassing aspects of my life. But, when people enquired if I was especially concerned about this, I could reply with honesty that I wasn't.

Writing such a personal account was, after all, a voluntary act, and it would seem more than a little disingenuous to protest too much about reactions to events and emotions I opted to disclose. Plus, one of the reasons I decided to write a memoir—a platform certainly more suited for celebrities or writers with a following—was because the material didn't, or couldn't, work appropriately as fiction. It was less a matter of accuracy (you either tell the truth or you don't) than an issue of aesthetics (you either engage the reader or you can't).

The project evolved as an anti-memoir of sorts, or at least a conscious rejoinder to the solipsistic stylizing that infested so many of the memoirs I'd read and found lacking. (This is not to imply I succeeded even in this modest objective.) Years earlier I'd jotted down something *Washington Post* book critic Jonathan Yardley—who tended to parcel out praise not unlike a disapproving parent—wrote while celebrating Neil Simon: "The autobiographical is meant to be a pathway to the universal rather than mere absorption in the personal."

While he could be accused of being both cranky and quaint on occasion, Yardley was not only on-target here, he was prescient, making this observation before the ubiquity of blogs, social media and reality TV forever closed—or at least obfuscated—the gap between the personal and the public. Writers, I've found, have (increasingly) edged into self-indulgence, finding that fullest possible disclosure is a short-cut to earned insight or authentic connection. The defense "but it's all true" might inoculate a memoirist in the most superficial ways, but *mere* truth is an inadequate approach, even for a work of non-fiction. (Of course, willful invention may appeal, at least initially, to more prurient readers, but is the strategy of a charlatan, as James Frey discovered.)

Despite my appetite for discretion (and, wherever possible, precision), I was not sufficiently prepared for the ambivalence my recollections tended to inspire amongst others whose experiences coincided, or clashed, with my perspective. Another quote, this one from Roger Angell, succinctly articulates what every honest writer won't hesitate to acknowledge: "Memory is fiction, an anecdotal version of some scene or past event we need to store away for present or future use."

Everything depicted in my memoir is true, but that does not necessarily mean everything I wrote is the *truth*. Being a recovered grad student with more than a few Cultural Studies classes under my belt, I come to the table with a predisposed appreciation for intent vs. execution, or interpretation vs. integrity, or ownership vs. textual authority, *et cetera*. For me, analyzing the myriad facets of creation, production and reception can be edifying, even imperative components of the reading—and writing—experience. As a writer, I am ultimately accountable to myself: so long as there's an honest attempt to engage, avoiding sentimentality and cliché at all costs, the rest is in the hands of whoever picks up the book. This idea might torture or terrify a literary theorist, but I continue to find it remarkably liberating.

A less pretentious way of saying all this is simply to suggest that as long as a writer is satisfied, relatively speaking, it follows that by even allowing the material to be received by anonymous readers, it has already overcome, however tenuously, the author's own doubts, insecurity, hysteria and windmill-tilting.

ii. Partly Truth, Partly Fiction

As I publish my novel *Not To Mention a Nice Life*, I find myself more, and not less, circumspect. This time around it's not so much what I'm ostensibly revealing that makes me wary, but what prospective readers may, understandably, suspect or suppose.

Which isn't to say I'm unduly concerned; when you write fiction employing a first person narrator who is roughly your age, ethnicity, etc., you are all but provoking—even daring—people to assume you're writing about yourself. (Generally speaking, the more obviously the writer wants the audience to associate the protagonist and himself, the more insufferable and lifeless the prose is likely to be.)

Then, of course, there's the fact that novels are not-so-thinly disguised delivery devices for the author's own obsessions and ideas. Aren't they? No, not really or, at least, it's seldom so straightforward. But that won't stop readers from drawing certain conclusions. In any event, don't feel sorry for a misunderstood scribbler, no one is compelling them to put their stories—real or imagined—into the proverbial court of public opinion. (Generally speaking, the more noble or lovable a protagonist that may *coincidentally* be confused with the author is, the less trustworthy and insecure the human writing the book is likely to be.)

On one hand, it's difficult to deny the accuracy of this observation by David Foster Wallace: "Writing fiction becomes a way to go deep inside yourself and illuminate precisely the stuff you don't want to see or let anyone else see, and this stuff usually turns out (paradoxically) to be precisely the stuff all writers and readers everywhere share and respond to."

On the other hand, Tim O'Brien—who, incidentally, has mastered both fiction and memoir—speaks with unassailable authority when he asserts "by telling stories, you objectify your own experience. You separate it from yourself. You pin down certain truths. You make up others."

A memoirist can invoke this explanation to illuminate, or justify passages that don't mesh accurately—or comfortably—with someone else's memories. A novelist cannot use the same shield, especially since fiction is, after all, entirely invented. Right?

"I want you to feel what I felt," O'Brien writes, addressing the reader (the audacity!) in his story "Good Form". "I want you to know why story-truth is truer sometimes than happening-truth."

One of the reasons *The Things They Carried* is such a singular, innovative work is that it skirts the unconventional even as it circles around itself, explicitly attentive to the traditional. O'Brien was one of the first, or at least most successful seekers of a new way to interrogate the always uncertain intersection of memory and truth. His authorial stance broke through the postmodern haze, updating Kundera's undaunted intruder and Vonnegut's awkward interloper, conceiving an honesty that is at once self-aware and unvarnished. It's the voice of the writer, yes, but more, the voice of the *writing*; the words between the written lines.

Speaking personally, and with appreciation, O'Brien helped me to filter and, at times, repurpose the creative and intellectual circles literary criticism had me spinning inside, during some tentative years when theory and deconstruction usurped much of the adventure and serene uncertainty fiction requires. If sober retention can't be trusted and there's no such thing as Truth, memoirs are illusions and novels are nihilism.

iii. Good Form

Take a guy. Let's say he's about my age: old enough to own his own condo and pay almost all his bills, who is young enough to be unmarried but old enough to understand he is not getting any younger. Add a fresh dose of alienation—not enough to be unhealthy, of course, but enough to enable him to function in a world full of a-holes, imbecility and indifference. Take this guy and provide just enough stability so that there are no excuses, but plenty of alibis. Maybe he's estranged from too many old friends, or aggrieved about an absent parent, or perhaps he is just emerging from the wreckage of a ruined relationship or, probably, he is utterly average in every regard, except for the uncomfortable fact that, unlike almost everyone else he knows, he is aware of it. He would love to mix things up and instigate some excitement into his own humble narrative. Unfortunately, a fight scene is not feasible, a car chase is getting too carried away, and a love interest appears to be out of the question. Also, he has to be awake and ready to work in the morning, just like everyone else.

And, he thinks: you'll never be *that* guy. The guy who sits on toilet seats without a second thought; who might use the restroom half a dozen times a day and look at himself in the mirror once, or twice, tops; who actually doesn't mind—or, perhaps, secretly prefers—lukewarm coffee (or, worse, decaf, or, worst, the kind served over ice for five bucks and change); who can eat bologna sandwiches and avoid meat (even bologna) on Fridays during Lent; who believes that God blesses America and that Jesus Christ is a capitalist; who can relate to anyone playing or providing commentary on a game of golf; who buys clothes—or food, or appliances, or fiancées for that matter—from a catalog; who is actually entertained by movies, or books, or albums, or *people* that put entertainment before aesthetic, or amusement before honesty; or sales before soul. You'll never, in short, be a normal person.

None of that actually happened, but it's the truth.

All of that is the truth. None of it ever happened.

(Anthony Burgess: "It is the novelist's innate cowardice that makes him depute to imaginary personalities the sins that he is too cautious to commit for himself."

Which is not to insinuate there are any discernible acts of derring-do in my novel. There aren't even many acts of derring-don't, though there is certainly plenty of derring-*dumb*.)

That's my story. But that's not me.

Maybe it's also your story. And that's the whole point.

Isn't it?

June, 2015

NEVER SAY NEVERMORE: A REAPPRAISAL OF EDGAR ALLAN POE

If Edgar Allan Poe—and his writing—has not aged well and seems more than a little passé for 21st century sensibilities, it's not entirely his fault. Like others who have done things first, and best, it's likely we grow more impatient with their imitations than the original.

In any event, Poe was a pioneer in almost too many ways to count. If his work and his life (and most especially his death) seem clichéd, dying young, debauched and with too little money was not yet the career move it would eventually become for other artists. With vices and an intensity that would give even a young Charles Bukowski pause, and would have buried the punk rock poseur Sid Vicious, Poe managed to be for literature what Miles Davis was for jazz: he didn't merely set new standards; he *changed* the course of subsequent art, perfecting entirely new paradigms in the process.

Some might claim Poe gets too much credit for pioneering (if not inventing) the American short horror story and detective story. The fact is, he doesn't get enough.

Perhaps the best way to gain historical perspective on the proper scope of Poe's achievements and influence is to consider an abbreviated list of legends who stood on his doleful shoulders: French poet Charles Baudelaire (who both championed and translated Poe), H.G. Wells, Jules Verne, Robert Louis Stevenson, Herman Melville, Arthur Conan Doyle, William Faulkner, Flannery O'Connor and a trio of tolerably impressive non-Americans: Fyodor Dostoyevsky, Oscar Wilde and Sigmund Freud. Suffice it to say, if your work has any part in shaping or inspiring authors who make significant contributions to the canon, your status is more than secure.

Arguably, no American figure has influenced as many brilliant—and imitated—writers as Poe. The entire genres of horror, science fiction and detective story might be quite different, and not for the better, without Poe's example. More, his insights into psychology, both as narrative device and metaphysical exercise, are considerable; he was describing behavior and phenomena that would become the stuff of textbooks several decades after his death.

He also happened to be a first rate critic, and his insights are as astute and insightful as anything being offered in the mid-19th Century (his essay "The Poetic Principle" comes as close to a "how to" manual for aspiring writers as Orwell's justly celebrated "Politics and the English Language"). Oh, and he was a pretty good poet, too.

When assessing Poe, 150-plus years after he died, it's imperative to interrogate and untangle that fact that not all clichés are created equally. Or, put another way, we must remember that before certain things became clichés, they were unarticulated concerns and compulsions.

When we talk about old school we typically call to mind an era that was pre-TV and even pre-movie. Well, Poe was writing in an era that was pre-*radio* and practically pre-daguerreotype. With no Snopes or MythBusters, encyclopedias not readily available and religion the common if inconsistent arbiter of moral guidance, Poe was not after cheap frights so much as uncovering the collective unconscious. Put more plainly, this was a time when being accidentally buried alive was something that might conceivably occur.

The reason Poe remains so convincing and unsettling is because he doesn't rely on goblins or scenarios that oblige the suspension of belief; he is himself the madman, the stalker, the outcast, the detective and, above all, the artist who made his life's work a deeper than healthy dive into the messy engine of human foibles, obsessions and misdeeds. He stands alone, still, at the top of a darkened lighthouse, unable to promise a happy ending and half-insane from what he's seen.

Here we celebrate Poe's ten greatest tales, but first, a brief sample of tales that don't quite make the cut, but warrant attention and approbation.

First and foremost, the almost unclassifiable (and Poe's only novel-length work) "The Narrative of Arthur Gordon Pym of Nantucket". Jorge Luis Borges loved it, Jules Verne was undoubtedly influenced and without this model, we may not have gotten our great (white) American novel. If it's good enough for Melville, it's good enough for everyone.

"Berenice" and "Eleonora", two character studies of doomed women, both epitomizing some of Poe's most persistent fixations (teeth, premature burial). There's also the whole "cousin thing".

The type of story O. Henry would make a career of, "The Oval Portrait" is an early "shocker" even though contemporary audiences will see the conclusion coming a mile away. Like "Pym", this one makes the cut if only for the eventual masterpiece it influenced, in this case Wilde's *The Picture of Dorian Gray*.

It might be a stretch to say that "Hop-Frog" presaged all the slasher dramas of the '70s and '80s, but it's definitely a quite satisfying prototype of the abused outcast getting his revenge, equal parts Michael Myers and (Black Sabbath's) Iron Man—with grating teeth.

Finally, "A Descent into the Maelström" is rightly credited as being an early attempt at a proper science fiction study, and the technique of an older, wiser sailor recounting his tale as narrative is an obvious antecedent to Conrad.

10. "The Gold Bug"

You almost have to transport yourself back to a time without electricity to fully appreciate Poe's achievement here. In terms of influence, Robert Louis Stevenson merrily declared he "broke into the gallery of Mr. Poe" (for the creation of *Treasure Island*), and the bug bite instigating heightened awareness anticipates both "Spiderman" and "The Fly". The extensive use of ciphers—cryptography being a big fad of the time—also may have inspired Zodiac (the killer and the subsequent movie). Even the appallingly dated dialect of Jupiter is a prelude for the cruder moments of *The Adventures of Huckleberry Finn*. The sheer effort of imagination alone in seeing this one through requires that it be regarded as an important work.

9. "The Facts in the Case of M. Valdemar"

Another one that must be properly appraised as a product of its time, the *fact* is that, upon publication, this tale caused a public uproar because it was sufficiently believable. This tale employs the ostensibly scientific case study of a hypnotized patient who, in his mesmerized state, is able to exist in a surreal, inexplicable condition where he's dead but… still alive. Once again, as preposterous as this sounds, today, and as outlandish as it clearly was, even in 1845, it's a credit to Poe's masterful description, pacing and use of suspense that he actually pulled it off.

8. "The Murders in the Rue Morgue"

Celebrated as the first modern detective story, Poe's hero C. Auguste Dupin is featured in two subsequent tales, "The Mystery of Marie Roget" and "The Purloined Letter", but "Rue Morgue" is the most famous, and best of the three. One of the many Poe efforts made into an inferior, and terribly dated, film, it works best on the page. Using his powers of deliberation, Dupin is an undeniable model for Doyle's Sherlock Holmes. Poe is in full command of his considerable powers here, employing the process of investigation and discovery, cleverly employed humor and terror, and a character that proves he's smarter than everyone else.

7. "William Wilson"

It seems impossible to prove that Dostoyevsky was directly influenced by Poe, but it's difficult to believe early novel *The Double* was not in some way informed by this compact tale that manages to invoke class, the concept of the doppelgänger, split-personality and the self-corrective of one's conscience (all themes Dostoyevsky would make his calling card, culminating in his masterpiece *The Brothers Karamazov*).

In only a handful of other stories was Poe so deftly able to balance shock and humor, albeit of a very dark variety. Cognizant that the narrator is a scoundrel, it's difficult to pity his plight even as we shudder at the humiliation he suffers. Although not often described as such, "William Wilson" is a tour de force psychological case study of an unreliable narrator tortured by a deservedly conflicted sense of self.

6. "The Pit and the Pendulum"

Darkness. Torture. Rats. Any questions? How about a slowly descending, foot-long razor ever-so-slowly descending from the ceiling, giving you plenty of time to think about how it will eventually (and ever-so-slowly) slice you open down the middle? And that's just a basic summary.

Here is a one of the author's most fully realized attempts at "totality". Poe creates a complete atmosphere of terror, where the narrator and reader understands it's not random, his captors are *very* aware of the conditions they've created, making the tension difficult to endure. Where other stories describe, in often excruciating detail, the anguish inflicted on an overly sensitive individual, in this one Poe makes the reader acutely aware of their own senses: unable to see inside the pit, smelling the rats as they gnaw at the ropes, hearing the deliberate hiss of the pendulum, feeling the sweat frozen by the fear of death.

5. "The Tell-Tale Heart"

Another one that's easy to imagine Dostoyevsky studying, this time in the construction of his underground man (*Notes from Underground*): an unreliable narrator, or a narrator so reliable—and truthful—that he indicts himself in the attempt to be understood, and pitied. As a study of horror, "The Tell-Tale Heart", perhaps Poe's most (in)famous story, seems tame to contemporary audiences. But as an examination of obsession and psychosis?

An amazingly compressed rendering of a pathology pushed to irrational extremes, Poe laid the groundwork for everyone from Fantômas to Norman Bates. The real fear an adult can derive from this story is not the narrator's brutality or even innocence, but his insistence that he's sane. With understated irony, Poe decodes the self-deceived stratagem of our most dangerous sociopaths.

4. "The Masque of the Red Death"

Although if *only* considered an unrivaled allegory of death (and its inevitability), that somewhat superficial analysis still sells this one short as a blistering critique of social stratification. Here Poe uses a rampant disease to illustrate not only the behaviors but attitudes of the haves toward the have-nots: actively walling themselves inside a fortified castle while misery wipes out the countryside, the superbly named Prince Prospero and his court can't be bothered with empathy for the afflicted, they have lavish masquerade balls to attend.

A masterful clinic of the Gothic aesthetic ensues as different-colored rooms are described, the air of revelry undercut with hourly reminders of mortality, courtesy of the ebony clock. Finally, there's the spectacle of a silent intruder who mockingly moves from room to room, until finally confronted by the unfortunate prince. And then, comeuppance courtesy of one of the great closing lines in literary history: "And Darkness and Decay and the Red Death held illimitable dominion over all."

3. "The Black Cat"

Self-loathing? Poe, at times, makes the Grunge and Goth movements look like ecstasy-addled raves. His irredeemable spiritual desolation was rooted not in anything like the info-overload pressure of too many choices we confront today, or finding the perfect partner or job, but fear of poverty, hunger and the unremarkable ailments that preyed upon humanity for so many centuries before sufficient medical advancements were made. He lived in a time when even libraries might not have the information you needed, so you wrote it down or took to sea or went insane as a matter of principle.

In "The Black Cat", when the narrator's abuse of the bottle becomes unmanageable, it seems not autobiographical so much as an expression of the author's greatest fear: that his appetite for alcohol would poison his personality and override his ability to create. It's also Poe's first extended interrogation of PERVERSENESS (all caps here, just like the story), which is described as an "unfathomable longing of the soul to vex itself—to offer violence to its own nature." The image of the corrupted narrator, hanging his beloved cat with tears streaming down his cheeks, remains among the most pitiful, and genuinely haunting images in the Poe catalog.

Once more, it's tantalizing to contemplate the ways Dostoyevsky may well have been developing the possibilities of an irresistible perversity driving one to self-defeat (which Poe himself expanded upon in "The Imp of the Perverse") in both *The Double* and *Crime and Punishment.* "The Black Cat", while quite successful as a spooky tale with an outrageous ending, presents Poe the psychologist at his most incisive—and unsettling.

2. "The Fall of the House of Usher"

If "The Masque of the Red Death" features one of the all-time great closing lines, "The Fall of the House of Usher" contains one of the most sublime opening passages: in one extended paragraph containing 417 words, Poe provides an enduring showcase for his "unity of effect" theory. Practically every image, every action, every word is dedicated toward the invocation of dread, and the suspense careens toward a conclusion that is literally shattering (in several senses of the word).

The tale concerns itself with the narrator and his childhood friend, Roderick Usher, as well as his twin sister Madeline. And yet the main character is the house itself. The narrator feels a palpable sense of dreariness and decay as he approaches the family mansion, a foreboding that comes full circle as the house collapses into itself in the final scene.

It's the impact of the house on its tenants, however, where Poe couples supernatural suspense with a human frailty to devastating effect. Sensitive to the point of intolerance to sound, Roderick has become an imploding specter of nervous energy and despair. As he confesses to his friend, "I feel that the period will sooner or later arrive when I must abandon life and reason together, in some struggle with the grim phantasm, FEAR."

With astonishing economy (this story could—and likely would, by a lesser writer—have easily been stretched into a novel, albeit with lesser punch), Poe manages to invoke his enduring preoccupation of live burial, split personalities, ruminate on the sentience of inanimate objects, and complicate the notions of art imitating life and vice versa, all while steadily orchestrating the ultimate confrontation (twin vs. twin, brother vs. sister, human vs. house, life vs. death). Tragic and absurd as the events become, the narrator is content to leave it as a family matter, hastily escaping as the history of the house and its occupants sink into nothingness.

1. "The Cask of Amontillado"

We've discussed a perfect opening section and a perfect closing sentence; "The Cask of Amontillado" is just perfection, period. It represents the consummation of so many of Poe's aesthetic innovations, crafted so each sentence builds upon the next (like an expertly tiered stone wall…), amping up the humor, irony and, finally, horror. Not a word wasted, an image unnecessary, a line of dialogue inessential and yet, despite the formal symmetry at its heart, a mystery.

What is the insult that drives Montresor's homicidal rage? It's never clear, and that only adds an element of menace. Is Montresor, like many of Poe's most inscrutable murderers, more or less insane?

Put another way, it's difficult to fathom, since he and Fortunato are still at least superficially cordial, any offense that would warrant live entombment.

As with "The Masque of the Red Death", Poe nimbly operates on multiple levels: there's an element of class disparity and resentment seething within the dialogue. When Montresor insists that he is, in fact, a mason (one of the delightful ironies, as he pulls out his trowel), it's easy to overlook Fortunato's offensive disbelief ("You? Impossible! A mason?").

There's also the not inconsiderable matter of Montresor's family crest, wherein "the foot crushes a serpent rampant whose fangs are imbedded in the heel." It's simple to imagine Montresor is the foot smiting the serpent, but it's possibly more appropriate to consider Montresor as the snake, refusing to die or, if he's to be defeated, fighting to the death. The motto "Nemo Me Impune Lacessit" (You will not harm me with impunity") is at once appropriate, yet repugnant.

A writer has succeeded if, in creating a story, a single unforgettable image is imprinted within the reader's mind. How many such scenes exist in this one short tale? The image of a drunken Fortunato (that name!), in motley—playing the clown, being played for a clown—insistent on proving his expertise, as he's drawn deeper into the catacombs; the aforementioned passage concerning whether Montresor is, in fact, a mason (producing the trowel, one of the great incidents of foreshadowing in fiction); Montresor, the mason, hurriedly piling brick upon brick; Fortunato, finally comprehending his plight, screaming inside the depths of his crypt, only to have Montresor, full of malevolent confidence, screaming back at him (no one will hear us down here, my friend).

And finally, the most cold-blooded line in Poe's collected works: "My heart grew sick—on account of the dampness of the catacombs." Is it, finally, the pang of human remorse? Or is it one last twist of the trowel, one final act of impunity to repay the insult made more than 50 years before? Like the insult itself, we'll never know.

October, 2015

FIVE: THE SPORTING LIFE

DO YOU BELIEVE IN MIRACLES?

Courtesy of *The New York Times:* On Feb. 22, 1980, in a stunning upset, the United States Olympic hockey team defeated the Soviets at Lake Placid, N.Y., 4-to-3. (The U.S. team went on to win the gold medal.)

If I'm not mistaken, there's only one cover in *Sports Illustrated* history that doesn't have a headline, or text of any sort. Naturally, it doesn't need any. There were certainly magnificent (semi-miraculous?) upsets in sports before (The Jets beating the Colts in Super Bowl III) and after (Rulon Gardner beating the unbeatable Alexander Karelin in the 2000 Olympics), but the import of this victory has to be considered within the context of the times. Pre-Internet (pre-VCRs, really), pre-ESPN (pre-cable, really), in an era when you really did get news on the radio. As in, driving in the car with your parents, during a commercial. Because in 1980 most Americans actually listened to the radio in the car (pre-Satellite, pre-CD changer, pre-cassette, really). 8-tracks were entering the last stage of their ascendancy, not even aware that they were already dead and subsisting on the last gasps of their magnetic fumes. And how many 8-tracks could one family own? How many could one family fit in a car? And so, by default, the radio still ruled. Some people may even have listened to that epic game on the radio, in their cars, in real time. That was less than thirty years ago.

Arguably, being nine years old, I was the ideal demographic to be fully impacted by this event. Not old enough to appropriate (or be unduly influenced by) the political implications, but old enough to understand that in winter Olympics games, the U.S.S.R. (and Eastern Europe) still held sway. We could not appreciate, or care too much about the irony of the big, bad U.S.A. casting themselves as underdogs, in *any* capacity. Two unavoidable facts: it was just a sporting event, and pure and simple, the U.S.A. *were* underdogs. Did this unanticipated and inexplicable victory tilt the scales in the escalating cold war? Arguably, if you measure political history by such standards as Rocky Balboa defeating Ivan Drago in *Rocky IV*, it makes all the sense in the world. More, if you are of the opinion (aided by propagandist historical revisions by certain, influential right-leaning folk) that the cold war was an even battle between two socially and economically equal parties, this cartoonish perception of Good vs. Evil is resonant, and revelatory. For younger, less politically impressionable viewers, this victory did, unironically; reinforce the genuine (if mythical) notion inherent in the American Dream: if you worked hard and played fair, anything was possible. It's not merely the ability to believe this claptrap that underscores the naiveté we lament losing as we get older and wiser, it's the ways in which real events, however fictionally applicable to real life, can inspire kids to believe in miracles.

February, 2009

BIRD AND MAGIC

1979.

It's been so well documented, and remains such a touchstone (it is still the most widely watched NCAA final ever, which—considering the inconceivably successful hype college and pro sports have promulgated in the last three decades—is genuinely astounding), yet it endures mostly as the introduction of Bird/Magic. Only two words, two names, have ever been necessary to sum up an entire rivalry. Michael Wilbon wrote a wonderful remembrance of this the other week; the piece is well worth reading, but here is the heart of the matter:

Michigan State cruised, more or less. Bird narrowly avoided losing to both Sidney Moncrief and Arkansas and Aguirre and DePaul. The most memorable scene from the title game is Bird, having lost for the first time as a senior, sitting with the white towel over his head, sobbing underneath it. That and Magic's smile while he hugged Heathcote after the 75-64 Spartans win.

More than 35 percent of all TV sets turned on that night were tuned to Magic and Bird. It was like a Christmas present in March, and it's something that could never happen today. We'd know everything about an undefeated team featuring any player as talented as Bird. A 6-foot-9 white kid from small-town Indiana who had driven a garbage truck and who had run from Bob Knight during a freshman year spent briefly at Indiana? Are you kidding?

And then it was on. On to the pros. East vs. West. Celtics vs. Lakers. The Green vs. The Gold.

How often do two players, particularly ones so indelibly linked from the start of their careers, have the opportunity not only to revive their respective franchises, but an entire professional sport? Approximately never. It's never happened before and it will never happen again. I'm not inclined to recap the entire Bird & Magic saga because everyone is already familiar with it (those that are not simply don't like sports). What a difference a year made: the Celtics went from worst to almost-first, with Bird taking Rookie of the Year honors, and Magic bookended his NCAA championship with the first of his five NBA titles. To say these guys took things to another level is like saying The Beatles made some pretty good albums. Simply put, nothing was ever the same once Bird and Magic made the NBA their personal playground.

So all of this ancient sports history is ambrosia for stat dorks obsessed with the great old days. But imagine if you actually *loved* one of those teams? I don't have to imagine; I was there. Learning to be a Red Sox and Celtics fan from my Boston-bred father (which is ironic because at the time the local Washington Bullets were coming off back-to-back appearances in the NBA finals and the Celtics were the joke of the league; following the Red Sox would be a masochistic family ritual countless souls from New England endured for another few decades), I remember being on board with Bird from the second he suited up. If you ever want to find out who actually followed the Celtics back in the day, wait until they finish name dropping McHale, Parrish, Dennis Johnson (R.I.P.) and Danny Ainge (the most hated athlete in the world in his day), and see if they have any idea who Cedric "Cornbread" Maxwell and Nate "Tiny" Archibald are. Then drop Quinn Buckner and Gerald Henderson (whose nifty hands secured the third most famous steal in Celtics history, after Havlicek and Bird—of which more, shortly).

So I loved Bird and the Celtics. And I *loathed* Magic and the Lakers.

As has been adequately documented elsewhere (and incessantly), it was a clash of two styles, two coasts, two philosophies. The Lakers were Hollywood (Showtime!), quick, flashy and their coach wore Armani suits. The Celtics were blue collar, methodical, stoic and crucially, quite possibly the most ugly assortment of athletes ever assembled on one team.

So when the Celtics edged out the Lakers in the seventh game of their epic 1984 championship series, it was the ultimate triumph of Good over Evil. Redemption for Bird! East coast over West coast! Substance over Style! Rocky vs. Apollo. You get the picture.

Did I mention that I *detested* Magic? The intensity of the disdain escalated exponentially in 1985 when Magic's Lakers got their revenge, on the sacred parquet floor no less, taking back the crown on the Celtics' home court. That hurt. What a bunch of punks the

Lakers were: Michael Cooper with his rolled up socks, James Worthy with his Kareem-Lite goggles, Kareem himself, that big whining sissy, Kurt Rambis, the resident honky who did the unthinkable and made Kevin McHale the *second* goofiest looking professional athlete of the '80s. And leading them all, Magic. I hated him. And Bird hated him, too. Seriously. That rivalry was for real. One can still see the barely-disguised animosity in their famous commercial.

Of course, the '86 Celtics were far and away the best team that ever suited up, and that subject is not open for discussion. It was the kind of year (the Celtics lost *one* home game over the course of the entire regular season) where Celtics fans were looking forward to the eventual Lakers rematch. There is no chance the Lakers would have won. None. It was therefore comical when the Lakers were upset in the western conference finals by the upstart Rockets (a young Hakeem Olajuwan and Ralph Sampson), but it was almost immediately anticlimactic; we wanted the Lakers that year and we *needed* the Lakers. It was not just going to be our turn on top of the revenge see-saw; it was going to be a bloodletting, a reckoning. It wasn't meant to be, and some of us actually felt cheated. But boy did the Celtics beat up on the Rockets, cementing their status as the big kids on the block.

No one had any doubt the two designated teams would meet again in 1987, and everyone was correct. It was not a finals so much as a formality. The Celtics were almost crippled by injuries throughout the season (especially the porcelain-kneed Bill Walton), and at times it appeared that Ainge and Parrish might come apart at mid-court. Famously, McHale played most of the post-season on a broken ankle: it undoubtedly shortened his career, but also earns him all-time stud status (normally only hockey players exhibit that type of grit and lunacy). And so the Celtics quite literally limped into the playoffs and the hungry young teams took their shots (including a sneak-peak at the increasingly explosive Michael Jordan, who dropped 63 points on the Celtics in the Garden). They barely beat the Bucks and it looked like the obnoxious, upstart Pistons (led by the always insufferable Isiah Thomas) might have too much juice for the suddenly torpid Celtics. Flash forward to Game Five, series tied 2-2: with seconds left on the clock and the ref (dubiously) awarding an out of bounds ball to the Pistons, the Celtics needed a miracle. And Bird provided one. This is it, for me: the most unexpected, sublime few seconds I've ever witnessed in sports. There are games that rank higher, achievements ultimately more significant, but in terms of the shock factor combined with the gratification, it was as though one of the Greek gods descended from Olympus just for my amusement.

Two unthinkable things occurred in the '87 finals: The Lakers won, and I (and many other Celtics fans) found myself unable to suppress a grudging admiration for how unbelievably great Magic Johnson was. Beyond appreciation, I was actually *almost* starting to like him. He won me over, not merely by the way he willed his team to win, but because he really did make watching the game more exciting. There was seldom any debate about whether Magic radiated more joy through the act of playing a sport than anyone else who has ever played at a high level. What he did in Game 4 with his improbable, and devastating, "junior" sky hook was a barbed wire ripping out the entrails of every Celtic fan's gut. But you had to admire it; you had no choice. Bird hit the three as if to say "That's what I have to say, what have you got?" And Magic responded. With two seconds left on the clock, Bird *did* get that last shot, and damn if it didn't just rim out (that is already one of the best endings of all time; if Bird had nailed that Hail Mary it would be considered the best playoff basketball game ever played).

We consoled ourselves knowing that we could count on many more years on the see-saw. Alas, that was it. The Celtics, slowed by injuries and derailed by the sudden and shocking death of Len Bias (that tragedy remains unendurable to this day), started to show their age, while younger, faster teams stepped into the spotlight. And I found myself ambivalent, in '88, watching the Pistons (who we hated so much, it's probable some of us would have done jail time in order for the opportunity to bitch slap Bill Laimbeer) and Lakers square off. I couldn't root for the Pistons, but I couldn't root for the *Lakers*. So I rooted for Magic. Well, I allowed myself to accept that it was better for Bird's rival to win. Or something like that.

In the meantime, Bird and Magic had gone from tolerating one another to building a genuine bond. So much so, when Magic realized he'd contracted HIV, Bird was one of the first people he phoned. Allegedly, Bird broke down and sobbed when he received the news. One more season and Bird, his body battered and his back an unrelenting source of misery, hung up the Converse Weapons. They needed one another, and for Celtics fans, it was like Batman had lost his Joker; it was time to walk away. Fortunately they did have the chance to play together on the "Dream Team" during the '92 Olympics. Watching the two of them talk about each other, in the years since (which they've done often) is always enjoyable and, no other word will do, heartwarming. They love the game and they love each other.

To consider that thirty years have passed since the night that changed everything is difficult to reconcile. On the other hand, it would be churlish to feel any emotion more than gratitude for having had the opportunity to watch that story unfold, in real time, savoring every second of it along the way.

April, 2009

A MIXTURE OF MISCHIEF AND CHEER: REMEMBERING BOB PROBERT

R.I.P. Probie.

Quick tally: #24, over 3,000 penalty minutes. Member, along with Joe Kocur, of the legendary "Bruise Brothers" tandem back in the days when the Detroit Red Wings were more feared for what they could do after the whistle stopped play. Participant in a handful of the all-time classic fights in hockey history. Man who inspired t-shirts that read "Give Blood. Fight Probert." Simply put, if one were to try and create the ideal enforcer (especially for an era that may not have been *the* toughest or most iconic era but was one of the most enjoyable), one could hardly imagine a more suitable cartoon character than Bob Probert.

As The Kinks once sang, Let's All Drink To The Death Of A Clown.

And lest anyone think I'm using the word *clown* carelessly or disrespectfully, it is in fact chosen with the aim of being both accurate and approbatory. (A Probie-tory, if you like.)

Think about what a clown does: he is the minor but essential character who shows up at a circus with the objective of instigating misconduct. Above all, his purpose is to entertain with a mixture of mischief and cheer. A superficial assessment might conclude that a clown is simply doing, in make-up, what any drunken idiot might do. But of course whether it is juggling, dancing or doing tricks, not just *anyone* could be (or would want to be) a clown. It's a job.

Think about what a hockey enforcer (what we used to call a *goon* just like we used to call *escorts* hookers or *stockbrokers* sociopaths) does: he is the minor but essential figure who shows up in an arena with the object of instigating misconduct (hopefully without receiving a *game misconduct).* Above all, his purpose is to settle scores and entertain a crowd while energizing his teammates. A superficial assessment might conclude that an enforcer is simply doing, in a colorful costume, what any drunken idiot might do. But needless to say, trading bare-fisted blows (sober or especially drunk) in a bar is considerably different than standing on skates and going toe to toe with an opponent who is well-prepared (and in some cases, well-paid) to kick your ass in front of thousands of people. Many people without athletic ability are very capable goons; only an extremely select group of individuals are able (much less willing) to abide by "The Code". It's a job.

It's difficult to talk intelligently with anyone about hockey because so few people watch (or care) about it. That goes double when trying to articulate the science of sanctioned pugilism. How can one possibly rationalize or defend the spectacle of adults engaging in behavior that would get them arrested out in the streets? (Indeed, fans are arrested nightly at hockey rinks all over the continent for imitating, albeit often drunkenly and with far less flair, the very behavior occurring in real time below them.) The answer is at once easy and complicated, like all truths tend to be. The easy part: there is no need to explain it. If you're not a hockey player, you can't hope to comprehend it; unless you are a fan, you have no hope of understanding or appreciating it. It's really that simple. Seriously. Just ask a hockey player. (And, as perspicacious commentators have pointed out for decades, one notices how nobody gets up to grab popcorn once a fight breaks out. While that may speak volumes about the distressing devolution of our species and our insatiable appetite for violence, there is something a bit more sophisticated going on.)

So what is complicated about it? For starters, hockey fighting remains a diversion that people who genuinely deplore violence (like this writer) endorse and get excited about. What does that say about us? I'm not certain. But I do know that unlike the "real" world, it is exceedingly rare for two hockey combatants to enter the fray unwillingly. Yes but, doesn't that make it a great deal worse, if they do it *because* they get paid? (Well, is boxing beautiful? Brutal? Your opinion here will go a decent way toward explaining your ability, or willingness, to negotiate the enigmatic charm of the expression "five minutes for fighting".) That gets to the not-so-easily explained sensibility of athletes (in general) and hockey players (in particular). Hockey players have traditionally been paid a great deal less than other athletes in more popular sports. It is, therefore, a bit ironic to consider that these players are more immune to pain and prone to play a regular season game like the world is on the line. It is, for hockey fans, refreshing that the players have an integrity that has been ingrained from generations and is remarkably resilient against the corrupting forces of salary, fame and product endorsements. Put in less exalted terms, people tend to get (understandably) cynical when, say, a baseball player with a multi-million dollar annual contract goes on the D.L. with a strained hamstring. That type of commonplace indifference is especially noticeable—and appalling—when one realizes that hockey players routinely return to the ice moments after receiving stitches, or losing teeth, or suffering bruised (and in some cases, broken) bones. Google it if you don't believe me.

None of this is to say that one might enjoy the sport more if one learned more about it, but a casual viewer (or hater) might be genuinely surprised to learn a few things about the history of hockey fighting. For starters, the opposing players seldom hate each other and in it is not uncommon for them to be friends off the ice (particularly if they are old teammates). Also, the aforementioned code does have a rather elaborate—and universally endorsed—system for the rules of engagement. Finally, and perhaps most significantly: not only are enforcers generally the most popular players (amongst the fans; amongst the teams), they tend to be some of the more thoughtful and soft-spoken ones. (For two obvious examples, consider the ever-humble Craig Berube, "The Chief", who toiled many seasons in the NHL including for my hometown Capitals and now is an assistant coach for the Flyers; then there is George McPhee who happens to be one of the more respected and successful GMs in the game.)

Of course, not all of them are model citizens, and for a variety of reasons (some understandable, some inscrutable), some of them have had very challenging and troubled lives.

Enter Bob Probert. Though it is debatable whether or not he (or any particular player) was "the best" enforcer in the history of organized hockey, not many people would argue with any credibility that he is not at least in the Top 10. For my money, pound for pound and in terms of longevity, respect, quality of opponents and success, Probert is the preeminent knuckle artist of the modern era.

Let the clichéd encomiums unfurl: he feared nobody. He fought everyone. Ultimate warrior. Ideal teammate. Crowd pleaser.

As Detroit (and Chicago) residents know, and as fans of the game remember, Probert battled the proverbial demons off the ice as well. His struggles with alcohol and substance abuse are amply documented. His occasional escapades drew the attention of law enforcement officials. He was, in short, a troubled man in certain ways, but he was always resilient, and never let his addictions keep him down (or out).

(The actual history of his difficulties is sufficiently reported that folks interested in more can easily find out with the click of a mouse. I also acknowledge that his livelihood may have done as much to exacerbate his issues as it did to ameliorate them. In other words, he quite possibly may have gone down certain roads whether or not he played hockey or threw a single punch. But I readily concede that there is an ugly side to sports, just like there is a sinister side to life, and all of us are constantly pushed and pulled by the momentum of necessity and choice, and the inexorable reality that we have to pay bills and obey laws. A more sustained—and serious— discussion of sports, hockey, hockey fighting and some of the casualties of this game (think John "Rambo" Kordic's tragic story) should occur at another time.)

If he had kept his act together a little better, he would have retired a Red Wing, possibly kissed the Cup, and pretty much owned the Motor City. Somebody could make a movie like that. Of course, somebody already did: his name was Bob Probert and the movie was his life. Not all movies have happy endings, alas. And like anyone who will be missed once they are gone, he gave us far more than we ever gave him.

July, 2010

JOE FRAZIER: REQUIEM FOR PHILLY'S FAVORITE SON

In typical 21st Century American fashion, the sad news of Joe Frazier's passing was quickly eclipsed by other big news; this week the unfolding—and sickening—Penn State scandal.

R.I.P., Smokin' Joe. Another casualty of The Big C; yet another instance where even the toughest amongst us can't overcome that greedy and too often indomitable disease.

In the day or so after the announcement of his death (which, his cancer prognosis having only been announced recently, I hope was relatively quick and as painless as possible) I came across several stories and tributes.

Most unfortunate, if inevitable, comment I've read: *Down goes Frazier!*

Most controversial, and poorly timed, comment: *Joe Frazier was the better fighter. And the better man.* Wow. Who died and made you (Don) King?

Most intriguing and worthwhile piece: *The Lonesome Death of Smokin' Joe Frazier*, courtesy of the always reliable Tom Junod at *GQ*. Junod does the near impossible and sums up his career and life, here:

"Hey Joe!" I said, and walked up to him as my father had 25 years earlier. He held out his hand horizontally, and held it still. "Hey Joe!" I repeated, and Joe, looking at his hand and then at me, said with a familiar smile: "Still steady."

He was saying that he had won. He was saying that while Ali was a rattling relic with Parkinson's Syndrome, he, Joe Frazier, was still steady, and capable of keeping his hand still. He was saying, above all, that wherever Ali was, he, Joe Frazier, put him there, and that he was vindicated by the split decision handed down by the fullness of time.

Now Joe Frazier is dead, and Muhammad Ali has once again miraculously outlasted him. But that's the thing about fighting your battles over the fullness of time: You fight when you're a young man, and you fight until the final bell. You keep fighting when you're an old man, and you keep fighting to the death.

There is a bizarre, more than merely ironic symmetry to the fact that once again, Ali managed to outlast Frazier.

Ali, who has been in notoriously difficult shape for over two decades now, keeps on keeping on (and we can hope he is leading as "normal" and/or happy life as his inner circle insists he is), and once again, Frazier gets counted out, this time permanently.

There is not much I can, or would want to try to add to the remarkable life story of Smokin' Joe. Whether it's the made-for-the-movies image of Joe pounding slabs of meat in a Philadelphia factory (see: Rocky Balboa), or the way-better-than-fiction melodrama of his relationship with Ali (the fights, the hype, the acrimony, the endurance, the bitterness, the not-fully-resolved antipathy), there has never been anything quite like Joe Frazier. And his relationship with Ali which, well....just watch the HBO documentary *The Thriller in Manila.* Beyond Sophocles; beyond Shakespeare. No bullshit.

Ali is rightly renowned for his courageous stand against Vietnam and the obvious inspiration he provided for countless black Americans (and white Americans; everyone). What not a lot of people are unaware of is that once Ali was out of boxing (during the "draft-dodging" controversy) Frazier rallied around his (then) friend, lent him money, and spoke out on Ali's behalf. It could be argued that Ali would not have gotten reinstated, or at least as soon as he did, without Joe's help. Of course, upon his return, who was Ali's first fight against? You really can't make this stuff up. You also can't overstate the almost sadistic cruelty Ali inflicted upon the man who assisted him, using unspeakable and totally out-of-bounds slurs like "Uncle Tom" and "gorilla". Of course, without the hostility this ensured, we may not have gotten that epic third fight; the fight that defined both men's life in profound ways.

When I watch clips from that fight, and think about what each man experienced, I have little option but concede I have no clue. For mere mortals like the rest of us, how could we begin to understand what it feels like to come that close to death in what could accurately be described as blood sport? In front of millions of eyeballs in real time. Preserved forever on tape. And that's just the (inconceivable) brutality that was inflicted and endured. What must it have been like for Frazier to know that he could and perhaps *should* have won that fight? You think you've had regrets in your life? How about knowing that Ali had no intention to come out for the 15th? I can scarcely comprehend how Frazier got out of bed each day with this thought gnawing at him like a rat feasts on a cold bone. It's likely that the same thing that defined him is what redeemed him: the stubborn, unflinching, brave and single-minded drive. To survive. To be the best. To be true to himself.

One need not denigrate Ali to elevate Frazier. It comes dangerously close to cliché, but it must be said that Frazier was a true champion. In many senses of the word. He was a fighter, but his biggest bouts always took place outside the ring.

It's a shame it did not happen while he was alive to see it, but it's long past the appropriate time for the city of Philadelphia to erect a statue for its favorite son. The one created in the dank, reeking gym where they build legends, as opposed to the bright, plastic city where they make movies. If there is a statue for Rocky, there damn well should be a statue for the man who inspired him.

November, 2011

APRIL 15, 1985: THE FIGHT

It probably says something about evolution that younger generations see the future as expansive, malleable and positive while the older generations eventually—and inexorably—see the past as safer, simpler and more sensible. Bob Dylan had it right, of course: the times they are a-changin'. But it wasn't a '60s thing: the times are *always* changing, it just depends on where you're standing and what you expect (or want) to see.

And so: athletes were less corrupted, politicians more honest, employers more human. Take your pick and add to the list, because it applies to everything and goes on forever.

But in the early '80s it really *was* a period of transition, perhaps unlike anything we've ever seen. Way before the Internet, obviously, but even before cable TV was ubiquitous and the news was a half-hour show you watched after you woke up or before you went to bed.

Looked at in the necessary continuum of history, it's easier to understand that the decade was simply straining toward the future, as we all do by virtue of being one second closer to death every time we exhale. And the '80s were faster and more—or less—complicated than the '70s, just as, in comparison, the '90s makes those years seem prehistoric. Example: at the dawn of 1980 nobody owned compact discs; by 1999 this revolutionary technology had already begun its death march.

Still, looking at where we are, now, and where we came from to get there, the '80s are somewhat suspended in time, a decade of transfiguration.

For me, nothing represents the shift quite like professional boxing. Baseball, football and basketball have not changed: they are still the biggest sports, only more so. But with MMA, ever-splintered affiliations and weight class rankings, DVD box sets and especially

YouTube (like porn, people prefer violence when it's cheap, readily available and as authentic as possible), the boxing game has changed. Few would argue it's changed for the better or that it can ever be anything like what it used to be. Certainly this has something to do with the star quality (of which more shortly), but mostly it involves the logistics of entertainment, circa 1980-something. A title bout was an event that got hyped, shown on live TV and was then…gone (like virtually all forms of entertainment until cable TV and then VCRs came along to save—and immortalize—the day). Before ESPN, before everyone could record everything, you had to make *time* to witness an event, because the show would go on, with or without you.

This, perhaps more than any other factor, illustrates the once-insatiable appetite for pay-per-view events: they were *events* and you not only invested your money, but your time to be a part of it (at least as much as any witness can be said to be a *part* of any activity). It may seem quaint now, but the pay-per-view model revolutionized by the boxing promoters of this time is a microcosm of what the world would become; a blueprint for the business model that is no longer confined to sports. Consider reality television or even the music and, increasingly, book publishing industries, wherein a washed-up rock star or talk show host or someone with a Twitter account can decree who matters and, more importantly, why—and how—they should matter to millions of people. It's equal parts hype, viral marketing and the machine of modern commerce: Everybody wants everything and whatever that thing is becomes the most important thing on the planet, at least while it's being watched.

The 1980's were, in short, the perfect time for immortals to roam our earth and ply a trade dating back to days when the loser became food for lions and being voted off the island meant public execution.

All of which brings us to Duran, Leonard, Hagler and Hearns. These men defined a decade and their fights function as Shakespearean works of that era: heroism, hubris, tragedy and, crucially, comedy—all delivered with lots of blood, ill-will and, considering what was at stake and how abundantly they rewarded us, honor. It was the neighborhood and schoolyard code writ large: the best fighters in any environment will inevitably find and confront each other. Before days when obscene dollars and unspeakable promoters did more to determine who fought whom for how much on what platform, these men sought one another to settle the simplest score: who was The Best and who could wear The Belt. Yes, there were malevolent forces, rapacious bean counters and outside-the-ring influences we can only guess about, but it's neither wrong nor naïve to assert, unselfconsciously, that it was a more unsullied age.

Exhibit A, which can serve as the Alpha and Omega of my formative sports-loving life: For years, I regarded the Hagler/Hearns masterpiece the way oral poets would preserve the ancient stories: I remembered it, replayed it and above all, celebrated it. Put one way: I can remember *everything* about the circumstances of that fight (Monday night, 9th grade, watched it in living room with Pops, etc.). Put another way: still many years before YouTube I was in a bar with a bunch of buddies in Denver. We were busy telling old stories, catching up on new ones and drinking. All of a sudden one of us noticed that the TV above us was replaying *The Fight.* Immediately, and without a word, we all stopped whatever else we were doing and focused in on the magic, relishing every second. If that sounds sentimental, it is. It's also something that could never happen today: in our mobile and connected world, circa 2015, this incident would be impossible to reproduce. And that's the whole point. Sure, there is nostalgia involved (but let's be clear: I would not change that world for a world where I can pull any of these fights up, for free, and watch virtually anywhere I happen to be), but more than that, this was an era where nobody who cared was unaffected and no one, looking back today, will trivialize. We saw the careers of Michael Jordan and Joe Montana and Wayne Gretzky, but those were extended marathons of magnificence, sporting miracles built like the pyramids: requiring time, sweat, blood and monomaniacal dedication. The great fights of the '80s were more like natural events, hurricanes that came, moving the earth and shifting the landscape, permanently.

***

Let's end the suspense and get this out of the way right up front: Hagler vs. Hearns on April 15, 1985 is the best sporting event I've ever witnessed.

First, some history: I'm not sure I thought so at the time; I had not seen enough yet. I've lived 30 years since then and savored lots of other great sports moments and the passage of three decades has only reaffirmed my verdict. Obviously I would never want to be put in the position of declaring what is *the best* sporting event (it's not unlike "the best" anything: does that mean most enjoyable, most important, most influential, most popular, etc.?), but if I want to stand up and be counted, for my money and based on what I've beheld, nothing can possibly top *The Fight.*

(To be a bit more clear: I did not have any money riding, I did not necessarily prefer either fighter—though I did/do greatly respect both—and in many senses this was not close to the most personally satisfying sports moment. It was not Larry Bird in Game 6 of the '86 finals, or Dennis Johnson shutting down Magic in '84, or any number of moments from the Red Sox World Series of '04 and '07, or what the Redskins did to the Broncos during the 2nd quarter of the '88 Super Bowl, or Riggo's 4th and 1 run in '83 vs. the Dolphins, or Dale Hunter's 7th game series winning goal vs. the Flyers, or the glorious shock of Mike Tyson fumbling around for his mouthpiece after Buster Douglas beat his ass, or any number of sublime moments from the various NHL playoff series in the last two decades, particularly the beyond-epic series between the Stars and Avs and then Stars and Devils during the 2000 finals or…you get the picture.)

Secondly, some perspective: in other sports, championship moments are often (or at least all-too-often) lackluster affairs. Consider how many mediocre Super Bowls, World Series and NHL (even NBA) finals we've hyped up and been disappointed by. And that is just referring to the ones that are either blow-outs or the function of one team demonstrating their dominance on a day when everything falls perfectly into place. Those are understandable, even inevitable. But how many other times have we been let down by a World Cup final or a boxing match, because one or both parties tried to avoid the loss rather than secure (and/or earn) the win? I think of Brazil in the '80s: those were the best teams and they probably should have won one or two World Cups (led by the incomparable playmaker named Socrates, but they could not restrain themselves and play it safe. Overwhelmed by their love of their game and their affinity for *joga bonito,* or allergic to the conservative style employed by the European powerhouses (like West Germany and Italy); they played with flair, audacity and because they could not help it, allowed a combination of chutzpah and zeal to expose their collective chins.

My passion for the World Cup is hardly diminished, but I regret seeing teams play too-safe and sit on small leads, resulting in lackluster games on the biggest possible stage. It has only gotten worse in recent years, but it's an undeniable recipe for success. As soon as Brazil reined in their aggressive and unbridled impulses they finally broke through, albeit it in joyless, aesthetically muted fashion. Their victories were, in many senses, objective fans' loss: to finally win they had to play mostly sterile and boring soccer. As such I retain a fondness and appreciation for the '82 and '86 squads and care—and remember—very little about the '02 team that won the prize.

The preceding paragraph might underscore why, in addition to loving the sheer entertainment spectacle *The Fight* provided, I appreciate and am humbled by the way Hearns and Hagler approached the biggest bout of their lives.

Am I supposed to do *The Fight* justice?

I will say, without too much irony, that in some ways I still feel slightly unworthy of what these two men gave us. I'm serious.

There is nothing in sports (is there anything in life?) that can match the three minutes of that first round. Not a second wasted, too many punches thrown to count, and a simple reality that transcends cliché: Hagler took Hearns' best shot and stayed on his feet. There is much more involved, but it can really be boiled down to that simple fact. Hearns threw the same right hand that had devastated pretty much everyone upon whom it had ever landed flush: he threw that punch at least a few times and not only did Hagler absorb it, Hearns *broke his hand on Hagler's dome.* At the same time, Hagler was inflicting unbelievable damage himself, and once Hearns' fist, then feet, were shot, it was just a matter of time. It's fair to suggest that Hearns made it through the next round and a half on instinct and courage alone. Hagler, for his part, used anger, resolve and willpower to, as he memorably put it, keep moving forward like Pac Man.

The second round allowed everyone, especially the viewers, to catch their breath. The gash that Hearns had opened up on Hagler's forehead fortuitously ran down his nose, and not into his eyes (that could have changed the course of the fight), and when the ref sent Hagler to his corner (even though at this point Hagler had all the momentum) in the third round, it's possible that this was what inspired—or scared—Hagler into deciding two things: The only person stopping this fight is *me*, and I need to stop it, *now*. There was simply no way he was going to let the fight get called on a dubious technicality, not after he had already taken the best Hearns could give him (and, it should be noted, for a man who was notoriously unlucky before and after this fight, it was almost miraculous that the blood didn't gush into either of his eyes; that would have been an obvious game-changer, or worse, may have given the ref sufficient cause to end the bout). In that classic finish, an almost-out-on-his-feet Hearns *jogs* away from Hagler, turning to grin (as if to say "that didn't hurt") but Hagler is already upon him, literally leaping into the air to throw his right-handed coup de grâce. Down went Hearns, up went Hagler, and both men became immortal in that forever moment.

***

It was hard to begrudge Hagler, who'd never been a media darling and had been done wrong by several judges and promoters over the years. This fight was his vindication, and it was sweet (the sour taste in his mouth, that he still carries to this day, courtesy of the controversial '87 fight with Leonard, remains an unfortunate footnote) while it lasted. I love Hagler for the guts, tenacity and resolve he displayed: he deserved to win. I admire Hearns for the respect he showed (to himself, the fans and the sport), willing to lose everything in an all-or-nothing strategy that would be unheard of, today. It was practically unheard of, then. More, he accepted the loss with grace and humor, and it remains moving to see the way he and Hagler embraced after it was over. The mutual respect the two men still have for one another is, understandably, unshaken.

What do we make of Hearns, who finished second in two of the best fights of the decade, both of which could easily be in the Top 10 (if not Top 5) of all time? In both instances, had he chosen to box instead of brawl he very likely could have won. He may still second-guess his strategy in the Leonard fight: if he'd been wise (or craven) enough to just dance away, he would have won handily on the scorecards. But he couldn't; he just didn't have it in him. I see this as neither cockiness nor recklessness; Hearns had a pride that was bigger than winning. I guarantee, despite his understandable regrets about being one of our most celebrated runners-up in sports history, he sleeps like a baby each night and is comfortable looking at himself in the mirror. He should be. In losing, especially the way he lost,

Hearns is more inspiring than any number of athletes who own the hardware, claim the victory, and have done little if anything to make anyone emulate them. I'm not suggesting that a go-for-broke approach is advisable, in sports or life, and as The Gambler reminds us, you've got to know when to hold 'em and know when to fold 'em. On the other hand, when the light is shining brightest, or perhaps more importantly when no one else is looking, you have to be willing to put it on the line and achieve something you'll be proud to remember.

April, 2015

SIX: POLITICS

BORN IN THE U.S.A. OR, EVERY DAY IS VETERANS DAY

I. Personal

Remember when *Born in the U.S.A.* was ubiquitous? The album and the song. Bruce was already big, but he wasn't over the top. *Born in the U.S.A.* put him over the top and, to a certain extent, he's stayed there ever since. Of course, people in the know understood he was already a legend before the '70s ended; in the early '80s *The River* and *Nebraska* cemented that status, but *Born in the U.S.A.* ensured that no one could ever ignore The Boss.

I already owned scratchy LP copies of *Born To Run* and *Darkness on the Edge of Town*, as well as original (and shitty sounding) cassette copies of the oft-overlooked but brilliant first two albums (*Greetings from Asbury Park, N.J.* and *The Wild, The Innocent, and the E. Street Shuffle*), so by the time *Born in the U.S.A.* hit the market, I was admittedly wary of the frenzied and new-fangled faithful joining the party. But other, more disconcerting forces were at play: the album, as good as it was, wasn't *that* good. "Dancing in the Dark", "I'm On Fire", "No Surrender", "My Hometown"? Eh. "Glory Days" was pretty much an instant classic, but (as is always the case with FM-friendly tunes, and never the fault of the artist) overplay hasn't helped its staying power. But the big hit, the title track, the song that seemed to shoot through the dial 24/7, that one was a love or hate affair. I hated it. If ever there was an arena-ready anthem, this was it. And the muscle-bound Bruce from the video? Give me the spindly Serpico clone from '78 any day.

(Interesting coincidence: Springsteen had a difficult time getting the track to sound the way he wanted it. Indeed, it was an outtake from his stark solo effort *Nebraska*. This is not unlike the origins of another overplayed song from the '80s, The Rolling Stones' insufferable "Start Me Up". That one was originally cut as a reggae-ish romp, before it devolved into the over-produced, if innocuous hit it was destined to be. "Start Me Up", to be certain, is a lark, and it was—for better or worse—fated to be recycled for eternity at sporting events. "Born in the U.S.A.", on the other hand, is actually a serious song and, as it happens, is much better than it *sounds*.)

Perhaps it's my own fault, but it took several years before I even figured out the words Bruce was singing; perhaps it's due to his overwrought delivery—equal parts marble-mouthed and shouting. Regardless, this is quite possibly Springsteen's most somber song—and considering the era (*Nebraska*) it was written, that is saying a great deal. (And for the curious, it's well worth checking out the (far superior) demo version that didn't make the cut for the *Nebraska* album.) It made all the sense in the world, then, when Springsteen hit the road for his subdued *Tom Joad* tour in the mid-'90s, he made the searing, stripped-down version of this song a centerpiece of the show. His hand pounding the acoustic guitar to simulate a heartbeat at the song's coda remains one of the most quietly powerful and emotional moments I've ever witnessed at a concert.

II. Polemical

Check it out:

Born down in a dead man's town
The first kick I took was when I hit the ground
You end up like a dog that's been beat too much
Till you spend half your life just covering up
Born in the U.S.A.
I was born in the U.S.A.
I was born in the U.S.A.
Born in the U.S.A.
Got in a little hometown jam
So they put a rifle in my hand
Sent me off to a foreign land
To go and kill the yellow man
(chorus)
Come back home to the refinery
Hiring man says "Son if it was up to me"
Went down to see my V.A. man
He said "Son, don't you understand"

I had a brother at Khe Sahn fighting off the Viet Cong
They're still there, he's all gone
He had a woman he loved in Saigon
I got a picture of him in her arms
Down in the shadow of the penitentiary
Out by the gas fires of the refinery
I'm ten years burning down the road
Nowhere to run ain't got nowhere to go

This song is, upon closer inspection, a staggering achievement. With few words and admirable restraint, Springsteen captures the cause and effects of the Vietnam War from the perspective of an ordinary American, the afflicted civilian. More, he moves the narrator into the here-and-now, making the uncomfortable point that the war never died for the people who managed to live. Movies like *The Deer Hunter* and *Coming Home* dealt with Vietnam's immediate aftermath—the dead or wounded—but not many artists (certainly not enough artists) articulated the dilemma of the working poor who returned from the front line to become the unemployed, or unemployable poor. The vets who ended up in jail, or hospitals, or sleeping under bridges. Or the ones always on the edge (this was, remarkably, a time when *shell shock* was still a more commonly used term than *Post Traumatic Stress Disorder* and, as George Carlin astutely pointed out, perhaps if we still called it "shell shock" it might be less easy to ignore), the ones who, by all outside appearances, could—and should—be finding work, and contributing to society, and staying out of trouble. As politicians of a certain party confirm time and again, you cease to be especially useful once you're no longer in the womb, or no longer wearing the uniform.

On albums like *Nebraska* and *Darkness on the Edge of Town*, Springsteen presented stories of the dirty and the desperate, the men and women straddling the line between paychecks and prison, the ones wrestling with the hope and glory inherent in the mostly mythical American Dream. All of them had a story, and many of them were archetypes from small towns and big cities all across the country. But "Born in the U.S.A." might be the first instance where Springsteen takes a topical dilemma and wrestles with an entire demographic: the veterans with "nowhere to run (and) nowhere to go".

Of course, in an irony that could only occur in America, none other than our PPP (proudly patriotic president), Ronald Reagan, (or, more likely, his handlers) utterly misread the song and tried to appropriate it as a feel-good anthem for his 1984 reelection campaign. Predictably, Springsteen protested. But what Reagan and his opportunistic underlings heard was, in fairness, the same interpretation so many other Americans shared. And who cares, anyway? It's just a *song* after all. And yet, it is a shame that such an effective, and affecting, observation was celebrated as representing the very facile values (unthinking nationalism, unblinking pride) it calls into question. Again, Springsteen and his band deserve no small amount of artistic culpability for marrying such stark lyrics to such a buoyant, fist-pumping, car commercial sounding song. People hear those martial drums and think of John Wayne instead of Travis Bickle.

III. Political

Why bring politics into it at all, one might ask? Music can be, and certainly is, enjoyed regardless of what it was intended to inspire. If a song moves you, or manages to make sense in ways that directly contradict the artist's design, beauty is forever in the eye of the beholder. On the other hand, as George Orwell noted, "the opinion that art should have nothing to do with politics is itself a political attitude". Put another way, "Born in the U.S.A." is still relevant because the issues it confronts are still relevant. We not only have (entirely too many) struggling veterans from last century's wars, we will have no shortage of men and women who have fought (or are currently fighting) in this generation's imbroglio. History only makes one promise, and it's that it will ceaselessly repeat itself.

And so, even as our ill-advised adventure in Iraq reaches its inevitable endgame, we will only be in the initial stages of dealing with the veterans who need care and attention. We won't count the ultimate cost of "mission accomplished" until we consider the lives lost and the walking wounded, tallied up alongside the untold billions of dollars. This is reason enough to be grateful for an Obama administration (the irony that a genuine war hero, had he managed to win, would have necessarily been obliged to overlook those in need of help to pacify the string-pullers in his party, was, thankfully, too outrageous even for America to make possible). The Democrats can't create miracles, but they can continue to ensure that the people owed the most won't get the least.

Remember this, when the small-government-sound bite hyenas crawl out of their tax-payer fortified foxholes to decry liberal "big spending" programs. Remember it's these programs that, in addition to paving roads, building schools and providing health care, attempt to secure some support and solace for our broken soldiers. And remember, in two, or four, or forty years, these same craven war pigs will once again wrap themselves in the American flag; these same armchair generals prepared to fight to the last drop of other folks' blood will be the ones seeking to slash the programs designed to save the ones burning down the road.

November, 2008

IT'S ALL PART OF *DER PROCESS*

From Roger Cohen, via *The New York Times*:

Of the 770 detainees grabbed here and there and flown to Guantánamo, only 23 have ever been charged with a crime. Of the more than 500 so far released, many traumatized by those "enhanced" techniques, not one has received an apology or compensation for their season in hell. What they got on release was a single piece of paper from the American government. A U.S. official met one of the dozens of Afghans now released from Guantánamo and was so appalled by this document that he forwarded me a copy. Dated Oct. 7, 2006, it reads as follows:

"An Administrative Review Board has reviewed the information about you that was talked about at the meeting on 02 December 2005 and the deciding official in the United States has made a decision about what will happen to you. You will be sent to the country of Afghanistan. Your departure will occur as soon as possible."

That's it, the one and only record on paper of protracted U.S. incarceration: three sentences for four years of a young Afghan's life, written in language Orwell would have recognized. We have "the deciding official," not an officer, general or judge. We have "the information about you," not allegations, or accusations, let alone charges. We have "a decision about what will happen to you," not a judgment, ruling or verdict. This is the lexicon of totalitarianism. It is acutely embarrassing to the United States. That is why I am thankful above all that the next U.S. commander in chief is a constitutional lawyer. Nothing has been more damaging to the United States than the violation of the legal principles at the heart of the American idea.

Let's face it; Orwell has become kind of a cliché. (No fault of his own; if the most sincere form of flattery is imitation, the most flattering form of sincerity is to have one's ideas transmogrified into clichés.) It's not just that Orwell was, in *1984*, writing about a futuristic dystopia; he was describing parts of the world that already existed. The best science fiction, of course, has always anticipated the future by channeling the present. History is obliged to repeat itself because the human beings who make history do so in such a predictable, patterned fashion. And so, Orwell has the curious fate of being over-quoted and under-read: everyone knows what *Orwellian* means because they've already seen what it means (in movies, in the news). More importantly, everyone understands that the horrors Orwell depicted are passé; totalitarianism is so 20th Century. Except for the fact that it isn't, and never was.

(It's tempting to point out another immortal text, one that is arguably second only to *1984* in terms of applicability and the type of cultural resonance that is so often invoked and so seldom analyzed. Nevertheless, it's all there in Conrad's fin-de-siècle classic *Heart of Darkness:* the dehumanization, for political purposes and/or the expedience of power, of the *Other*; an "other" that is assigned this designation necessarily from a position of powerlessness (powerless to protect, powerless to define). The naked will of brute force for the ostensible purpose of "exterminating the brutes" invariably involves religion or money, but either way, it always involves a struggle for power. Sadly, few seem to have actually bothered *reading* Conrad's novella, but everyone has seen *Apocalypse Now*, so it's a wash.)

But there is an exposed nerve running from Conrad to Orwell that might be best explained by considering the two Russian masters who connected the dots in between them: Yevgeny Zamyatin and Mikhail Bulgakov. The former's novel *We* (1921) and the latter's *The Master and Margarita* (commenced in 1928, completed in 1941) deal directly with the dehumanizing repercussions of totalitarian rule. Focusing more on the (very human) consequences of identity destruction and the suppression of self—a paramount objective of those in power, and a necessary condition of remaining in power—these novels are quite literally notes from the underground, infused with the verisimilitude of an insider's experience. They lived it and they wrote about it.

Orwell took that torch of truth and continued onward even as the scope of Fascism cast an ever-enlarging shadow over other parts of other continents: again, his work resonates because he is depicting (then, and now) realities that anyone who has lived inside an autocratic regime can easily recognize. And as Americans, we quickly apprehend the causes and effects of totalitarianism because, our history books austerely inform us, we did much to eradicate them. And so we did. But it was well before 9/11 that certain segments of society (usually the dreaded leftist types who work in universities or for newspapers, or even worse, the ones who write fiction or poetry or music) perceived the subtle and not-so-subtle ways in which even this most democratic society has at times unintentionally and at other times willfully revealed a dark heart that contradicts its own Constitution.

Here's the thing: people have read Orwell even if they haven't (because the author of *Animal Farm* is a *de rigeur* point of reference for any writer, particularly a politically oriented writer, who hopes to be taken seriously), and they've *watched* Conrad (or at least a sensationalized action-epic that delivers visually even if it severely lacks the scope or coherence of its inspiration), and few people have any interest in reading dead Russian writers not named Tolstoy or Dostoyevsky (and those that do are already ensconced in English graduate programs). Fortunately, for better or worse, we nevertheless have an author (and text) that covers everything already mentioned (the fiction, the non-fiction, and the considerable overlap in between them both, otherwise known as History). The good news: his name is, if possible, even more incessantly invoked than Orwell's. The bad news: even fewer people have actually read him. If that seems *Kafkaesque,* it's because it is. Well, actually it *isn't*; but that is the point: as an adjective, *Kafkaesque* is misused with greater abandon than *Orwellian.* Or, to put it slightly less pessimistically, it has been bludgeoned into submission. Put slightly more pretentiously, *Kafkaesque* awoke one morning from uneasy dreams it found itself transformed in its bed into a gigantic Cliché.

Check it out: an unassuming citizen is informed, one day, that he is accused of a crime. He has committed no crimes that he is aware of, but that is all but irrelevant, since a description of the crime is not given. He spends the rest of his harried life making the futile attempt to exonerate himself or, short of that, have the specific charges explained to him. Immersed in a Byzantine maze that is at once inherently bureaucratic and at the same time nonsensical, his will slowly dissolves in this irrational paralysis. When, ultimately, he is executed, it comes almost as a relief.

Sound familiar?

Of course, it scarcely suffices to look at what we've wrought at Guantánamo and abroad and call it *Orwellian* or *Kafkaesque*. It is both of those, in equal measure, but it's also something quite a bit more appalling. Partly because it's true--this has actually happened; partly because we've done it before and claimed we would never do it again. Mostly because, while it was happening, there were actually people (quite a lot of them) who raised the alarm and found themselves scoffed at, or threatened. Some were actually disenfranchised; most were simply dismissed. Eventual (inevitable?) progress has been sickeningly slow in coming, but at least there is a miniscule crack in the one-way glass. Once that hole gets bigger (and it will, as it always does) many of us are going to be disgusted at what we see (what we did, who was responsible for organizing it all, what was done in our name by others we paid to do what we couldn't quite bring ourselves to do). Some will defend it all, naturally: the acts, the people who undertook them; it is, after all, just good business. Others will, obviously, decry the (demonstrably *liberal*) media that seems to take so much pleasure pulling back the curtain to reveal the cretins scurrying into the cracks. Same as it ever was. And finally, there will be the newly-awakened, who'll shake their heads and lament that extraordinary times occasionally inspire atrocious activities. But never again, at least. At least we'll have learned that much. Again.

A cliché: those who do not learn from history are doomed to repeat it.

A tragedy: those who do not read literature are doomed to inspire it.

December, 2008

FOR BOROWSKI, MESSIAEN AND THE MILLIONS THEY SPOKE FOR

2009 is young, but I believe I already have a contender for essay of the year: a lengthy piece by Christopher Buckley, concerning his visit to Auschwitz. It's not easy or pleasurable reading, owing to its subject matter. The devastation of what he describes is augmented by how well he writes; it's at once unbearable and indispensable.

It would be recommended reading at any time, but seems particularly pertinent owing to the sorry spectacle of Prada-rocking Pope Benedict XVI, who (and when it comes to brass balls, you have to tip your mitre to the sallow old fucks who hold sway at the Vatican) has recently made it a point to "rehabilitate" Bishop Richard Williamson. Buckley begins his piece by making the understandable inquiry "Why on earth would Pope Benedict XVI want to rehabilitate a Holocaust denier?" This being Buckley, one is forgiven from wondering if that query is a tad over the top. Unfortunately, it's nothing of the sort. For anyone who has had the displeasure of seeing Williamson soil his fetid soul on national TV, it is readily available online.

I need not add my disdain to the proceedings (others far more eloquent than I have weighed in on this matter; indeed some have made careers out of it), and I'm happy to cede the spotlight to Buckley who acquits himself, for everyone's sake, as close to perfectly as possible. It is a long piece, and any number of sentences could be lifted to represent the whole. For me, this one conveys the scope of the horror succinctly enough:

On one side of the rail platform was the women's camp. "When the trains came," Jarek says, "women would shout to the women arriving, 'Give the baby to the granny.' That way you might not be selected for the gas chamber. This was the choice."

It's unlikely Williamson would be swayed too much by Buckley's account. That's fine. But I'd take the opportunity, if it existed, to recommend some light reading for Williamson. It's a book written by a man named Tadeusz Borowski, and his book (which would almost sound like something Mel Brooks might make up, were it not so sickening), is entitled *This Way for the Gas, Ladies and Gentlemen.* Borowski was a Polish writer apprehended by the Nazis at the age of 21. Over the course of two years, he spent time at Auschwitz and Dachau. Liberated in 1945, he wrote about his experiences in the book that is now considered a masterpiece. If Buckley's article is painful reading, Borowski's is almost intolerable. But it's essential, for all the obvious reasons. Against all probability, Borowski writes his eye-witness inspired accounts and manages to infuse them with humor and even irony. This effectively humanizes the unimaginable.

Perhaps Williamson, and Ratzinger, would be jarred from their smug, ecclesiastical apathy to know that Borowski, unable to cope with what he'd experienced, took his life. At the age of 28. By sticking his head in a gas stove. Perhaps this would move them. Perhaps not.

If, indulging in my scenario, I were able to compel these two men of God to read Buckley and Borowski, I think it would be a fitting touch to have some music in the background. Maybe *Quatuor pour la fin du temps (Quartet for the End of Time)*, a chamber quartet by French composer Olivier Messiaen. This music was not merely inspired by the concentration camps; it was created, and performed there. True story, and worth looking up. Of course, Williamson refers to the various "experts" he has consulted in his pursuit of truth (he actually says this); perhaps he could go directly the source (physically, as Buckley did, or artistically, courtesy of Borowski and Messiaen). Perhaps it would make a difference. Perhaps not.

January, 2009

FEBRUARY 19, 1942

On this day in 1942 Executive Order 9066 was issued. That is, the infamous presidential/executive order that, validated by America's state of war, gave a president (FDR) the power to consign various ethnic groups (see: the Japanese) to internment camps. Not too coincidentally, the individuals targeted happened to be Americans belonging to the ancestry the U.S. was concurrently fighting in WW II (the aforementioned Japanese, as well as Germans and Italians). Over *100,000* Japanese-Americans were spirited away to these camps. Not unlike the concentration camps, one thinks about this period in history and thinks (hopes?) it was far back in our past. Considering the 20th Century was already half-over puts it in immediate, and painful, perspective. About sixty years ago, millions of Jews were being slaughtered in Germany and tens of thousands of Japanese-Americans were being forcibly sent to internment camps. Less than two generations. On good days, we look at this and say "how could it have happened?" On other days, we look at Guantanamo and it's difficult to feel too proud of the progress we've supposedly made.

There's a picture that has haunted me ever since I first saw it, over a decade ago.

A Japanese family, en route to an internment camp. Neither defiant nor indignant (they couldn't afford to be), they are quite obviously eager to illustrate their solidarity. Acquiescence. Approbation. The miniature American flags, the victory signs, the smiles. The fear behind those forced gestures. (Not forced because they were fake, but because they were obligatory; imperative as the bare minimum to ensure that the worst was not automatically assumed.) Look closely at how the father sets the tone: he understands the score. Smile, this is your life. The kids are either too old to protest (the older daughter) or too young to fake it (the son). But it's the young girl in the middle (middle of the picture, middle child in the family) that conveys the intolerable hypocrisy and inhumanity of the situation: she's the only one without a smile on her face or a flag in her hand. She is old enough to understand, but young enough to be petulant about her circumstances. No matter her age, she *knows* this unwilling exodus is unnatural, unacceptable. And her face (more than a million subsequent words decrying the conditions that led to this embarrassing moment in U.S. history) is able to convey the very human cost of counterproductive policies begat by hysteria.

Never again, one thinks, looking at that picture. It was unfortunate, but that was half a century ago, we've evolved into e-mail and instant communication across the globe, certainly we shan't act that rashly again. Surely we've seen enough of this appalling history to ensure that it's never repeated. Obviously we have made amends and are stronger, as a nation, for what we commissioned in the name of national security. Clearly we could never dive into the deep end again, indulging the uglier side of our collective sensibility. Fortunately we've come a long way since the dark ages of our (parents') infancy.

Haven't we...

February, 2009

CANCEL MY SUBSCRIPTION: AN OPEN LETTER TO THE WASHINGTON POST

To those too clueless to be concerned:

First, let this letter serve as my formal request to cancel my subscription, effective immediately.

Second, let me express my ardent hope and expectation that I am one of hundreds (thousands?) who shall officially cease helping fund your publication. A publication that has tilted ever rightward in the last two decades, culminating in the unconscionable firing of Dan Froomkin yesterday.

Third, let me tell you a little about myself. My family has been rooted in northern Virginia since the early '70s and I began reading *The Washington Post* to get my daily fix of *The Far Side*; later, to get my fix of Sports; later still to get my fix on events political and otherwise. I started subscribing as soon as I lived on my own, in 1994, and have paid to receive the paper each day ever since. Indeed, even as it became increasingly easy to access content online, I chose not to read *The Post* online; at first out of habit, later because I wanted to do my part to help sustain the struggling print industry. I continued to pay, even as the size and scope of the coverage decreased; I continued to pay, even as it seemed that every new Op-Ed writer was not merely right-of-center, but hardcore conservative. I continued to pay, even as the insufferable Fred Hiatt and his merry band of neocons refused, after shamefully pimping out the Iraq invasion, to own up to any mistakes or admit any culpability. Indeed, I continued to pay even after the editorial page doubled down on its disgraceful stance and maintained that despite some obvious ineptitude (wow, what a concession), the right choice had been made to invade. I continued to pay even after *The Post* made the truly insulting decision to employ Bill Kristol, once his intelligence-insulting stint at *The New York Times* came to an overdue end. I may even have been talked off the ledge after immediately deciding to cancel, in the wake of the announcement that Dan Froomkin had been summarily dismissed (of which more shortly). But on the day after this ignoble decision *The Post* saw fit to run an Op-Ed from Paul Wolfowitz (*Paul Wolfowitz!*)—that thoroughly discredited buffoon who did as much as anyone to turn the Iraq adventure into an epic catastrophe—lambasting Obama, as only the most shameless neocons are capable of doing, for his ostensibly ineffective diplomacy. That, as they say, is the final straw.

While it is a thoroughly debunked farce that the mainstream media in America has a discernible liberal bias, it is nevertheless undeniable that *The Post* has carried a stigma second only to the venerated (and disdained) *New York Times*. Doubtless this at least in part due to the historical scoop Woodward and Bernstein uncovered, leading to the Watergate story and Nixon's subsequent resignation. (To think that actual reporting done by real human beings to prove that crimes were being committed in the White House somehow signifies any type of liberal agenda is both amusing and appalling.) Nevertheless, there were two unfortunate aftershocks from the Watergate revelations. One, because Nixon was a Republican, it gave GOP operatives ample, if facile, ammunition to charge that *The Washington Post* had a strategic and systematic disdain for conservative politics. Two, the success of this hysterical and myopic (but quite successful) talking point, second only to the blind fetishization of the free market in terms of the force and frequency with which it is employed, has caused timid publications, like *The Post,* to tremble like the cowed and co-opted enterprises they truly are.

The decision to fire Froomkin stinks so badly, on so many levels, it's hardly worth discussing in detail. Suffice it to say, despite the fact that Froomkin is unarguably one of the most popular and respected writers *The Post* employs, his services, somehow, are no longer deemed necessary. Really? Good luck with that, Graham. As your paper hemorrhages money, you decide to terminate (in transparently petty and politically-calculated fashion) one of the handful of writers who inspired loyal readers to keep you afloat. This is beyond hubris and seems practically a dare to your readership: *What are you going to do about it?* I'm going to cancel. Now.

My condolences,
Sean Murphy

June, 2009

THE CATHOLIC CHURCH IS DECADENT AND DEPRAVED

Part One: Abandon hope all ye who enter here...

First, and appropriately, a confession.

The title is both a tribute to, and an outright plagiarism of Hunter S. Thompson's masterful essay "The Kentucky Derby is Decadent and Depraved." And if, with that piece, he could be accused of shooting some very wealthy and insular fish in a bourbon-scented barrel, somebody had to do it. The pompous and circumstance of a spectacle like the Kentucky Derby needed to be sent up. And the thing about the good doctor during his prime, when he decided to do something, it *stayed* done.

The Catholic Church, on the other hand, has been assailed from all sides, so any new criticism will be neither original nor particularly surprising. So what. It remains essential to single out hypocrisy and maleficence when it is condoned or perpetrated by people or places wielding power. And despite the fact that its influence has been waning, the Catholic Church is still an appallingly influential and imperious organization. To put things plainly, it's frankly because so many millions of innocent (and unknowing) human beings are impacted by this institution that its self-righteous posturing be paraded as openly and often as possible. That's all.

Aside from Richard Dawkins, the most vocal and coruscating critic of late has been the indefatigable Christopher Hitchens. His seminal book *God Is Not Great* would be required reading in a sane world; but a sane world would not require that such a book be written. Of course, Hitchens correctly does not limit himself to just the Catholic church: he sets his sights on the entire notion of a Big Guy upstairs, or more specifically, our farcical and self-serving conception of same. To be certain, Hitchens does not waste his time and energy poking holes in the fairy tales and phantasmagoria that all organized religions are predicated upon. Any half-witted college freshman with a semester of Logic or Composition 101 can handle that light work. Rather, Hitchens trains his sights on the considerable violence, repression and ignorance the various religions have instilled and propagated, spanning the last two centuries. He assails the clergy, and the historically inconsistent, often hysterical dogma that they cling to for their specious moral autonomy. Hitchens argues that, for all the good deeds religion is regularly credited for inspiring, the scales are quite heavily tilted toward the negative in terms of wars, moral terror and child rape—just to pick some of the low-hanging fruit. Speaking of fruit, it remains hilarious and more than a little pathetic that grown men dressed in fancy pajamas invoke words written centuries ago as an inviolable decree to guide the contemporary affairs of mankind. (And I understand that this simple-minded insistence of following "God's word" is the convenient catchall acting as a kind of ecclesiastical flypaper to ensnare all troublesome inconsistencies and intrusions of logic or inconvenient Truth; suffice it to say, until I see any of these disciples actually living by the letter of the onerous and inconceivable edicts of the Old Testament, I'll remain wary and skeptical.)

Hitchens has recently engaged in a series of debates about whether or not Catholicism is a positive force in the world. This, it seems to me, is ultimately a proposition that remains largely unprovable and not particularly relevant (prolestyzers on either side of that argument can—and will—produce what they consider immutable testimony to advance their case; and both sides have sufficient ammunition). With no choice but to (belatedly, begrudgingly) own up to some of the more colossal outrages it has perpetrated, the clergy draws a line in the sand with the following concession: for all its faults, the church does endeavor to fill more potholes than it causes.

The enduring question remains: does it?

For every pedophilic priest one can point to (and the unforgivable, institutionally sanctioned cover-up of these atrocities), you also have humble men and women making genuine and heartfelt contributions to society. The vocation, whatever manifold psychological impulses it answers (or quells), seems genuine enough to have attracted hundreds of thousands of young men, at least some of whom have remained celibate and faithful. That warrants consideration, leaving aside any understandable questions about the spiritual duress and denial such a lifestyle entails.

And yet. At the end of the analysis, while it's easy for anyone with an IQ approaching triple digits to poke fun at the snake handling or spaceship-seeing outliers on the religious spectrum (despite the considerable damage the more extreme, and whacko, religions do to its most earnest and unenlightened parishioners), it is difficult not to suppress a special distaste for the fathomless myopia that underscores Catholicism's sensibility. One look at The Vatican (in Vatican *City*) is enough to salivate at what Jesus would make of *that* temple. No money lenders there; these are straight up faith pimps, trading favors for forgiveness going back several centuries. What these charlatans are able to pull off, in tax exempt fashion, is the apotheosis of all Ponzi schemes. But, like the simple saps that Madof ensnared, few tithers throw their sheckles in the collection jar without a preconceived quid pro quo: it's an ecclesiastical installment plan, and Catholic guilt—inbred from an early age—creates a collective bank account that accrues interest at unprecedented rates. The Catholic hierarchy's ultimate legacy is successfully establishing a cadre of spiritual stockbrokers.

Part Two: The Soup Kitchen Nazis

So, with so much to mock about the self-satisfied piety of the RCC, why now?

What brings the RCC out of the cloister? War? The outrages of Wall Street? Humiliation over its involvement in generations of profligate buggery? Of course not. Only the *really* crucial and relevant issues prompt such expediency: abortion and gay marriage! These are the conjoined crises that impel the otherwise oblivious foxes to slink out of the holy henhouse.

To summarize for those with short-attention spans or quick gag reflexes: in recent weeks the Catholic brain trust has picked public battles with Patrick Kennedy and D.C. area homeless. In the first instance, the smug and odious Bishop Thomas J. Tobin castigated Kennedy over his support of abortion rights. It is, the robe-wearing one whined, "a deliberate an obstinate act of will... (and) unacceptable to the church and *scandalous to many of our members*" (emphasis mine). Scandalous? Really? That anyone in a position of authority within the Catholic Church would have the audacity to use the word *scandalous* tells you all you need know about how truly clueless and shameless they have become.

This grandstanding, naturally, recalls memories of certain priests getting involved in the '04 election, reminding their parishioners that voting for a man (Kerry) who didn't have the appropriate pro-life bona fides was tantamount to heresy. This while the incumbent was actively waging preemptive war and shrinking the middle class to levels not seen since, well, the Great Depression. We all know how that one played out.

But you almost expect that type of intransigence, that level of obliviousness, from the men who have evolved from the bad old days when they burned scientists at the stake. What inspires the ongoing outrage is the fact that the Catholic Church—this tone-deaf, intellectually devoid, bullying organization—ceaselessly finds ways to outdo itself. Take, for instance, the real and present outrage playing itself out, right now, in Washington D.C.

To recap: the (ultra conservative) Catholic Archdiocese of Washington has recently made ugly noise about withholding support for the homeless (about 70,000 individuals) due to its "principled" opposition to D.C.'s same-sex marriage bill. Let that one sink in for a moment. The church, ostensibly doing the work Christ instructed, is grandstanding said work over an issue that Christ never made a single mention of in the scriptures (go ahead and look it up; we'll wait for you). Welcome to the Catholic sensibility! This is bigotry disguised as rectitude, but what else is new? Aside from the sickening hypocrisy (that word again, it's unavoidable), this jumps so many sacred sharks it is difficult to keep track. For starters, these same churches that continue to enjoy *tax exempt* status are sticking their nose into the affairs of the government. Really? These same churches that are more than happy to accept government funding think it's acceptable (legal?) to ignore said government's laws, should they pass? The Catholic lemmings, following their Prada-wearing pontiff, have descended to the level of being soup (kitchen) Nazis.

As ever, to fully grasp the illimitable duplicity of the church, one must inevitably turn to the costume-clad church elders. (Not for nothing, and with an irony that no objective reader of biblical scripture can avoid noting with a particular pang of nausea, it is the same well-fed and unreflective old men that Jesus had a special disdain for.) Look, let's not sugarcoat the underlying issue at hand:

with the world moving ever further away from biblical flights of fancy and despotic mind games; this is the sign of a desperate institution indeed. You only see this in politics and religion: when things start to spiral out of control, double down. In this instance, the decaying infrastructure and waning sway the church holds over humanity at large, makes its actions resemble those of a cult. Isn't it funny how people (understandably) feel no compunction poking fun at the ludicrous precepts of Scientology, but bristle if anyone snickers at the apparent seriousness with which Catholics (and many other cults) regard that virgin birth thing or the notion that the Pope speaks infallibly (no, really). Farcical, sure, but also insulting, considering the man Catholics look to as an arbiter of morality, Thomas Aquinas, was last seen levitating in that cathedral (no, really).

In closing, allow me to directly address anyone (Catholic or otherwise) who applauds (or remains merely unmoved by) the appalling positions the church is clinging to. The abortion issue is, at least, a tangible (if complicated) dilemma that people can wrestle with for spiritual and secular reasons. The open hostility toward and discrimination against homosexuals, on the other hand, is something that simply cannot be tolerated by anyone pretending to endorse the Declaration of Independence as well as the New Testament (you know, *What Would Jesus Do?).*

The prayerful prejudiced can hide behind the bogus claim of faith and fidelity, but in the final analysis, a bigot is a bigot. Congratulations on being, once again, on the wrong side of history and the righteous shift of love over fear.

And for the Catholic-Lite weekend warriors who don't have the guts or the brains to, at long last, cut the cord, understand that you continue to associate with—and, to a certain extent, intellectually and spiritually prostrate yourself to—an organized religion that goes several steps farther than these ignorant, opportunistic politicians who use pro-life positions to garner votes. The Catholic Church, despite any real evidence in the bible (!) abominates not only the practice but *existence* of homosexuality. Despite the much-discussed (but ever astonishing) fact that it harbors more than a fair share of closeted, (and not-so-closeted) in its cloister. Despite the fact that this obsessive and intolerant dogma is the fulcrum upon which these political types fortify their indefensible positions. Despite the fact that, even knowing—if failing to come to grips with—the hypocrisy and mendacity that exists in its own sullied garden, this craven institution uses its brute force and reliably backwards (see: women, blacks, gays just to name the unholy trinity) clerical acumen to tyrannize anyone susceptible to its influence. The world that includes the powerless and dispossessed who cower, and especially the useful insects who apprehend and *acknowledge* this moral fascism (yes, fascism), and either choose to whistle blithely past the truth or, in inimitably Catholic fashion, obey the rules that fit and overlook or rationalize the ones that cause discomfort. Avoiding that discomfort at the expense of your innocent brothers and sisters is an abomination. It is also the essence of Catholicism.

But hey, who knows, maybe one day you'll stand before your white, Republican Jesus and explain to him that you were only doing what he instructed you to do. Good luck with that.

November, 2009

RUSH LIMBAUGH: DON'T HATE THE PLAYER, HATE THE GAME

Beneath contempt? Of course.

Shameless? Obviously.

A ludicrous, cowardly clown? Clearly.

A bullying blowhard? Yup.

A self-aggrandizing huckster who sells snake piss to imbeciles and laughs all the way to his drug dealer? You know this.

Are we really surprised by his latest lowering of the bar?

I'm certainly not.

(Which isn't to say I almost caught myself shaking my head, not quite in disbelief but in a kind of awed amusement: there he goes again. Seriously, when you not only live in the slimy detritus of talk-radio sewage, but make a (very remunerative) living doing so, there is literally no bottom, nowhere further to sink. Indeed, the gig almost necessitates a blind, ceaseless strain to burrow further and deeper, getting to darker places. In other words, Rush's latest outrage is merely another day at the office.)

For centuries, Punch and Judy shows were all the rage (literally). Our appetite for self-destruction is neither new nor novel; we've been perfecting ways to taste the pain for as long as we've been upright (and before that we swung from trees throwing shit at each other; before that we crawled in the primordial ooze and threw up on one another). The closest thing we have to these spectacles today is Reality TV and Talk Radio. While some humiliation, desperation and a whole lot of narcissism makes the Reality TV carousel go round, there is an element of selfishness that cuts the inexorable humiliation. In other words, it's an equal opportunity farce: it's like gambling or playing the lottery, chances are decent you'll gain nothing, and the rules could not be clearer. Talk radio, on the other hand (as has been discussed and documented many million times by critics more astute—and interested—than myself) is predicated upon an uneven playing field. The prophets of fury and despair (like so many religious hucksters) offer the illusion of solidarity to their disenfranchised followers. By preying upon their real (or affected) sense of dispossession, these self-declared saviors offer solace by validating the ignorance, prejudices and pains of their flock.

We see it with Limbaugh, we see it with Glenn Beck and we'll see plenty more of it from Sarah Palin now that she has fulfilled her destiny by getting a platform on Fox News, the purest source of propaganda money can buy.

So what?

Should we protest (and play right into his hands) Limbaugh? Of course not, that will only empower him and augment the sanctimony of his shtick. It's not often you can call someone a vampire *and* a whore at the same time, but more than anyone in modern times, Limbaugh is the worst possible combination of everything we despise in humanity. And here is the thing, unlike virtually all the other vermin who fatten their wallets by fomenting unrighteous indignation, there is not a single redeeming value in anything this clownish swine says or does. Nada.

But this was all abundantly obvious almost two full decades ago.

If you want to get fired up, if you really want to feel frightened, consider the fact that Rush's ratings will skyrocket after today's shitstorm. Think about that. And be truly mortified for where we are, as Americans. What is most repugnant, when you stop and contemplate it, is that there would be even a single person who might hear Limbaugh's calculated and cynical hogwash and agree. Or, worse, feel inspired by the way their chosen one brings the hate. The plain, putrid reality is that there are hundreds of thousands, perhaps millions, who do. And will.

Just like there are tons of people who will walk over rusty glass for Sarah Palin. If Limbaugh or Palin were offering these people (the bigots, the uneducated, the willfully ignorant, the impotent imbeciles, as well as the doctors, lawyers, teachers and parents) anything—money, peace, progress, *hope*—it would just be politics as usual. Or as they used to say, That's Entertainment.

But the fact of the matter is, nothing is being offered. And the worst part of the whole deal is that the most (superficially) faithful and dedicated believers are being sold a bill of goods that is straight-up nihilism. While Fox News gets their Fascist on, and Rush gorges his fat ass on profitable cynicism, these has-beens and never-will-be's find the voice that never answers them in church, or at the office, or in their cars, or in the bedroom or—worst of all—in their own dark and empty heads when the lights go out.

It is, and always has been, a game. Let's stop laughing at it (or ignoring it) and start hating it back.

January, 2010

SOME DAY A REAL RAIN WILL COME: WHAT TRAVIS BICKLE CAN TELL US ABOUT TUCSON

Voices In Our Heads

You talking to me?

It is the pivotal scene in Scorsese's *Taxi Driver* and it remains one of the seminal moments in movie history. Not so much because of its improvisational nature, or the uncanny way Robert De Niro (playing the alienated and ultimately violent Travis Bickle) disappears into this character, managing to seem invisible and menacing all at once. Most important, this short scene echoes a question that all of us, to a certain extent, ask the world every day.

"Are you talking to me?" we ask, and the tone may be inquisitive, rhetorical or defiant. It may be those and many other things. Mostly, as we interact in a mechanized, sped-up and increasingly unreal reality, we want to make sure people know we are there. We use our voices, our eyes, our frowns or smiles, our horns, our phones, our e-mail, our clothes and a thousand unspoken thoughts to affirm that our presence does not go entirely unnoticed.

In a way, it was easier a few decades ago, around the time *Taxi Driver* (1976) was released. There was no Internet, no texting, no cell phones, no cable TV, no electronic anything. If you needed to reach out and touch someone, you had to do just that. It's possible that with the proliferation of devices and toys, in our information-overload moment (which, as it relates to art, content and information, is definitely not a negative thing), we are lonelier than ever before. This ground has been well-covered and there are compelling arguments on either side. On one hand, it can be conjectured that by remaining indoors, behind a glowing screen, we've effectively cut ourselves off from old-fashioned interaction and our communication—however ceaseless—lacks intimacy and engagement. On the other hand, people who in another era (including this one) may be best described as socially awkward (due to a variety of societal and self-imposed factors) have myriad opportunities to connect that simply did not exist even ten-to-fifteen years ago.

And the above observations almost entirely relate to action as opposed to reaction. It's difficult to accurately gauge precisely how a constant bombardment of content, opinions and steadily louder voices is affecting our perception. Not too long ago it was a common joke to talk about (either in celebratory or castigating tones) how we had one hundred channels to choose from via cable TV. Now we have *hundreds* of channels, as well as streaming video, social media, blogs, and a dedicated website for every news channel, program and talking head in the world. And all of these voices are trying to tell, or sell, us something. Always urgently, never off message, constantly competing with all the other noise to get inside our heads and influence our opinions in one way or another.

Who Owns The American Dream?

You're in a hell, and you're gonna' die in a hell like the rest of them.

It was horrifying enough when we had Travis Bickle types who, for their various reasons, sought violent ends to make some type of statement or try and quell that voice screeching non-stop in their ears, like a demented wasps' nest. *Taxi Driver*, though wrongly or at least simplistically described by too many as the story of a psychopath, is very much a cautionary tale about what can happen when an alienated citizen has no one to talk to. The fact that it's set in one of the busiest cities in the world is less ironic than tragic: anyone who has spent time in a bustling urban environment can confirm that it's sometimes—if not often—the case that one can feel most alone when surrounded by millions of people who don't know or care about them.

Loneliness, alienation and even violence are sufficiently commonplace as to be unremarkable facets of American existence: watch the news or consider your own life story. This certainly holds true in any society, particularly our plugged in but often disconnected post-millennial era. It seems safe to suggest these conditions are most rampant and profound in the United States. There are countless reasons and/or symptoms, and they are rooted more in myth than reality. For instance, while America does not have the rigid and stratified class systems that still plague Europe, we do have a collective addiction to the white-washed fantasy also known as the American Dream.

Lest that sound like a facile dismissal of a very complicated and, in many ways useful illusion, there are undeniably certain aspects of the American Dream parable that are provable and worthwhile. The ceaseless influx of grateful immigrants is sufficient testament to the inherent promise of an ostensibly free society. The same promise luring men and women to illegally enter our country is the same impulse that served as a siren song for Irish, Italian and other immigration movements through the 19th and 20th centuries. And yet, this speaks to the dream of America itself more than what we call the American Dream. Being able to do *something* is altogether different from being able to do *anything*. Most of these immigrants (then, now) are obliged to work excruciating hours doing horrific work at woeful wages, and the only thing making it tolerable is that it is (usually) better than the alternative.

The proposition that any of us, regardless of who we are and whatever our initial station in life can, with the correct combination of industry, initiative and luck, ascend to a status of wealth festers as one of the more powerful, if poisonous fictions our country has produced. More, it is not merely promulgated but actively *inculcated*: history books and sentimental movies tend to tout the exceedingly rare rags-to-riches allegory while ignoring, denying or conveniently dismissing the typical reality, which is that the working poor are likely to remain exactly where they are. In fact, as we've seen in the last few decades, this is more—not less—the case in a political and cultural system that has steadily ensured that those who have more will get more, usually directly at the expense of those who have little.

This dichotomy between what we see on screens or inside magazines is not new, but commercials, ads and websites telling us how can be or who we should be are incalculably more prevalent and powerful in today's world. Thus, the same types of alienating forces that the lonely, angry and outcast citizens have historically been subject to are alarmingly more intense in a 24/7 info-tainment unreality. Which brings us to the Republicans in general and the Tea Party in particular. The GOP has auto-piloted the Horatio Alger story to the extent that counties receiving the most federal aid will lash out most indignantly (if ignorantly) about the perils of "big government". Indeed, generation after generation illustrates that those who benefit most from higher taxes (and who have the least likelihood of ascending to the upper tax brackets) are consistently fanatical about keeping taxes low for those who earn the most. There are an unfortunate number of tragedies we commit as Americans, but this is one of the more profound examples.

Someday A Real Rain Will Come…

Loneliness has followed me my whole life…there's no escape. I'm God's lonely man.

One of the more devastatingly poignant (or poignantly devastating) scenes in *Taxi Driver* occurs when Travis sits, silently in his apartment, watching the attractive and fashionable folks dancing on TV. Alone in his sweltering studio walk-up, the look on his face—at once longing, frustrated and confused—reveals the hastening recognition that he will never attain the easy, if superficial, security he sees on the screen. With subtlety and lack of sentimentality (the script is actually somewhat slight, which only underscores the astonishing work De Niro turns in), we see that Bickle is the ultimate loner, an underground entity who is as much insect as human, scurrying in and out of his pointless and preordained routine.

Add to this the fact that he is a veteran, perhaps the most overlooked, yet prescient touch of the film (flash forward thirty-plus years to see how we treat our soldiers when they return from the wars we ask them to fight; little coincidence that it's the same party that salutes the flag most tearfully who are quickest to slash and burn the programs designed to provide physical—and especially mental—assistance). The result of these circumstances and lack of choices provide us, circa 1976, with a character sketch of someone who, if one thing leads to the next, might opt for a more sociopathic solution to his problems. Importantly, Bickle is not revealed as a man destined to snap; while he is far from blameless for his predicament, he is very much a casualty of the world (the real one and the manufactured one) that he can't master but must exist in. Therefore when he decides "my whole life is pointed in one direction…there never has been any choice for me", it is both a confession and a one-man verdict, his indictment against this world.

There is some irony, looking back on the candidate he turns his grim attention toward: Palantine, running under the campaign slogan "We Are The People", seems to espouse a very optimistic (if clichéd) message. (Further irony in that this notion of a collective synergy only amplifies Bickle's isolation.) Imagine all of these elements contributing to Bickle's disintegration placed in the context of our contemporary culture, with venom being spewed 24/7 by charlatans and circus clowns like Beck, O'Riley and Palin. Imagine Travis Bickle watching Fox News each day. If you can, you may begin to see why the concern and loathing of the Tea Party movement had much more to do with what happened this week in Arizona and little to do with comically misspelled signs and morons telling the government to stay out of their Medicare.

Travis gets his guns after a frightening encounter in his cab (and having heard about the violence fellow drivers have suffered). Only after he feels himself finally out of options does he contemplate using his gun on an innocent person (and later, people). Even in 1976, this was sufficiently compelling commentary on the ease with which Americans get access to guns. Today, appallingly, gun laws are looser than ever (and—shocker!—one political party defends this madness with the same tenacity they bring to cutting taxes and eliminating federal aid programs) and instead of a lone madman with one round, we have the sickening spectacle of semi-automatic weapons. Flash forward to Columbine, Virginia Tech and Tucson.

It slowly comes into focus: it is easier, now, for more people (except perhaps the politicians and mainstream media, the two most culpable parties) to understand the calculus that made this weekend's tragedy predictable and, perhaps, inevitable. There are and—as ass-covering TV talking heads remind us—always will be lunatics in our midst who will kill and maim others and there is little we can do (other than disarm them). That said, it is way too easy to suggest this was an ambivalent act with random victims: in the same state the cretinous Sarah Palin put gun-sights on in a map of "targets". It's not necessary to pile on Palin, no matter how much blood she has on her carefully manicured hands; it is every bit the supine and opportunistic media's fault, since they have breathlessly provided this imbecile with a public platform every step of the way. Special disgust, certainly, must be reserved for the reprehensible propaganda machine at Fox

News: that so many Americans receive their "information" (and/or marching orders) from these scavengers debases us all.

And so, while the GOP gleefully fed the ill-conceived ire of the Tea Party faithful, they continued to double down on the very things that have caused so many of these folks to feel genuine hardship. It would almost be comical, except for the immorality and the guns. If someone in a red (or blue) state wants to endorse candidates who blithely promise to increase the collective misery, one can only laugh—unless one can't help but cry. But when we see these candidates urging "Second Amendment remedies", we need not wring our hands and ask how we all share the blame. No, the bulk of the blame can easily be laid at the spit-shined shoes of the pied pipers leading these rats to the water's edge. That, an older and/or more cynical observer might suggest, has always been the case. Except now these rats are packing heat and they don't mind taking out as many of us as they can, smiling as they do it.

January, 2011

RUSSELL BRAND, REVOLUTION AND THE AUDACITY OF APATHY

Russell Brand's most recent foray into sociopolitical observation (about abstaining from politics) is going viral, prompting all sorts of justifiable, encouraging commentary. While his eloquent and witty rant does some heavy lifting in the service of exposing the Royal Scam of manufactured democracy (etc. etc.), and I endorse much of what he says, I do take serious exception with the statement he thinks he's making by declining to vote. Apathy, or better yet, the type of cultivated disgust that leads to "both sides do it" equivocation is almost certainly what the people pulling the proverbial strings want our default settings to be.

I always get nervous, and ultimately frustrated when I hear intelligent people asking the rhetorical question: Why bother?

Why bother getting invested in politics?

Why bother reading all those papers and blogs and magazines?

Why bother since politicians are all the same?

Why bother voting at all?

Well, there are lots of good reasons, some of which are immediately evident to anyone who is even moderately informed. Not to mention aware of not-so-complicated concepts like *cause* and *effect*. That the policies of our former administration combined with the ideology informing those policies bankrupted our nation and— this is the toughest one to grasp— made us *less* safe is not a matter of opinion. There is no room for any possible nuance. There is only one type of Socialism being practiced in America today and it has been in effect for longer than five years. It's Corporate Socialism. For evidence to support this claim, I submit every action taken by every Republican politician since 1980.

There was probably not a more irascible yet articulate comedian who spoke the Truth to Power in the last quarter-century than George Carlin. He made you laugh, but the topics were often ugly and dead-serious. He dissected the greed, opportunism and collective culpability of a super-sized America as well as anyone has but, like Twain, his indignation eventually (inevitably) took a turn for the bitter toward the end. Not that there's necessarily anything wrong with that. If any famous public figure—an artist, no less!— went as ungently into that not-so-good night, I can't think of one; eternal kudos to Carlin for keeping it real until he flat-lined.

The one beef I had with Carlin was similar: he famously refused to vote as well. And while it's difficult to quibble with any of the points he makes in the video below (wherein he proves that he still had both his fastball and spitball up until the last pitch he threw), it is in the 21st Century—and after what we've just witnessed with one party fighting for the right to default—disingenuous to deny that the other party even bothers to pay lip service to working Americans.

I'm not certain if it has anything to do with what one studies in college, or the type of person one already is (of course the two are not mutually exclusive by any means) but speaking for myself, I suspect that if one is a certain age and not already convinced that God is White and the GOP is Right, reading a book like *The Road To Wigan Pier* changes you. Reading a book like *The Jungle* changes you. Books like *Madame Bovary* change you. Books like *The Second Sex* change you. Books like *Notes From Underground* change you. Books like *Invisible Man* change you. Then you might start reading poetry and come to appreciate what William Carlos Williams meant when he wrote "It is difficult to get the news from poems, yet men die miserably every day for lack of what is found there." These works alter your perception of the big picture: agency vs. incapacity, history vs. ideology and the myriad ways Truth and History are manufactured by the so-called winners.

Put another way, even if one is open-minded and receptive to various sources of information, if your studies focus on economics, business or political science, you are already being inculcated into an established way of thinking. Liberal arts education, if it has anything going for it (and it has plenty, thank you very little!), reinforces and insists upon what Milan Kundera called a "furious non-identification." This does not mean to imply that all, or most, or even some of the students who embrace (or abscomb from) the ivory tower remain inquisitive and objective. It does mean that reading works from different cultures and different times inevitably denotes facts, even if couched in fictional narratives, which are largely outside of time and agenda.

It is, therefore, easier to make connections between Irish immigrants who worked the coal mines in Pennsylvania and Lithuanian immigrants who worked in the meatpacking plants in Chicago and Mexican immigrants—especially the illegal ones—who labor in sweltering kitchens and frigid fields all across our country. It is impossible not to put human faces and real feelings alongside this suffering and start connecting the dots that define how exploitation works. All of a sudden, it's less easy to espouse the impartial axioms of the Free Market and the immutable forces of commerce or especially the notion that (in America anyway) everyone starts out at the same place and those who work hard enough and say their prayers and drink their milk will attain vast fortunes without breaking laws, stepping on innocent faces, or engaging in the oppressive *pas de deux* with Authority. Then, presumably, it goes from being merely disconcerting to outrageous that the Weasels of Wall Street are back in business with billion-dollar bonuses (thanks taxpayers!) while unionized public school teachers and middle-to-lower class workers' pensions are being blamed for America's current deficits.

One must concede that when it comes to bumper-sticker braggadocio, no one sloganeers for the soldiers, country, and Christ like Republicans. Of course, we won't count the ultimate cost of "Mission Accomplished" until we consider the lives lost and the walking wounded, tallied up alongside the untold billions of dollars our adventure in Iraq has put on the ledger. And isn't it amusing how seldom *the war that would pay for itself* comes up during discussions of the big deficits racked up during the last decade? Remember this, when those hoping to drown government in a bathtub crawl out of their taxpayer-fortified foxholes to decry liberal "big spending" programs. Remember it's these programs that, in addition to paving roads, building schools and providing health care, attempt to secure some support and solace for our broken soldiers.

The Democrats are not immune from the corrupting influence of their donors and corporate masters, but they can continue to ensure the people owed the most won't get the least. It's up to enlightened citizens to ensure the Dems don't dance with the devil and sell out Social Security. It's the obligation of those who know better to remind their disgruntled or oblivious buddies that Obamacare is almost entirely a plan designed by Republicans! Listen to right-wing radio or the rhetoric of men like the Ayn Rand acolyte Paul Ryan, who will happily sign off on savage cuts to food stamps, and persuade their supporters to inquire, *What Would Jesus Do?*

There will be haters, and it's easy enough to feel their pain, to a point. Yes, watching the Democrats try to govern is an often painful and occasionally pitiful spectacle. Of course, in their defense, a reasonable person understands that actually *attempting* to govern is messy, difficult and frustrating. More than ever, as our nation has become increasingly ignorant, self-absorbed and childish, we don't want any government interference. We don't want to pay taxes and then wonder why the Free Market isn't sorting out these pesky problems that won't take care of themselves. Put still another way, if you don't share the view that giving the wealthiest one percent even larger tax cuts is not an antidote for what ails us, you *should* vote and there is one party you should never vote for.

This is why we have to choose sides. This is why we can't to let the super-affluent and well-insured with the least to lose lull us into a state of impotent rage or, worse, apathy. Because aside from the ceaseless class warfare they will instigate, their ultimate ambition is to render the literate and sentient amongst us fed up and indifferent. Without awareness, and with no resistance, they can more easily continue their unchecked assault on our collective well-being.

Your vote matters, and is vital, so whether it's the disarming charm of Russell Brand or the transparent mendacity of the puppet-masters, resist the temptation to walk away: the only hope to win what feels like a rigged game is to remain on the playing field.

November, 2013

THE WORST PERSON IN AMERICA: DICK CHENEY

Motherfucker has so much blood on his hands he makes Lady Macbeth look like Snow White.

He makes Nixon and Kissinger look like the Hardy Boys.

I'm not sure what it says about me, but I've gone on record declaring, at times, my fervent wish that there was a God.

Because if there's a God, there might be something, somewhere, approximating what we imagine Heaven to be. And if so, the existence of Hell would be unnecessary and irrelevant, because God could choose to exclude whomever She wanted, and by default, those denied entrance would spend eternity in a dark, cold place with nothing but memories of their misdeeds to neither console nor distract them.

To be clear: I yearn to see the Evil punished more than I hope to see Good rewarded.

Good, as we know, is often its own reward, but Evil, especially in America, not only tends to go unpunished, but unrecognized. Indeed, in a world where power trumps due process and wealth equals winning, Evil can wrap itself in the flag and cudgel sanity, occasionally even reality, into submission.

(Because in my vision, just about everyone can or should get into heaven. Even the murderers and rapists, who demonstrate some measure of penance or remorse. Or else, after prison or the simple passage of time, they come to understand the error of their actions. And, while some sins are unforgivable and some acts unimaginable, there is usually a greater injustice at the root of all senseless activity, including extreme violence and depravity. Concerning those who lead lives of crime, who are we –as well-fed and educated citizens– to declare Right and Wrong in any philosophical sense? In short, I don't fancy being Judge and Jury to anyone's eternal soul, or to act as some divine arbiter of forgiveness and forgetting. That, after all, is God's job. Which is why we invented Him.)

But I do reserve the right to wish, against reason and the better angels of my very human nature, for something quite biblical in its simplicity and perfection. I wish that the rare individuals who do unto others what none could do unto them (i.e., the untouchable), and express nothing close to regret and can't bring themselves to feign a gesture of introspection, face –at long last– some entity that humbles them irrevocably, incessantly. For those who are typically given the most and therefore expect *more* and commission the greatest ill against their fellow citizens, I possess indignation and disdain that yearns for an Ecclesiastic Imperative.

On my rather long list of most despicable people to pollute the planet during my lifetime, Dick Cheney goes straight to the top, no one particularly close to second place. In terms of rapacity combined with cowardice (nothing quite like a chicken hawk who actively avoided battle, blithely sending young soldiers to die and okaying the obliteration of hundreds of thousands of innocent civilians; nothing like being in bed with Big Oil and profiting from policies that devastate the environment; nothing like being head of the company that wins the sole right to "rebuild" the infrastructure you did the most to help destroy, etc.) it's difficult to imagine an American who has done greater harm while getting his pale bloated paws over as much filthy lucre as he could count.

A coked-up Kafka, plagiarized by Orwell on acid, run through a filter of Hunter S. Thompson with a suitcase full of narcotics, could not begin to articulate, could not even hope to *imagine*, a Hollow Man who epitomizes the worst humanity is capable of. Dick Cheney is many things: a half-assed Iago to Bush, a postmodern Rasputin with a borrowed heart, a bloated Robespierre without the wig, a self-styled Jove realized by illicit funds, treasonous friends and the bravado of back room deals.

***

Some are born into it; some are paid to do it. Some, like the irredeemably despicable Liz Cheney, are born into it *and* get paid (quite handsomely) to do it. But to single these cretins out is like blaming rock musicians for the dumbing down of American culture. The fact of the matter is that if people weren't willing or able to be duped by clowns like Karl Rove, then clowns like Karl Rove would have to find another line of work.

And then there are the sociopaths, the ones who you actually fear believe not only in the apocalyptic fantasies they peddle, but feel they are the appropriate (even the chosen) ones to answer the challenges. Here you have the Kissingers, Weinbergers, Fleischers, Gingriches. These are seldom the ones behind the wheel (although some of them would jump at the chance), these are the ones riding shotgun, whispering not-so-sweet nothings into the impressionable ear of the idiot in charge (think Reagan, think Bush), the ones content to practice their dirty work long distance.

I have a special hatred in my heart for these smirking maggots, these duplicitous political hacks who reside inside the fortified cocoon of spin and subterfuge. The ones who are neither powerful enough to make the decisions or brave enough to do the damage; these are the ones who put on business suits before hitting the battlefield, talking points echoing around their half-empty heads. Their masters, the flies, crawl into the shit to lay their eggs, they are merely the spawn that emerges from this waste, camera-ready smiles frozen on their faces. They are not born into this, but they are bred for it (or, even more disgustingly, breed themselves, semi-human dung-beetles getting their coprophagia on), never capable of playing on the field or willing to cheer from the sidelines, they are the equipment managers, the ones who want to be near the action but not close enough to get caught in the crossfire. These are the spokespersons and professional apologists; the career insiders.

And, finally, there are the rare ones who, through a gruesome combination of timing, connections and monomaniacal compulsion, *will* themselves to power. To be certain, it's always, in the end, about money (access to it or people who have it, and the truly American ability to make a great deal more of it if you can discard your conscience and avoid any actual consequences). But for the exceedingly singular individuals (Nixon and Reagan come to mind, a kind of yin and yang of will vs, skill coupled with venality and psychopathy), it requires a will to power that even Nietzsche would be at once impressed and appalled by.

Throw all that shit in a blender, add all the stale piss and vinegar, dirty money, fetid air of ill-intent and unimagined misdeeds from our country's collective unconscious, and out comes Dick Cheney, *sui generis*, unclassifiable, undefinable even, the leering, recalcitrant sum total of everything we are capable of being, at our worst.

***

Don't hate the player, they say. Hate the game.

Well I do hate the game. But I also reserve the right to despise. And crave the prospect of comeuppance for the players who bulldozed this world like it was their personal playpen. For the horror movie monsters who laughed at the carnage they caused. Because they could. Because no one down here could stop them.

Is there someone out there, somewhere, who can ensure there is some type of reckoning for these irredeemable swine?

It's almost enough to make you pray.

Then again, we'd have to invent a whole new type of hell to house Dick Cheney.

July, 2014

THE POWER OF POLITICAL NARRATIVE, PART ONE: THE GOP

i. Magical Thinking and the Memory Hole

Like most everyone else I know, I grew up—*really* grew up, if I've ever actually grown up—in the Reagan 80's. Take my childhood, please. Actually, it wasn't all that bad, at least for the middle class kids. During the extreme periods of Boom and Busted, Pro and Convicts, the majority in the middle seldom feels the pain; they rarely see the cocked fists and hoisted heels. It's the people on the poles playing out cause and effect: the haves doing things the have-nots don't have the voice or power to protest. The have-lesses can afford to ignore the news or else lay back like so many frogs, believing the boiling pan is actually a Jacuzzi.

Question: How else can you get people to consistently vote for policies that devastate them, counter almost each admonition of the (white, muscle-bound) Jesus and stagnate growth for every sector except, of course, the obscenely wealthy who rewrite the rules as they go along?

Answer: The power of magical thinking. It's the fulcrum upon which most religious and political momentum swings: all it requires is uncritical, unblinking fealty and it's amazing how simple, and ceaselessly restorative this exercise can be for the unenquiring mind. All of a sudden the world shrinks, Santa Claus exists, America is God's favorite country, regulation is anathema, raising the minimum wage kills job creation, *et cetera.*

Capitalism isn't wrong, but neither is intelligence: you cannot spend money and make money; someone is always paying the tab (and it's usually the poor suckers who can't spend it who take it in the you-know-where so that anonymous, ancient board members can pulverize their portfolios). It's all about numbers. Like an army, like

America. Whether you're a company or a cult (like an army, like America), you simply want to amass enough affluence that nothing else matters.

Which brings us to the looming midterm elections. If Obama has been sufficiently underwhelming to induce depression, at least he staved off a Depression. If we have nothing else going for us, no one wants to return to the bad old days when W. took us on a (dry) drunk drive into the ditch, right? The silver lining of falling so far is the full and final repudiation of a greed-first ethos so aggressively sold for thirty-plus years. Isn't it? Oh…

Instead of putting his boot on the squirming corpse of Reagan's revolution, Obama postulated that we should *heal*. Instead of accountability for the Masters of the Universe who insisted the ensuing debacle was not possible even as they gorged at the trough, Obama appointed some of them in charge of the clean-up. Instead of a reckoning—and the welcome spectacle of some well-warranted tar and feathering on Wall Street—we suffered the indignity of a gigantic reset button, paid for by the taxpayers whose 401(k)'s got fucked. The super-connected swindlers whose idea of trickle-down economics is pissing on the collective heads of the middle and lower classes bounced right back into the saddle. Check them out: their fattened wallets broke their falls.

The Democrats, who had a once-in-a-generation opportunity to rebrand (reestablish?) themselves as the party that not only cared, but governed for the 98%, snatched defeat from the jaws of victory as only Dems can do. More egregiously by far, the GOP, who have dedicated six years to temper tantrums and intransigence, stand poised to retake the Senate and retain the House.

How did this happen? How is it possible? The power of political narrative.

ii. The Power of Political Narrative

Understanding, and exploiting, the power of Narrative is the impetus that unites such unlikely—and antithetical—endeavors as Art, Business and Politics. The ones that can tell a story about what you need to know are important; the ones who tell you a story about what you *want* to hear can become immortal.

Our country was founded on the Narrative of The Future (City upon a Hill, anyone?): always looking toward what we could be, collectively, if we appealed to the better angels of our Nature, our Natural State being invariably democratic, tolerant of disparate faiths—including those without faith—and apparently unperturbed by the genocides inflicted upon our Native and African American brethren. Some eggs, after all, had to be broken in the service of this great experimental omelet called America.

Eventually, it required a Civil War to determine if we would keep looking forward or be cleaved forever into (at least) two countries, one peering over its shoulder, pining to preserve a way of life that never existed in the first place, at least for the majority of the people. (Sound familiar?)

Flash forward one hundred years to the Civil Rights Movement: a generational and geographic divide that once again found us at a crossroads of progress and reactionary segregation. History, as the cliché goes, is ghost-written by the winners. Looking at American history, for good or ill we've tended to define our triumphs as events that unified us, moving us along a progressive path from *there* to *here*, consistent with the founding notion—however fanciful—that we were collectively edging toward improvement and inclusion.

Two of the big "wins" of the 20th Century involved presidents named Roosevelt. First, Teddy, who took on Big Business and monopolies, instituting some overdue governmental oversight. His Square Deal regulated out-of-control American industry in the name of safety. A few decades later, his cousin Franklin ushered in The New Deal, ensuring that, for the next several decades government would, on balance, be seen as an institution that did more good than ill. Until the '80s, both of these developments were generally considered positive for all citizens, regardless of their political affiliation. Books like Sinclair's *The Jungle* or indelible memories from the Great Depression reminded people—and their heirs—that government was the last thing standing between them and unfettered market forces. The notable exception, as ever, being the wealthiest percentile, whose disdain FDR all but celebrated ("I welcome their hatred"), a provocation Obama might wish he'd emulated in 2009.

In an exploit that still resonates for its audacity, Ronald Reagan drew a conservative line in the sand, assailing the presumption of government as an constructive agent, not by nitpicking but taking aim at its *raison d'être* .With a country still reeling from the apathy and cynicism of the post-Nixon nadir, he pre-empted that anger and uttered the immortal words: "Government is not the solution to our problem, government is the problem." And for the first time in half a century the Republicans steadily assumed control of a new narrative. It was simple as it was shameless; it was the most facile strategy fathomable, and the GOP finally had a patron saint to make it sacrosanct. Needless to say, it worked brilliantly.

iii. The Ill Communicator

The greatest trick the devil ever pulled, Baudelaire once wrote, was convincing the world he doesn't exist. Well, the greatest trick the GOP ever pulled was convincing its flock that the devil *does* exist. The way to keep the Evil One at bay is to close your eyes and never, ever question The Man—unless he happens to be a Democrat.

All some Americans need is a person to play the part and tell them how great they are, how amazing we are, and then, no matter how much the unemployment rate and the deficit spike, it's all good because we *feel* good. It is too easy and that is too simple. But the more one looks at Reagan (the man, the myth, the legend—literally), the more difficult it becomes to reach any other conclusion.

Along came St. Ronnie, the actor who made a fortune making awful movies, parlaying this into a career that put his acting ability to the summit of its purpose, circa second-half century America. Rich, he became a lot richer turning his back gleefully on his past, transmuting from an admirer of FDR to a True Believer who hit the trail for the repugnant Barry Goldwater. From a man who saw the country ravaged by the Great Depression, and therefore endorsed the New Deal, he subsequently did more than any president to undo the legislation that helped stave off a genuine catastrophe and fortified the middle-class for decades.

Now it's an open competition to see which Republican can invoke him most often and they can't name buildings after him quickly enough. Reagan has become the conservative alternative to Che Guevara. As we've seen in the short time since his death (indeed, in an initiative that kicked off years before he even kicked the bucket, by those who stand to profit most from his hagiography), a very intense and deliberate effort was undertaken to beatify and whitewash a legacy that was far from undisputed in the late '80s.

The Reagan Revolution built its momentum on a shameful vilification of America's poor and lionized (some would say fetishized) the wealthiest percentile and transformed them into folk heroes. Because Michael Douglas turned in such an effulgent performance (in a rather mush-mouthed, typically ham-fisted Oliver Stone screenplay), few people—then; now—understood that Gordon Gekko was not "merely" a bad guy; he was a sociopath. In less than two terms, Reaganomics and Wall Street vandalism laid waste to the working class and put us on a path where the richest of the rich were entitled, by Divine Right, to pay ever-smaller tax rates. Meanwhile, young pillagers in training, like Mitt Romney, perfected the business acumen of bankrupting companies for profit into a repugnant performance art.

Despite an inconvenient eight year blip on the radar, where taxes were raised and the economy soared, the GOP, led by Dick "Deficits Don't Matter" Cheney, had eight years to use the country as a demented sort of lab experiment. The result: 2008 and the cratered economy Obama inherited.

iv. The Five Commandments

After the disgust and disbelief settles, one feels obliged to give props to the Republican ratfuckers. Over the last few decades while they have dabbled in the vicarious thrill of foreign occupations and the odious gutter-dwelling of racial and sexual identity politicking, the cretins behind the curtain have focused on a handful of tactical battles in which they have more or less achieved their ends. This strategy has many moving parts, but can be boiled down to a handful of inviolable commandments, the enforcement of which ensures that no one is ever off script. And make no mistake, this script is like religion—only belief is not optional. The first and foremost commandment, propagated to the extent that it's literally received as gospel—no matter how repeatedly disproven it is in practice—is that any taxes at any time are always a deplorable idea.

The second is that the mainstream media has a liberal bias. They've succeeded so thoroughly in this monomaniacal mission that once first-rate newspapers like *The Washington Post* now police their content excessively enough to render them neutral, if not neutered. The Op-Ed page has for more than a decade been patrolled by whacked-out hardliners who would have been laughed out of conservative circles only twenty years ago; back in the days when the

GOP was devising health care reform that is now successfully considered socialism.

The third, which has been accomplished with considerable assistance from an increasingly reckless, ambitious and soulless Democratic party, is the demonization of unions. Long, sad story in one sentence or less: during the last half-century—but with a vengeance beginning in the '70s—unions lost influence while Democrats simultaneously abandoned them to court wealthy financiers to fund their increasingly lavish campaign expenses. Why the Republicans want to eradicate the same movement that helped bring us regulation, forty hour work weeks, overtime and collective bargaining is beyond no-brainer. Why the Democrats have allowed this to happen, abetting it more often than not, is owed to an opportunistic cynicism that has gutted the sensible and effective backbone of the Progressive cause in ways both myopic and tragic.

The fourth is that public education fails us, that teachers are overpaid and underachieving, and that while no cuts to any military spending are conceivable, all manner of funds and aid to public schools are forever on the table.

The fifth, final and cheekiest involves the mantra that government does not work. It's a neat trick in which, when Republicans take power, they spend their time ensuring this assertion is true, all while consistently expanding the size of government along with the size of the national debt. Then, like clockwork, once the people have finally seen enough, a Democrat comes in with the thankless task of cleaning up the mess, and the disloyal opposition becomes a cadre of small government deficit hawks. That this same farce was pulled off so spectacularly after our recent recession says as much, if not more, about the aforementioned media and the supine Democrats as it does about the unabashed GOP.

v. Faith in Something Bigger than God

To see the full flowering of this psychosis, one needs look no further than the recent passing of James Brady.

Brady, for those who weren't alive in 1981, is the unfortunate aid who had the bad luck of being mortal, and getting in the way of some bullets that could never have killed Reagan anyway. Before Brady died I might have been embarrassed to write something so churlish; a cursory glance at the comments section of any of the Brady obits confirms that there are a *lot* of people out there spouting shit like this, if even sardonically. Don't kid yourself, beneath the sarcasm is a sincere reverence, the type of veneration we typically reserve for saints (and members of the Kennedy clan).

It's a matter of Faith: Reagan wasn't meant to be assassinated. And by Faith, of course, I don't mean God (Reagan didn't need God), I mean the Free Market. If the Free Market had wanted him to die, he would have died.

Speaking of faith, freedom and folly: the only force of nature more powerful than any of the fixations previously mentioned is that of the gun fanatics. Maybe, *maybe*—coming as it did less than half a year after John Lennon was murdered—if Hinckley's assassination attempt had been successful, we might have had a national consensus of sorts. This, after all, was *the* moment, where we could—and should—have rallied around sensible gun control. It was the moment when all forces came into focus; it was, after all, their hero in the crosshairs.

Naturally, nothing of the sort happened. Brady became an advocate for a more sane approach to gun ownership, earning him the enmity of idiots who should have never ceased appreciating him. These, after all, are the same sorts who will swear up and down that Reagan did as much as anyone not named Rocky Balboa to defeat the Evil Empire.

How then, was any of this possible and how can such farce still hold sway over a sizable portion of our populace? The same technique that ensures certain stories get told and taught centuries after they are composed: the power of good narrative. That the Iran-contra affair is glossed over the way we never talk about our drunken uncle in the retirement home, or that taxes are actually lower during Obama's tenure than Reagan's, or that the First Couple regularly consulted an astrologist never tends to come up in not-so-casual conversation is part and parcel of the almost entirely successful enterprise to consecrate The Gipper.

The moral, as it applies to our contemporary political scene, is straightforward as it is distressing: risible dialogue delivered by a screen-tested salesman will always win more votes than substance offered up, however earnestly, by a substitute teacher. This helps explain the (mostly) refreshing phenomenon of Bill Clinton and underscores the inestimable potential squandered by Barack Obama:

when the Democrats have a personality commensurate with their common-sense policies, they have half a chance.

There have, of course, been elections won and lost by both parties, PR initiatives shifting momentum (and money, always money) from the haves to the have-mores and there is little new under the sun. But if we look back at the last three decades, the Biggest Victory—transcending all the skirmishes fought during the last several presidential terms—and the enduring legacy of the Reagan Revolution, is the impervious *story* it continues to tell, and sell. It informs our craven political discourse; it intimidates an increasingly incurious media and bulldozes an ever credulous Republican base.

Data, facts and near-depressions be damned, we have seen one side nominate a succession of buffoons who should only have inspired bad fiction instead of engineering ever-more-implausible reality. Against all probability, that's their story and they're sticking to it.

Against all tolerability, the rest of us might remain stuck to it.

September, 2014

THE POWER OF POLITICAL NARRATIVE, PART TWO: THE DEMOCRATS

i. Ridic, Redux

Last month I wrote about The Power of Political Narrative and the ways Republicans have kept it simple (stupid) and mostly stuck to an inflexible script for the last thirty years. No matter how flawed that script is, in reality, and no matter how many times reality makes a point of pointing out that virtually every talking point—taken as Gospel and enforced as Scripture—results in the opposite of what it claims (Clear Skies Act, etc.), a reckoning never occurs.

As such, we saw austerity when we desperately needed stimulus, coddling of Wall Street cretins when perp walks were well-warranted, craven acquiescence on the Guantanamo catastrophe, "Death Panels" instead of a public option, *et cetera.* Not that these are the results Obama (or the left) wanted or predicted, but because of—at least in part—the ability of the other side to sling the same excrement at every policy, proposal or achievement, defying a twice-elected leader to bring about change we can believe in. Or pocket change for the middle class. Or something.

Certainly, it sucks to see a party whose signal accomplishment the last two years (doubling down what they did the previous four years) was acting petulant and saying *no* like a paroxysm rendered Reductio ad absurdum, smug and certain they are about to retake the Senate. By refusing to govern they are likely to be rewarded, not because anyone (even Fox viewers) particularly likes the results, but because they have stuck so steadfastly to the scheme: lay blame on Obama, Democrats, and Government, respectively. At best tolerated (at worst abetted) by a degraded mainstream media they have done this repeatedly, and mostly with impunity.

And because we expect less than little from the intransigent GOP, how can we resent them for proving the cowardice of their convictions? Particularly when the profiles in courage *not* on display by their political opposition is so…typical. My concern is—and has been for some time—the ways in which Democrats are congenitally incapable of articulating their achievements, and crafting a message that is either compelling or consistent. The shame of it is, all they have to do is tell the truth and it would set them (and the rest of us) free.

I'm not suggesting it's easy, or that it would be embraced—at least initially. As I argued last month, it's a hell of a lot less demanding to pick a handful of platitudes and recite them like zealots at a Sunday service. But this is not a matter of formulating counterpoints or rebuttals; it's about crafting a narrative that is consistent and, as no less a salesman than Henry Kissinger once said, has the added advantage of being true. Naturally, telling the truth does not come *naturally* to elected officials who are often paid for before they take the oath of office, and this circumstance is further complicated by the question of how many of them really believe in left-of-center principle in the first place. Still, any introductory class in marketing or communications (or English Literature for that matter) will emphasize the importance of narrative; the necessity of telling the story you want to tell.

It's not that difficult to imagine, and this shit practically writes itself. One speech, early in '09, wherein Obama declared: "not only am I going to fund these projects, no American who wants to work will go without on my watch. I'm going to spend this money, because it is an investment on *people*, and you will be able to measure the results immediately. This is a mission on behalf of our well-being, and if you want to judge me in four years, I will take those odds. And if I'm wrong, the worst case scenario will be an early retirement where I can drive across this great nation over new roads and rebuilt bridges, and take advantage of the radically improved infrastructure that these projects made possible. I'll walk away from the Oval Office happy and proud, because I'll know we made a difference, and that is what I was elected to do."

Obama was either too clueless or (worse) haughty to believe he actually *needed* to make a case, and be ready to fight back against the full-scale war the GOP declared on him the second he was elected.

(His refusal to bother himself getting involved in the health care brawls all summer of 2009 is the second largest blunder of his presidency: he not only allowed the malevolent Republicans to define the narrative (wrongly), he let the Tea Party lunatics get a foothold and, with the lack of any consistent, intelligible message, determine that opposing government was the correct, patriotic thing to do. By the time he saw the grammatically-challenged writing on the signs, it was arguably too late. Meanwhile, against all probability, the masses with their pitchforks and flames, had—for lack of a tangible target for the ire—latched on to the Fox-spewed propaganda filling the inexplicable vacuum of what passes, these days, for political discourse.

ii . Coal Mines, Sean Connery and (of course) George Orwell

In *The Road to Wigan Pier*, George Orwell's masterful investigation of the English working class, he makes the following observation: *Watching coal-miners at work, you realize momentarily what different universes people inhabit.*

That succinct, typically clear-eyed assessment has stuck with me because, like so much of what Orwell wrote, it is not tied to any particular period of time. As I get older, I realize this quote can be applied to any number of professions. Put simply, money and means enable certain people to reside in entirely different realities. After one has read Orwell—hopefully at an early enough age that it makes one allergic to relativism and libertarianism—one can't help but view the world through a sociological lens.

Quite by chance, I just watched an old classic that had been languishing in my Netflix queue: like St. Peter allowing a purgatoried soul into heaven, I finally brought it to metaphorical salvation via my DVD player. It's one of those movies I've heard about many times and hear referenced often enough that I've had it on my to-do list for entirely too long. Plus, the notion Richard Harris sharing screen space with Sean Connery was, suffice it to say, enticing. The movie in question, *The Molly Maguires,* did not do well upon its release and has become something of a cult classic—with an emphasis on the cult.

The story, in a nutshell, involves the gruesome exploitation suffered by Irish immigrants (and workers in general including, of course, young children because this was before Teddy Roosevelt, horrified by the depictions in books like Sinclair's *The Jungle*, got inspired to seize some manner of control from Big Business and introduce those quaint concepts of regulation and workers' rights: in other words, this story takes place precisely in the era that today's GOP is aggressively working behind the scenes to bring us back to) toiling for paltry pay in the coal mines.

If you are imagining an environment where safety was tenuous and the conditions were barbaric at best, you are not incorrect. It is also a workplace where the owners controlled everything, including the breaks not given and the payment not rendered. In one illuminating scene the new employee (Harris) stands in line to get his weekly wages: the boss adds up the coal collected and announces the amount; Harris smiles. Then the boss subtracts the damaged tools, the wear-and-tear (a 19th C. version of "administrative fees") and the final amount is reduced from nine bucks and change to just change. As Harris stands in disbelief the boss, flanked on either side by police officers, glowers at him and says "Next!" If that sounds too much like a bad out-take from *It's A Wonderful Life,* check yourself: these are the conditions that absolutely existed, as men like Sinclair (and later, George Orwell, of course) observed and reported.

The reason the movie was probably unsuccessful, and the reason the timing of my first viewing is serendipitous, is because of the subject matter: way before unions existed; circumstances were suitably dire that the use of drastic measures were required, and understandable. As a result, a group of protestors (or terrorists, depending on what century you live in and what newspapers you read) took to undermining the mine's profitability by using incendiary tactics, literally. Harris, the "good guy" is a paid detective assigned to infiltrate this mob and help the honchos crush the uprising by killing the culprits. If this sounds a bit familiar, the story is based in large part on true events inspired by the reprehensible actions of the Pinkertons, who operated kind of like union busters before unions existed.

The movie is clever: by making Connery grim and uncharismatic (no mean feat considering this is Mr. *Shaken, Not Stirred* we are talking about) and playing up Harris's roguish charm (yes, that is a cliché but if anyone could ever be said to possess roguish charm it's the ever-ebullient but burly Harris), the viewer is almost conned into empathizing with, and rooting for the putative protagonist. Only after the film concludes does it finally—and fully—occur to the viewer: if the movie had been shot, or written differently we would be pulling for the "bad guys" all along. And that is the point. If the movie was told from the alternate point of view, it would have been preachy, unconvincing and free of emotional conflict. Which is exactly why it's a good movie and most likely why it did not set the box office on fire. It also might make one recall the other chestnut (speaking of clichés) about history being written by the victors, the power of language to shape story and the mechanisms always at work to manufacture how reality is perceived.

iii. The Medium Remains the Message

As we stare down the ignoble specter of the GOP taking back the Senate next month, it is at once exasperating yet simple to see how we got here. Yes, the Democrats' incompetence at crafting an actionable narrative has, at best, enabled the Republicans to proselytize their fealty to an ever-more-free market. But at least when they try (see: Clinton and Obama in campaign mode), they can compete, and occasionally win (!). The deeper and more disturbing issue is the way they've abandoned the very middle class their policies demonstrably support.

What has long befuddled me is that, even if you can cynically concede that even Democrats tread lightly before their corporate masters these days, it makes *political* sense to maintain a healthy relationship with unions. During the Tea Party shenanigans in '09, I kept asking myself: when is our chronically aloof commander-in-chief going to start reminding everyone that this big bad government has historically been the bulwark between the people and an Industrial Revolution lifestyle? Does it need to actually get to the point where the Republican Party *literally* says "let them eat cake" before people start to realize wages are stagnating, prices are rising and the only people getting fat are the wealthiest one percent? Apparently it does.

Feel-good (or, feel-bad) lip service is paid to the undeniable, growing discrepancy of salaries paid and taxes not collected on the *makers* vs. the *takers*, but the song remains the same (see: a dose Romney, a dash of Ayn Rand and an unhealthy smattering of Religulous paranoia to expedite a state like Kansas acquiescing itself into fiefdom). And we've not come to terms with the fact that the wealthiest percentile don't just look down on—or worse, ignore—their lesser brethren. They neither understand nor want to understand: they contemplate the impoverished the way many of us might ponder serial hoarders: we see it, are disgusted by it, and wouldn't ever want to be like them, but we simply can't fathom *how* they got to be that way; what happened to make them so unreasonable.

What Orwell articulated so well, in part because it was (is?) so stark and systemic across the pond, is the way class is at once an explanation and excuse for imbalance—not only in practical and political terms, but as ingrained disposition: things are this way because they've always been this way. After a while, injustice just seems to be the natural order of things. Okay, but it's supposed to be different in America. We ostensibly have laws and systems in place to prevent unchecked stratification. That we can't quite challenge—or even believe—what our lying eyes tell us is, again, what the Reagan Revolution has wrought. However much he has disappointed, it's certainly not (only) Obama's fault that his party has generally avoided the entire issue of class for practically half-a-century.

But even if the seemingly unsophisticated battle to prove the relative benevolence of government (or compassionate conservatism—ha!) seems a non-starter in 2014, it should not require too much PowerPoint proficiency to compile a quick commentary about what unions have wrought: minimum wage, forty-hour work weeks, health insurance, pensions, vacations, sick-leave, etc. All of the things people assume exist as an evolved conciliation, or were always just sort of there; or best of all, were the inevitable rewards of laissez-faire philosophy until big government came along and screwed everything up.

Regardless of her short-term political (e.g. presidential) aspirations, Elizabeth Warren—and the Yes-We-Can-type approbation she's accruing—is, if nothing else, an indication that at least one notable liberal understands the power of going back to the future. The fact that someone like her (or Bernie Sanders, for that matter) exists is encouraging, but the fact that people are responding to this message should translate to a broader game plan, the sooner the better.

No matter what happens next month, it can hopefully provide sufficient momentum for the marble-mouthed Democrats to cobble together some cohesive messaging en route to 2016. One would think the mere act of pointing out the truth would not require heavy-lifting and soul-searching (but those without souls, admittedly, can have difficulty here). Again, I do not count on any of these center-left pols to suddenly find religion, so to speak, but presumably they can grasp that there is a purely political advantage to being on the right side of the middle class, not to mention history.

October, 2014

SORRY, CHARLIE: ON ART AND EXTREMISM

i.

Of course religion is the problem.

For anyone who, understandably, would say it's a political issue and not a religious issue, I aver that so many of our political difficulties exist because of and not in spite of religion. And we muddle the matter if drawn into a debate about whether Religion-with-a-capital-R is ultimately a force of Good or Evil. I know how I feel and you know how you feel. More importantly, religion isn't going anywhere, so we heretics must remain skeptical, and vigilant. And if there's one thing that unites East and West it's the chasm between those convinced more religion is the answer and those for whom the less the better.

It has become a tad too fashionable these days to pit believers vs. non-believers (and there are few things more exasperating than proselytizers playing the victim card). Let me stand up and be counted as someone who respects—in theory and practice—anyone's right to believe anything they choose. Indeed, I'm relieved we have a handful of commandments, however randomly obeyed, to keep would-be-sociopaths in check, their eyes on an eternal prize. The problem, as always, involves those amongst us who would initiate mayhem, compelled by the imperatives of their faith.

We do ourselves a great disservice by failing to acknowledge the role religion has ceaselessly played as either an instigator of, or cover for, violence. In this regard, a similar impulse connects what happened in Paris and what happened during the Crusades and that disaster porn saturating the Old Testament: perceived righteousness in the name of divinity. Yes, clever commentators can point out that, at least in some instances, religion is a cynical shield for atrocity. It has always been thus.

We have, at least, advanced culturally (one might say we've evolved) to the extent where no one can be taken seriously for condoning massacre of innocents. That, in any event, is not the crux of the matter before us. What we see, and what has been polluting the discourse these last two weeks, is a refusal to denounce, without reservation, the religious rationalization signaling—then seeking to explain—such acts.

A single quote resurfaced in several news stories last week, and it crystallizes the cause and effect so many are struggling to see with clarity. Nasser Lajil, a Muslim city councilor in France, had this to say regarding the slaughter of 11 journalists: "I want to make clear that I completely condemn the attack on Charlie Hebdo. *But I think freedom of speech needs to stop when it harms the dignity of someone else. The prophet for us is sacred.*" (Emphasis mine.)

Two simple points need to be made. One, any sane argument begins and ends with a declaration that under no faith-related circumstances is murder of human beings ever acceptable. Two, if your faith is capable of being threatened by a cartoon, your faith *is* a cartoon.

ii.

Which brings us to Charlie Hebdo. Our collective reaction requires more *J'Accuse* and less *Je ne sais quoi.* Anything other than a full-throated and unequivocal denunciation of such carnage renders one a coward. When it comes to free speech and matters of life and death, you are either an advocate or an accomplice; there can be no middle ground. Satire is not possible without someone's sacred bovine being savaged; the complication is that so many of us are equal opportunity instigators until it's *our* cow getting cudgeled. Free speech, in short, is not an à la carte arrangement.

It is, therefore, dispiriting to see anyone, especially (if predictably) the liberal intelligentsia, so cavalier about throwing down what's typically a trump card. *Is Charlie Hebdo racist?* It's an interesting question for curious minds to ponder, but irrelevant in this context of assassination and presumptive self-censorship. Even if, however hysterical the argument, we concede that this magazine exists only to offend, does that in any way legitimize the act of murder?

More, it's precisely because so many of these cartoons are juvenile that we must defend their right to exist. It's generally painless to rally around literature we consider sacrosanct, and feel smug doing so, but if we don't allow the claptrap to function as an aesthetic caboose, we risk being elitists as well as defeatists. How revolting, then, to read pundit after political analyst after Op-Ed arbitrator stroking their chins and opining that the images were, after all, in questionable taste. Or, if you provoke certain groups often enough you have to expect some type of reaction. Really?

Any form of suppression, especially as it pertains to someone else's faith, is an act of accommodation. Full stop. These intellectually bankrupt rationalizations, in effect blaming the victim, smack of our rape-enabling semantics. Some of the self-righteous comments sullying our newspapers and blogs call to mind the familiar formulation: "Yes, she was brutally raped but should she really have worn that skirt?" Translation: *Rape is awful, but maybe next time she'll think twice about the decisions she makes.*

It's situations like this that help me understand what pushed Christopher Hitchens, the erstwhile socialist, over the edge. It was occasionally perplexing to see him stand alongside (figuratively and sometimes literally) the architects of Iraq and unrepentant exploiters of America's underwear-wetting sensibility concerning all-things-terror post 9/11. But even then, while I couldn't forgive it, I could fathom it. Here was a dude who talked the belligerent talk, but also walked the uncompromised walk: he spent considerable time in the very hot zones he wrote about, and bore witness to the atrocities we excoriate in editorials.

And while many lamented his ostensible act of betrayal and/or expedience in the years before his death, he had political and creative skin in the game. Also, and this is important: it quite clearly wasn't a game for him; whatever else one can say about The Hitch, he had the courage of his convictions and they were not easily earned. His good friend Salman Rushdie, one might recall, was targeted for the infamous fatwa—a price on the author's head equal parts medieval and postmodern—and, it's quite worth noting, this occurred several years before the *first* Iraq war. As such, he saw the reaction of the literary community, which ranged from muted to craven. Everyone, it seems, is all for artists' rights until it's their ass in the crosshairs.

It obviously galled him, over a decade later, to see the usual suspects, secure in their tenured offices and café latte circle jerks, sniffing about imperialism and why our Big Bad Empire had come to bring all this grief upon ourselves. Nevermind the fact that these internecine quarrels predate the founding of America by several centuries. (Look it up, it's in the Bible.)

And that is the real (dark) heart of this matter: of *course* it's about religion. Invariably, it's always about religion. (It's always about money, too, but the two are not mutually exclusive; indeed, it's arguably the lack of money—and resources, education and democracy or at least unregulated thought—that makes one susceptible, if not ravenous for what religion promises to those who can't find heaven or even a hint of transcendence here on earth.)

iii.

Let's be clear: our collective hands, in the West, are far from clean as it pertains to policies and actions antithetical to our own beliefs (due process, drones, etc.), and certainly there are myriad dots that must be connected before we can hope to comprehend the resentment we've allowed—if not enabled—to fester. In so many ways, we have so much to answer for. Nevertheless, the underlying symptom, religion, was alive and unwell long before our current, clichéd clash of civilizations.

We can respect, or at least tolerate the existence of, cultural mores (see: subjugation of women; lack of walls between church and state, and so on) that seem odious or at least antiquated to our Western eyes. We can also acknowledge that perhaps it's not our place to interfere, particularly when we have our own complicated quandaries of race, class and sexuality in the states. But we can, and must, judge. If we abdicate our obligation to denounce such archaic attitudes we are derelict, rationally and morally.

Here is an affair, at long last, that should serve to unite the Left and Right: a genuine atrocity that's at once easy to understand, and revile. It has done so, to an extent, but for the wrong reasons. The only thing more hypocritical than conservative Christians becoming convenient allies of Muslims only because they can't stomach denigrations of their own faith is the faction of liberals who disparage All Things America even as they bask in the very freedoms their country provides them. (Want a laugh? Contemplate how long any of our textbook radicals would linger in the offices of Charlie Hebdo after the first death threat.)

A commitment to free speech inexorably allows bigots an opportunity to spew sewage, all in the name of ill-will. But that is precisely the price we pay for free speech, and hurt feelings are an exceedingly small price to pay, especially compared to the body count accumulated in religious conflicts throughout history. But there is a silver lining: allowing, even encouraging, morons to get their outrage on does us the collective service of isolating the antisocial and potentially psychotic amongst us. Free speech is, like it or not, an all-or-nothing proposition. Where are we, as Americans, if we agree the KKK must be allowed to legally march, but draw the line at religious satire?

Are we actually in a place, circa 2015, where we unthinkingly submit to X-ray scans at airports but confiscate cartoonist's pens? We soil ourselves if a color-coded terror alert goes into effect but don't see that "Terror" really *is* winning if we let extremists dictate the terms of engagement—artistic or otherwise? If we are at war, even metaphorically, what is the fight about if we can't agree that unfettered expression is inviolable?

This debate can—and should—continue, but on the topic of faith-based violence, the concern should be plain and pure: free speech is a non-negotiable precept. It has everything to do with everything we talk about when we talk, often speciously, about American exceptionalism. Ironically, or not, it was free speech that enabled early Americans to practice the religion of their choice (!); it is the guarantee of free speech that underpins our Great Experiment and gives Americans the freedom to *not* believe. It is, ultimately, free speech that ensures the pen is mightier than the sword, and that no one has to die proving otherwise.

January, 2015

ACKNOWLEDGMENTS

The easy part: I sincerely thank anyone who has ever read anything I've written.

More difficult: wanting to give credit and appreciation where it's due, knowing I'll inevitably leave some folks out. You all know who you are (no, really: if you know me, or have ever read my work, you probably know how grateful I am; if not, you know now).

As always, props to my pops: Jack Murphy. He not only had to raise me, he's read pretty much all these pieces in real time; the same long-suffering man who tried, with mixed results that are entirely a reflection on his son and not him, to tutor me through several math and science courses. How do I repay him? By obliging him to read pieces on foreign films and rock bands he's never heard of.

To my sister, Janine, who also has read as much of my work as would be fair to expect or hope for. Thanks again, sis, for being involved and encouraging all these years. Thanks to my brother, Scott, for reading, responding and mostly for being himself. Madeleine and Anthony: there will be a test, so get reading!

Mark Seferian remains, and always will be, my oldest friend, ideal reader and brother from another mother. There actually aren't words to express my gratitude and love and, fortunately, none are necessary (does anyone speak Micronaut?). Add lovely wife Laurel and your two amazing kids (Elliotte and Ash) to the mix and you continue to be the gift that keeps giving.

Like an equilateral triangle with four parts: Mike Shields, Rob Simms, Jamey Barlow and Matt Canada defy the rules of friendship and even geometry. Thanks, again, for the solidarity and the sustenance I receive from you each.

Mark Hanlon and A.J. Hernandez, two of my best, old school friends: among many other things, thanks for reminding me I never need to worry or even ask if you've got my back.

Thanks to consigliere emeritus Beth Wolfe, for being *that* person, even if only we understand what it even means.

Special gratitude to Jane Friedman (again), Mary Esselman, Ed Cyzewski and Renée Malloy Ludlam. Beth Bates and Mandi Perry also get too many high-fives to count.

Extra special thanks to Justen Ahren for befriending, supporting and even surprising me. (Also for being a great poet and even better person.)

Thanks again to Sarah Zupko and Karen Zarker, for all your editorial blessings.

Love and a raised glass to my partners in crime at Noepe, especially Zia Wesley, Ronnie Citron-Fink, Linda Flaherty Haltmaier, and Jack Sonni.

Julene and Randy Slusher for a list of unpayable debts that grows, seemingly daily.

John and Lisa Santoro (and Riley and Logan!), for everything, and other stuff too.

Snoop, Ass, Ferg-Dawg, Papa, Boo-Boo, Drewsoph, Jughead, The Don, The Muns, The Legend, Happer, Grease, Mistah P-Flam: thank you for allowing me to rename you all, and for being the pro quo to my quid.

Robert Rodriguez, Cerphe Colwell and Whit Matheson, I thank you all for support and inspiration.

To a short but essential list of writers who influenced these pieces, I offer you both praise and apologies: Milan Kundera, Martin Amis, Christopher Hitchens, Michael Dirda, Jonathan Yardley and Stephen King.

Heather Sherard, thank you for showing me that loneliness is neither necessary nor advantageous for a wannabe artiste. Thank you for making me a better writer, a better man, and a happier human being. Thank you, above all, for being yourself: a lovely, kind, intelligent, supportive and beautiful (inside & out) woman. Looking forward to happily ever after!

Finally, as always, I'm happily obliged to name my mother, Linda Murphy, as my number one fan and all-time favorite person. Without you I'd never be here on both literal and figurative levels. Allow me to repeat myself: I'll never stop trying and I'll always have faith because your love provides an inextinguishable light.

ABOUT THE AUTHOR

SEAN MURPHY has been publishing fiction, reviews (music, movie, book, food), and essays on the technology industry for more than twenty years. He has appeared on NPR's "All Things Considered" and been quoted in *USA Today*, *The New York Times*, *Forbes* and *AdAge*. In addition, he is an associate editor at *The Weeklings*, where he contributes a monthly column.

He writes regularly for *PopMatters*, and his work has also appeared in *The Village Voice*, *The Good Men Project, All About Jazz, AlterNet, Web Del Sol, Empty Mirror, Elephant Journal* and *Northern Virginia Magazine.* His best-selling memoir *Please Talk about Me When I'm Gone* was released in 2013 and his first novel *Not To Mention a Nice Life* in 2015. He has been nominated for a Puschart Prize and plans to publish a collection of short stories in 2016. He is presently the writer in residence for Noepe Center for Literary Arts at Martha's Vineyard. Visit him online at seanmurphy.net.

www.ingramcontent.com/pod-product-compliance
Lightning Source LLC
Chambersburg PA
CBHW060820170526
45158CB00001B/39

9780989880534